the Legacy of The Blackwood Brothers

By Paul Davis

Authorized Biographies of
Cecil Blackwood &
James Blackwood

The Legacy of the Blackwood Brothers
Authorized Biographies of Cecil Blackwood & James Blackwood
Copyright © 2000 Paul Davis

Published by
Blue Ridge Publishing
427 Wade Hampton Boulevard
Greenville, South Carolina 29609 USA
Phone: (864) 235-2434
Toll-free: (800) 209-8570
Fax: (864) 235-2491

Ambassador Productions, Ltd.
Providence House
Ardenlee Street
Belfast BT6 8QJ, Northern Ireland
Phone: 028-90450010
Fax: 028-90739659
E-mail: info@ambassador-productions.com

Website: www.emeraldhouse.com

Cover design and book layout by
Timothy Artus for Dye & Son Printing, Inc.

Dedicated to:
My Dear Wife, Hazel

Our Wonderful Children & Grandchildren:
Sue & Wes Davis
Laura & Paul Ewers
Anita & Ed McGirr
(& Nathanael and Rachel)

Our Faithful Parents:
Helen & Tom Davis
Rose & Walter Scott

Our Loving Church:
Leighton Christian Fellowship, England and Worldwide

All Our Friends:
In The World Of Music

Acknowledgments:
Miriam and James Blackwood
Francine and Cecil Blackwood
Karlene and George Beverly Shea
Bill Gaither
Jerry Arhelger
Anne and Cliff Barrows
Adelaide and George Hamilton IV
Samuel Lowry
Joy and Samuel Purdy
Jim Guild
Laura Ewers
and Hazel Davis

CONTENTS

FOREWORD
by
Bill Gaither

INTRODUCTION
by
George Beverly Shea

Chapter	Title	Page
1	ADMONISHING ONE ANOTHER	9
2	THE OLD HOMESTEAD	11
3	PIONEERING HARDSHIP'S SONGS	19
4	COUNTRY MUSIC SEEDS	23
5	CHILLING WINDS OF DEPRESSION!	33
6	COURTSHIPS AND BROADCASTS	39
7	STORMY WAR CLOUDS	45
8	BACK TO THE BIBLE BELT	51
9	THE GOSPEL TRAIN	57
10	SUNSHINE STUDIO MEMORIES	65
11	FLYING HIGH AND CAREFREE	69
12	THEN TRAGEDY STRUCK	73
13	DEEP SHOCK	77
14	OUT OF DESPAIR	81
15	MISSION RESTART	85
16	CONVENTION BIRTHPANGS	95
17	NIGHT AND DAY	101
18	THE NASHVILLE SOUND	109
19	MULTIPLE AWARDS	117
20	HOMECOMING INSPIRATION	125
21	CRITICISM AND CONTROVERSY	133
22	MR. GOSPEL MUSIC	143
23	THE FAMILY VOCATION CONTINUES	149
24	THE LEGACY THAT REMAINS!	155
25	THE BLACKWOODS BROTHERS' VOICE	159
26	LONG-PLAY ALBUM DISCOGRAPHY	161
27	VOCAL PERSONNEL 1934-2000	189

FOREWORD
by
Bill Gaither

I was fourteen years old when I first heard the Blackwood Brothers on record. I could not wait to get home from school in the evening to play them, and I had dreams to one day be able to sing like that. I still have many of those old 78-rpm records over at my house.

As a boy I can not begin to tell you the impression those records made on my young life!

I will never forget when my dad and mom took me to Nashville for the first time and I met James Blackwood personally. What a thrill that was for this young Indiana farm boy. That was many, many years ago!

Later when I was in college and our Bill Gather Trio had started singing, we sang on the same program with the Blackwood Brothers in a northern Indiana town. Afterwards we went out to a restaurant to eat. I remember that James complimented us and said that he thought that we had possibilities and some very interesting new ideas. He encouraged us to continue on. That too was many, many years ago!

Now, although the personnel of the Blackwood Brothers' Quartet have changed from time to time, the group is still singing and thrilling audiences all over the country. I am so happy that they chose to sing so many of our songs. I am also happy that they are our friends.

BILL GAITHER

INTRODUCTION
by
George Beverly Shea

The saga of the Blackwood Brothers is an enthralling story that is worth telling and worth reading. So I am pleased that my friend, Paul Davis, decided to put pen to paper and ask me to do this introduction.

Throughout the twentieth century, the name of The Blackwood Brothers has been a long lasting institution in Christian music. It is amazing to recount that they first began their ministry in 1934 and that it continues into the third millennium.

The Blackwood Brothers have during this time had countless opportunities to evangelize by singing the gospel message in untold, different locations to millions. That privilege, in itself, must have been, for them a wonderful blessing. Added to that, they have had the great joy of recording numerous albums of hymns and gospel songs that have reached the hearts and homes of so many millions more.

I remember well, with great affection, when we recorded our 1967 milestone album entitled Surely Goodness and Mercy for RCA Victor. Inspired by King David's psalm, this title song, by John Peterson has proved to be so prophetic particularly with reference to our respective singing ministries. "Surely goodness and mercy shall follow me all the days of my life: and I shall dwell in the house of the Lord for ever." (Psalm 23:6)

I am convinced that often where preaching has failed, Christian music has still touched hearts for the Lord. A good Christian song can touch the soul of even the hardest of men. I sometimes say that music with a Christian message can reach the heart in a hurry!

I know that when the message of Jesus Christ is lifted up in a song (particularly when sung by a singer who has experienced the One of whom he or she sings about), then hearts are made ready to receive The Word.

The Bible says in Romans 10:17, "Faith cometh by hearing, and hearing by the word of God". What a great privilege it has been for the Blackwood Brothers to have been used by God as instruments in helping to inspire faith in the hearts of so many, many men and women.

My prayer is that the Blackwood Brothers example may inspire many others in years to come to follow in the gospel music ministry tracks that they have so diligently laid down over many decades.

GEORGE BEVERLY SHEA

1 ADMONISHING ONE ANOTHER

The LORD is my strength and song, and He is become my salvation: He is my God, and I will prepare Him an habitation; my father's God, and I will exalt Him. Exodus 15:2

As the new Christian millennium dawns in the world of Gospel Music the Blackwood Brothers remain unique, legends among their peers, successors and fans alike. In retrospect, evidently their early rock and roll sounds preceded the secular music industry revolution by three or four years.

Their undoubted effect on the mainstream of popular music is often understated especially with reference to their considerable influence on the young King of Rock and Roll, Elvis Presley.

Their inspiring story reads, amazingly at times, as if it were fiction. It is a human tale full of passionate and heart-warming sentiment, spiritual idealism, and blood, sweat and tears! The story has its balanced share of achievements and mistakes.

Throughout the second half of the twentieth century, the illustrious Blackwood name became synonymous with excellence in their particular field. They set the ever-rising standard all other aspiring performers that followed have tried to exceed.

Their lengthy career-struggle really started in the depression-beset thirties, yet it was not until their two winning appearances on the Arthur Godfrey Talent Scout Show on national TV that they became household names in the early fifties across North America.

According to country singer, Barbara Mandrell, it is impossible to think of gospel music without thinking of the Blackwood Brothers. She says that they have given so much to so many through the years.

Ask any gospel music fan in the world the question, "Which group most epitomizes for you the best Southern gospel quartet style of singing?" and it's a safe bet that the Blackwood Brothers would be top of the list!

Their evangelistic, edifying, yet unashamedly entertaining performances brought their unique talent to general public attention. Among the viewing, listening and record buying public they gained huge followings at their concerts, All Day Sings and Dinner on the Grounds. The public enthusiasm never waned.

Many of the parents who, with their families, attended the Blackwood Brothers' All Day Sings now lend support to the nostalgia and sentiment of the Gaither Homecoming video concerts. Their enthusiasm for the Blackwoods was passed down the generations to their children. These children well remember being taken to the Blackwood gospel events. Research has found that the gospel quartet fan of today is still essentially the gospel quartet fan of thirty years ago.

Record company giant, RCA Victor astutely recognized the Blackwood Brothers' commercial potential, signing them up in 1952 and keeping them on contract for twenty-one years! These plentiful RCA Victor recordings became immensely popular, earning the Blackwood Brothers' numerous Gospel Music Association Dove Awards and nominations. Such recognition was a strong affirmation of the high esteem in which the music industry and gospel music enthusiasts held the Blackwood Brothers alike.

The Blackwood Brothers' were among the first gospel quartet groups to secure a recording contract with a major record company, and their recording artistry is evident in these early recordings. Just listen to the piano wizardry of pianists such as Wally Varner and Jackie Marshall as they took their turn with other noted musicians, to enhance the boys' phenomenal vocal-harmony acrobatics.

The essential part played by these quartets in the formation of what became termed as the Nashville Sound should not be underestimated. Like their celebrated peers, the Jordanaires, the Imperials, the Statesmen and the Stamps, the Blackwoods were most proficient at quality back-up vocals. Their masterful album recordings with Hank Snow, Porter Wagoner, Barbara Mandrell and George Beverly Shea display this ability to the full.

Truly, they achieved the kind of reputation, following and fame from which legends arise. The Blackwood Brothers' panoramic vocal-vistas, complicated harmony-techniques, and ear-catching arrangements gave the quartet a distinctive quality that stands out from among other groups of this genre.

Years later, as one listens back to their exciting, original master-recordings in the crystal-clear, clean, crisp miracle of CD sound, one cannot help marveling at the quality of their music. No wonder there is a continuing longevity to the popularity of their waxings. One appreciates afresh just why the Blackwood Brothers are renowned and revered among the finest quartets that have ever performed...or still are performing today.

At the dawn of the new millennium, Cecil Blackwood, is the present, effervescent leader of the Blackwood Brothers. Heading for his golden jubilee with the group, he is as enthusiastic as ever about what he sees is a God-given vocation.

Let the word of Christ dwell in you richly in all wisdom; teaching and admonishing one another in psalms and hymns and spiritual songs, singing with grace in your hearts to the Lord. And whatsoever ye do in word or deed, do all in the name of the Lord Jesus, giving thanks to God and the Father by him. Colossians 3: 16-17

2 THE OLD HOMESTEAD

Choose you this day whom ye will serve...
but as for me and my house, we will serve the LORD.
Joshua 24:15

As James wandered round the homestead,
Many a dear familiar spot
Brought within his recollection
Scenes he'd seemingly forgot;
There, the orchard - meadow, yonder-
Here, the deep, old-fashioned well,
With its old moss-covered bucket,
Sent a thrill no tongue can tell.

Though the house was held by strangers,
All remained the same within;
Just as when a child he rambled
Up and down, and out and in;
To the attic dark ascending
Once a source of childish dread-
Peering through the misty cobwebs,
There! He saw his cradle bed.

Quick he drew it from the rubbish
Covered o'er with dust so long;
When, behold, he heard in fancy
Strains of one familiar song,
Often sung by his dear mother
To him in that cradle bed;
"Hush my dear, lie still and slumber!
Holy angels guard your bed!"

While he listened to the music
Stealing on in gentle strain,
He was carried back to childhood
He was now a child again:
'Tis the hour of his retiring,
At the dusky eventide;

Near his cradle bed he's kneeling,
As of yore, by mother's side.

Hands are on his head so loving
As they were in childhood's days;
He, with weary tones, was trying
to repeat the words she says;
'Tis a prayer in language simple
As a mother's lips can frame:
"Father, Thou who are in heaven
Hallowed, ever, be thy name."

Prayer is over, to his pillow
With a "good night" kiss he creeps,
Scarcely walking while he whispers,
"Now I lay me down to sleep."
Then his mother, o'er him bending,
Prays in earnest words, but mild:
"Hear my prayer, O heavenly Father,
Bless, Oh bless, my precious child!"

Yet he was but only dreaming:
Never he'll be a child again;
Many years has that dear mother
In the quiet graveyard lain;
But her blessed saintly spirit
Daily hovers over his head,
Calling him from earth to heaven,
Even from his cradle bed.
Traditional. Arranged by Wes Davis / © New Music Enterprises 1999

Dressed in a simple gingham gown, Mother Blackwood's graying hair was tied back in missionary-bun-style. Small in stature but mighty in influence, she was the epitome of her nineteenth century's pioneering stock. Young James Blackwood and his brothers adored their dear mother. Humanly speaking, she was a very small, insignificant individual but her devout Christian life played a powerfully decisive and very crucial part in their early development.

"I can see her now in our humble Mississippi log homestead," reminisced James. "Early in the morning, after doing the breakfast dishes and sweeping the floor, she would make the beds. Then in a disciplined fashion, she would stretch to get her Bible down from the shelf. It was time for her to wander down by the garden fence. It was a daily, divine appointment she made sure she never missed!"

With loving devotion, there the demure figure would reverently kneel, slowly open her well-fingered Bible and read from it sometimes aloud to the backdrop sounds of God's creation. The birds twittered sweetly while the farmyard creatures enjoyed their morning feed. Then, usually without warning, she would gently roll into sacred song, an Ira Sankey-type standard such as *Oh,*

How I Love Jesus!

> *There is a Name I love to sing,*
> *I love to speak its worth;*
> *It sounds like music in my ear,*
> *The sweetest name on earth.*
>
> *Oh, How I Love Jesus!*
> *Oh, How I Love Jesus!*
> *Oh, How I Love Jesus!*
> *Because He first loved me!*
>
> *It tells us of a Savior's love,*
> *Who died to set me free;*
> *It tells me of His precious blood,*
> *The sinner's perfect plea.*
>
> *It tells me of One whose loving heart*
> *Can fell our deepest woe;*
> *Who in our sorrow bears a part*
> *That none can bear below*
>
> *It bids my trembling heart rejoice,*
> *It dries each rising tear;*
> *It tells me in a still, small voice*
> *To trust and never fear.*
>
> *Jesus, the name we love so well,*
> *The name we love to hear!*
> *No saint on earth its worth can tell*
> *No heart conceive how dear!*
> *Frederick Whitfield /Trad. arranged by Wes Davis / © New Music Enterprises 1999*

She would always conclude her worshipful vocalizing with the blind, Fanny Crosby's plaintive plea, *Close to Thee.*

> *Christ our everlasting portion,*
> *More than friend or life to me;*
> *All along our pilgrim journey,*
> *Savior, let us walk with Thee.*
> *Close to Thee, close to Thee*
> *All along our pilgrim journey*
> *Savior, let us walk with Thee.*
>
> *Not for ease or worldly pleasure,*
> *Nor for fame my prayer shall be;*
> *Gladly will I toil and suffer,*
> *Only let me walk with Thee.*
> *Close to thee, close to Thee,*
> *Gladly will I toil and suffer,*
> *Only let me walk with Thee.*

Lead me through the vale of shadows,
Bear me o'er life's fitful sea;
Then the gate of life eternal
May I enter, Lord, with Thee.
Close to Thee, close to Thee
Then the gate of life eternal
May I enter Lord, with Thee.
Fanny Crosby /Trad. arranged by Wes Davis / © New Music Enterprises 1999

It was still early in the beautiful, Mississippi morning and now with her personal thanksgiving and worship over it was time to lovingly remember family and friends. Tearfully, she would gather up her anxieties and cares in prayer.

Focusing her weary eyes on the far off hills, the little lady breathed out her fervent supplications. As she would say to her watching boys, she was taking her burdens to the Lord, her Friend, in prayer.

With her spiritual priorities met she was refreshed and ready for whatever the tiring daily chores of a wife and mother would bring! The tough work of the dirt farm was often challenging and backbreaking, but she would tell her family at every opportunity, "Just like the Good Book says, I have learned, in whatsoever state I am, therewith to be content. I know both how to be abased, and I know how to abound!"

Her positive, optimistic outlook rubbed off with great effect on the young brood she cared for with whole-hearted devotion.

With her daily duties fully met, later in the fading sunset and twilight of the evening, the united Blackwood family would gather. Around the crackling, stone fireplace, by the light of the flickering, kerosene lamp they settled. No matter how tired they were, either mama or papa would devotionally read the allotted portion from the Family Bible. When the inspiring scripture reading concluded, the family would all fall on their knees and spontaneously bubble forth in song and prayer!

The ethos of home and mother was burned deeply into the memories, motives, and values of James Blackwood. During his long life, he was destined to travel many, many thousands, perhaps millions, of miles. He traversed many rivers and many mountains from the mid-thirties to the close of the second millennium. Whether in carefree sunshine or severe storm, that country boy's old Mississippi homesteads's realistic, down-to-earth piety fully prepared the man for a lifetime of Christian service.

When speaking about his humble roots on that small, sharecropper farm in Mississippi James Blackwood said, "I had rather be raised in a home as poor and humble as ours was and Christ be there than to live in the finest mansion of a monarch and God not be there!"

On the ice-cold, Christmas Eve of 1900, on that humble farm near Ackerman, Mississippi, Carrie Blackwood, wife of sharecropper William Emmett, painfully travailed in childbirth. She finally gave home-birth to the first of her three sons, Roy. Sons, Doyle in 1911 and then James in 1919 followed him. Home was not, however, an absolute, male domain. The three brothers had a sister to contend with! Named Lena, she was born in 1903.

These three Blackwood brothers, along with the addition of R.W. Blackwood, Roy's son, were to become the original members of the Blackwood Brothers Quartet.

> *To Him shall endless prayer be made,*
> *And praises throng to crown His head;*
> *His name like sweet perfume shall rise*
> *With every morning sacrifice.*
>
> *People and tribes of every tongue*
> *Dwell on His love with sweetest song,*
> *And infant voices shall proclaim*
> *Their early blessings on His name.*
> *Isaac Watts /Trad. arranged by Wes Davis / © New Music Enterprises 1999*

These Mississippi country boys would determinedly start to mount the steep stairway that would eventually lead them to the top of the gospel music world and to unprecedented music industry recognition for a Christian act.

Father and Mother, Emmett and Carrie stressed hard work as a lifestyle ethic and earnestly tried to sincerely foster an atmosphere of love and appreciation for Christian values in their children. This dedicated commitment evidenced itself further when they joined the Baptist church in Fentress, Mississippi. Later, they affiliated themselves to Pentecostal denominations of the Church of God and the Assemblies of God.

"Music and prayer," James recalled, "were important everyday parts of life, even if money and ease were not."

Despite the dire privations life was good! There was still a song to sing! James's older brother Doyle, who was eight years his senior, bought himself a mandolin and when he became proficient on the instrument the two brothers sang together and hence commenced their early singing career. Doyle sang lead and James sang alto.

One fine sunny day, their dad's brother, Uncle Rema from Jackson, Tennessee, visited the humble family homestead. With persuasive enthusiasm, he suggested that the young brothers, Doyle and James sing for him. He was genuinely so impressed with their fledgling talent that he asked their proud mother if he could take them to a "Singing" at the court house in Jackson the following Sunday. Mother too was proud and pleased at the suggestion, but it posed one big problem. They did not have enough smart clothes to go to something as imposing as that! "Don't you worry about that! I will make sure the boys have some new clothes!" declared Uncle Rema determinedly. Nothing was to stand in the way of his plans.

Sure enough, Uncle Rema was as good as his word. The car ride was a real treat for the boys, as their parents did not own a car then. After a seemingly unending 175-mile journey in his rickety old car he stopped at an appropriate clothing store. There he sacrificially bought the excited boys each a sport coat, trousers, shirt, tie and shoes.

"Boy, did I feel dressed up!" recalled James. The two excited brothers paraded before the store mirror in all their new finery. They strutted back and forth proud as peacocks!

"Come on boys!" shouted Uncle Rema, "We're gonna be late! We've still miles to go!"

With the demure James perched up on a simple, wooden dining-chair to give more height, the two brothers boldly sang their hearts out! They were a big hit at the courthouse that day.

The success brought immediate awards. Impressed, one of the other quartets there suggested that the two boys should sing on their radio program on the local station, WTJS. It was the duo's first introduction to performing on live radio, a medium that they would eventually take by storm.

Back then, singing schools were a very popular and pragmatic means of learning the rudiments of gospel singing, Southern style. In the early nineteenth century, popular-music training in America was centered in so called 'singing schools' - schools that were characterized by their strong spiritual, as well as musical, emphasis. These schools soon became an important part of the social fabric of the small towns and rural communities of America. Each 'singing school' was strictly a one-man operation usually enterprisingly run by a musician of some degree of musical ability. These itinerant teachers traveled from place to place, organizing and teaching classes. They then collected their fees at the end of each session. In some of the poor, farming communities the fees were often paid with farm produce instead of cash. These classes were most often held in the evening and consisted mainly of learning how to sight-read and how to conduct a choir. In country schoolhouses, churches, or town halls, the students would usually sit in rows on planks of wood hung between chairs. Pupils were taught how to sight-read using the tonic sol-fa (a system of solmization that replaces the normal notation with sol-fa syllables /e. g. do-re-mi). Each student was also made to beat time for himself while singing by moving his hand and arm in a prescribed pattern. Many musicians of this period in the USA started out their musical careers as singing school teachers. Their tradition lasted more than one hundred years, regenerated by the hugely successful videos of Bill and Gloria Gaither in the Nineties. Thus it is enjoying a revival in popularity among enthusiasts of Southern Gospel quartet style of music in the USA. This particular genre of music relied heavily in its infancy on learning harmony through this method of teaching. These schools also had a profound effect on the quality of congregational, harmony-singing and music produced at home.

When James was about ten years old news started to spread in the community that someone was coming to start a singing school at the Clear Springs Baptist Church about three miles from the Blackwood home. He pleaded, "Oh Mama, please can we go? We'll make sure the chores get done first!" He yearningly spoke up for both himself and his brother with a look on his pensive face that melted his mother's heart!

The tuition fee was a mere $3 each for the ten nights, but their hardworking parents were too poor to be able to afford the $6 for the two boys. On hearing her two boys discussing their disappointment at not being able to go, their loving mother, at great sacrifice, secretly sold some of her chickens and gave the delighted boys the $6 they needed.

Each tiring day, the keen boys worked diligently in the Mississippi fields and then rode borrowed mules each night to the Clear Springs Church. There they passionately learned to read music; the *Do, Re, Me's*, sight-reading, ear training, and other rudiments of music. The patient music teacher was Vardaman Ray. He was so impressed by the boys' natural talent, he tentatively asked them to join him in forming a new gospel quartet. Of course, the boys were delighted and their answer was an immediate, "Yes!" After finding a bass singer, Gene Catledge, and with Ray to sing lead, Doyle (baritone) and James (alto), they were ready to win the world!

James recalled with great affection how his dedicated teacher, Mr. Ray had a profound influence on his life. The inspiration of his mentor instilled in the young Blackwood the desire to sing gospel music on a serious, career basis.

Their first public performance was at an 'all-day singing' at the Concord Baptist Church that was five miles south of Ackerman, Mississippi. Once there, they eagerly practiced their sacred songs in the cool shade of a tree by the church.

Be ye filled with the Spirit;
Speaking to yourselves in psalms and hymns and spiritual songs, singing and making
melody in your heart to the Lord; Giving thanks always for all things unto God and the
Father in the name of our Lord Jesus Christ;
Submitting yourselves one to another in the fear of God.
Ephesians 5:18b-21

Somebody asked them what the quartet called themselves and the name The Choctaw County Jubilee Singers was hurriedly invented.

By this time, the eldest of the Blackwood boys, Roy, pastored evangelical churches in different parts of the rural locality. It was his wise practice to have a local gospel quartet sing in the service each time he ministered. Usually his son, R.W. sang alto, he himself sang lead, and two other persons from the local church would make up the quartet singing baritone and bass.

It was at Christmas time when the younger Blackwood brothers heard, for the first time, phonograph records of the professional gospel quartets of the day. Enthralled, they could now sing along to the progressive harmonies via the 78-rpm records brought to their home by big brother, Roy.

Frank Stamps and his All Star Quartet, the Owens Brothers and Ellis, and the Vaughan Quartet began to be an all-consuming influence. Through constant listening and practice-singing along to V.O. Stamps' rendition of He Bore It All, James remembered how he learned to sing after-beats.

More and more, the young Blackwoods were sensing and responding to nothing less than a divine calling on their lives.

Take our lives and let them be
Consecrated, Lord, to Thee;
Take our moments and our days,
Let them flow in ceaseless praise.

Take our hands, and let them move
At the impulse of Thy love;

Take our feet, and let them be
Swift and beautiful for Thee.

Take our voice, and let us sing
Always, only, for our King;
Take our lips, and let them be
Filled with messages from Thee.

Take our love; our Lord, we pour
At Thy feet its treasure store:
Take ourselves, and may we be
Ever, only, all for Thee.
Frances Ridley Havergal / Trad. arranged by Wes Davis /
© *New Music Enterprises 1999*

Although they did not know it at the time, Frank Stamps was to play a very influential part in the Blackwood Brothers' aspiring vocation. Inexperienced but steadily improving, the keen quartet members continued to passionately pursue their harmony singing around their hometown community.

3   PIONEERING HARDSHIP'S SONGS

We have known and heard of the Blackwood Family for years
but meeting and performing with them on stage has certainly enriched our lives!
Roy Rogers and Dale Evans

History documents the priceless debt Americans owe to the Christian Faith. It was the continuous, ready supply of strength, comfort and assurance. It gave life meaning, a purpose for existence in the stark face of heart-breaking disappointment and struggle in the wilderness of the new frontiers. In the early pioneering days of the New World, an individual's faith blossomed and grew strong under the pressures and strains of hardship and deprivation.

The sturdy, pioneering families of the North American continent, like the Blackwood family, would love to gather in those old-fashioned days for Divine worship. In their nearby churches and tent-meetings, All-Day-Sings and Dinner-on-the-Grounds were top of the relaxation agenda.

Come let us join our saintly songs
With angels round the throne;
Ten thousand thousand are our tongues,
But all our joys are one!

Christ is worthy to receive
Honor and power divine:
And blessings, more than we can give,
Be, Christ, forever Thine.

Let all that dwell above the sky,
And air, and earth, and seas,
Conspire to lift His glories high,
And speak His endless praise.

The whole creation join in one
To bless that sacred name
Of Him that sits upon the throne
And to adore the Lamb.
Isaac Watts/ Trad. arranged by Wes Davis / © New Music Enterprises 1999

Midweek, it was the popular practice to gather around the cosy Blackwood fireside with neighbours, friends and loved ones on cold, winter nights for a heart-warming sing-a-long.

"Come on in! Y'all welcome!" Mother Blackwood would cry out loudly as she beckoned relatives and friends enthusiastically over the humble threshold. Luxuries were very scarce but the family fellowship was rich and warm. "We ain't got enough chairs but yur still mighty welcome. Some of you young uns are gonna have to sit on the floor!"

In the summer, the same family and friends, young and old would take to sitting outside on the porch. Somebody was sure to get out a banjo or guitar and the whole company would enjoy harmony singing. The dear old gospel songs and community folk songs would provide wholesome inspiration, relaxation and entertainment in the cool of the evening.

The Blackwoods were typical of the hard-working pioneers who doggedly settled the thirteen original States. Later, some families were to adventurously migrate even further westward encountering even more hardship and danger. To ease the daily pain of their deep struggles and dire deprivation they would sing songs of inspiration as they journeyed. As they broke new ground and finally settled in humble homesteads, the front parlor's piano or organ became the family gathering place. To the accompaniment of a piano or organ, they continued to enjoy, testify and sing of their Savior's keeping power and daily blessings.

Throughout ever-expanding territories, new churches and tabernacles sprouted up wherever people settled. It was not long before each church community would develop its own particular style of what they called "music ministry". Choirs, quartets, and soloists sprang up, blossomed and flourished. Where ecclesiastical buildings were not yet available, itinerant ministers and musicians carried the gospel into the primitive backwoods, hills, and ranges.

Calls to worship in the neighborhood surrounding the Blackwood homestead nearly always meant the surrounding congregation joining together in singing the gospel. Musical accompaniment was generally quite simple. Down-to-earth sincerity and heart-felt identification with the sentiments of the songs from the ardent performers flavored the fledgling genre with genuine emotion later to be described as soul.

> You servants of God!
> Your Master proclaim,
> And publish abroad
> His wonderful name;
> The name all-victorious
> Of Jesus extol;
> His kingdom is glorious
> And rules over all.
>
> Trad. arranged by Wes Davis / © New Music Enterprises 1999

Real country harmony-singing prospered in the Blackwood community, sometimes backed by traditional stringed instruments such auto-harp, five-stringed banjo and guitar. The five-stringed banjo is reputed to be the only instrument to have originated in North America. From generation to generation, it was handed down from the bluegrass traditions of the eastern mountain states.

Predictably, the home-based instruments used in gospel music mirrored those used in country music. Inevitably, country artists raised on a diet of religious music from a very early age included an ample selection of such in their regular entertainment programs. Cross-fertilization between the two music styles has, in the opinion of country hit maker, George Hamilton IV, produced a rare art form.

"Country music and gospel music have always been closely linked. I was born in North Carolina in what they call the 'Bible Belt'. It is the section of the States that is very religiously orientated. The area has lots of churches and most people are actively involved in church activities.

I'm grateful for the influence of inspirational songs. They have blended into the country music culture that happily mixes Christian values with entertainment. They have made a great contribution to my emotional development since I heard them as a young child growing up in North Carolina. Ever since the first Sunday School songs I heard, I have grown to love the grand ole gospel songs of the church."

Blessed Assurance, Jesus is mine:
Say! What a foretaste of glory divine!
Heir of salvation, purchase of God;
Born of His Spirit, washed in His blood.

This is our story, this is our song,
Praising our Saviour all the day long.
This is our story, this is our song,
Praising our Saviour all the day long.

Perfect submission, perfect delight,
Visions of rapture burst on my sight;
Angels descending bring from above
Echoes of mercy, whispers of love.

Perfect submission, all is at rest,
I in my Saviour am happy and blessed;
Watching and waiting, looking above,
Filled with His goodness, lost in His love.
Fanny J. Crosby/ Trad. arranged by Wes Davis / © New Music Enterprises 1999

"You will often find this ole country boy", George IV continued, "settling down in the front parlor of his Nashville home in his favorite armchair at the end of a hectic, busy day. There I just relax to the sweet uplifting and inspiring sounds of gospel music. It's the kind of music I like to hear after the evening's TV newscast has told me the worst of the daily headlines. Gospel music dispels the depression and the worry and puts new tread on my tires!"

During the Twentieth Century, gospel music became universal and now comes in many diverse manifestations. There is, however, at least one common denominator, quality songs are handed down from one generation to another. Trained and untrained voices professionally made and homemade instruments, all became conduits as successive generations learned to pick and sing.

A familiar example of music tradition and culture being conducted down successive generations, is that of the black Americans. The Blackwood family deeply appreciated their poor black neighbors' rich inheritance of spirituals developed from hardships endured in the dark days of life and work in the slave fields.

The white settlers later adapted many of these simple, spiritual expressions of Christian truth. Later still, entertainers and evangelists blended them into the mainstream of popular music and hymnody. Cross-pollination has been a constant factor between the black and white traditions, the north and south traditions, and even the west and east traditions. The Blackwood Brothers called upon all these diverse traditions and cultures to form their own unique repertoire

Gospel music has now secured a prominent position in the musical arena. Many professional artists, black and white, have adopted it into their personal musical repertoire. The Grand Ole Opry and other music shows, plus radio and TV, have added emphasis and popularity to this growing genre.

This heart-warming trend of music has always been in essence a home grown or church grown commodity. Yet over the decades, a commercially acceptable spectator form of the music has swept across the world to capture the attention and devotion of millions in all walks of life. Inevitably, the fusion of entertainment and evangelism, and the blending of ministry with business, causes on-going debate, tension, and occasional controversy. The Blackwoods found themselves often in the thick of the battle!

This tired old world may no longer be the simple place it used to be when the heart-warming gospel songs were conceived and articulated in time past. Indeed, as is truthfully said, "Things ain't what they used to be and never will be!" Nevertheless, today millions of ordinary people in almost every walk of life, whether they regularly attend church or not, still enjoy singing or listening to the message of the gospel. It caused their ancestors to sing and endure to the end. Like them, our peers too find genuine inspiration and peaceful consolation in the music of the gospel.

The preaching country gospel singer, Jerry Arhelger astutely assessed the situation in his telling remark. "Christianity is at the core of the America's culture and people. Middle America is down-to-earth, unpretentious, and happy to wear her religion on her sleeve. She enjoys sentimental music that tugs at her heart, moistens her eyes, sets her feet tapping, and her voice humming!'

Behold, God is my salvation; I will trust, and not be afraid:
for the LORD JEHOVAH is my strength and my song; he also is become my salvation.
Therefore with joy shall ye draw water out of the wells of salvation.
And in that day shall ye say,
Praise the LORD, call upon his name,
declare his doings among the people, make mention that his name is exalted.
Sing unto the LORD; for he hath done excellent things: this is known in all the earth.
Cry out and shout, thou inhabitant of Zion:
for great is the Holy One of Israel in the midst of thee.
Isaiah 12: 2-6

4   COUNTRY MUSIC SEEDS

While the earth remaineth, seedtime and harvest, and cold and heat, and summer and winter, and day and night shall not cease.
Genesis 8: 22

The wide circulation and specifically the publication of contemporary gospel songs and hymns had their real beginnings in North America. In 1737, the English preacher and founder of Methodism, John Wesley, surprisingly, published his first songbook in what were then the colonies. The printing was done in Charles Town (now Charleston, South Carolina) for the blooming Methodist Church.

John and his song-writing brother Charles, planted the first musical seeds that were to grow into a tremendous harvest by the end of the Twentieth Century. That first hymnal, published in America, was surprisingly the first book of hymns and gospel songs for the use of the Church of England in Great Britain. It was the musical mainstay of evangelical Christianity for nearly a century.

O for a thousand tongues to sing
Our great Redeemer's praise,
Our great Redeemer's praise!
The glories of our God and King,
The triumphs of His grace!

Jesus! the name that charms our fears,
That bids our sorrows cease,
That bids our sorrows cease;
'Tis music in the sinner's ears,
'Tis life, and health, and peace.

Our gracious Master and our God,
Assist us to proclaim,
Assist us to proclaim,
To spread through all the earth abroad
The honors of Thy name.
Charles Wesley/ Trad. arranged by Wes Davis / © New Music Enterprises 1999

Other denominations in Great Britain and the United States later issued numerous collections of hymns and gospel songs suited to their particular needs down through the years. Their policy was to include all worthy contributions in their books no matter what the denominational source. Initially, the hymns of Charles Wesley and Isaac Watts generally dominated, outnumbering those of any other writer. Every possible source of suitable material was explored.

Open-air preacher, John Wesley established a practice of including gospel song translations from other languages, especially German. Other selections came from the Scottish Psalter plus items from Latin, Greek, Scandinavian, Welsh, French, and even Jewish derivations. By the early Twentieth Century, the blossoming field of sacred poetry had a lively display of contemporary writers, singers and musicians. The young Blackwoods searched high and low for suitable material to add to their growing repertoire.

The spiritual revivals of the Nineteenth Century had opened the way for a new form of Christian musical expression. Not excluded from the Blackwood community were the fires of revival. Christian music was affected accordingly.

Esteemed hymnwriter, Isaac Watts conformed to familiar metrical schemes, namely long, short and common, for tunes already known. Charles Wesley wrote hymns regardless of any known tunes. The enthusiastic, new revival converts to Christianity were from the common people and were keen to introduce familiar, singable melodies into their worship.

Composers before that time, writing for the church, tended to be educated musicians from the establishment. A new genre of writer and singer was to spring up as a result of the revivals. The emphasis became the creation of a more folksy, singable type of Christian song that the Blackwood family embraced. The evangelicals, puritans and pentecostals, being democratic and "of the people" in philosophy, embraced these radical changes with some enthusiasm.

As evangelical and Pentecostal denominations became more and more acceptable by the establishment, the further use of popular tunes was extended. The newly converted common people had, within a generation, succeeded in introducing spirituality into their every-day poetry and music. History documents that this musical movement helped Christianity to move nearer to the soul of the common people.

Folk style rhyme and music have successfully blended into the cosmopolitan character of all denominations. By the end of the Nineteenth Century, gospel music was emotionally and culturally impacting as never before on individuals and even upon society as a whole. Even the great popular composers of the secular field were contributing to the blossoming field of popular hymnody.

Great gospel personalities started to emerge. Two of the greatest spanned the end of the nineteenth century and the twentieth century. Fanny Crosby was to epitomize the best of the newly evolving gospel songwriters and Ira Sankey was to fulfil the same role as a gospel performer.

More than any other songwriter, blind Fanny Crosby captured the attention of millions (including Mother Blackwood) in the latter half of the nineteenth century with her simple yet meaningful gospel songs. Frances Jane Crosby Van Alstyne was born in 1820 and was blinded six weeks later by the blunder of a quack doctor. She lovingly devoted her life to transposing the great spiritual truths of the Christian faith into singable rhyme and melody. Fully persuaded of those truths, her life enjoyed and radiated *Blessed Assurance*, to quote her famous song. She was always keen to give God the glory!

To God Be The Glory! great things He has done!
So loved He the world that He gave us His Son,
He yielded His life an atonement for sin,
And opened the life-gate that we may go in.

Praise the Lord! Praise the Lord!
Let the earth hear His voice!
Praise the Lord! Praise the Lord!
Let the people rejoice!
O come to the Father through Jesus the Son;
And give Him the glory, great things He hath done!

Yes! Perfect redemption, the purchase of blood!
To every believer the promise of God;
The vilest offender who truly believes,
That moment from Jesus a pardon receives.

Great things He has taught us, great things He has done,
And great our rejoicing through Jesus the Son:
But purer and higher and greater will be
Our wonder, our worship, when Jesus we see!
Fanny Crosby Trad. arranged by Wes Davis / © *New Music Enterprises 1999*

Fanny rose to be a social guest of six presidents yet she humbly accepted only about two dollars for each of her compositions and deliberately chose to live simply and soberly. She entered the New York Institution for the Blind at thirteen years of age where she was first a pupil, and then a teacher. It was there that she developed her skills as a poet and writer. One of her teachers was Grover Cleveland who later went on to become the President of the United States. In 1858 she met and married a fellow blind musician, Alexander Van Alstyne.

Fanny was a great supporter of home and foreign missions and so her many associates included such people as Dwight L. Moody the greatly renowned Victorian evangelist and his song leader, Ira Sankey. Other songwriters, George C. Stebbins, William H. Doane, George Root, Robert Lowry, Philip Phillips and William R. Bradbury were also among her contemporaries she considered to be friends. Fanny Crosby's emotion-tugging songs of personal, subjective salvation still attract world attention and have been translated into many languages. Wes Davis' impressive, biographical ballad of Fanny Crosby entitled *Her Story, His Song* has been sung by Jerry Arhelger, Pat Boone, and George Hamilton IV.

In Putnam, New York State, Francis Jane was born
In the year of 1820, in the coldness of the dawn
And the doctor saw the child in the sixth week of her life,
And in trying to prevent it, he took away her sight

And life was very hard and many said unkind,
For it gave her in her innocence a mountain hard to climb.

But she never was alone and she never climbed unheard,
For her loving heavenly Father held His hand in hers

One Broadway, New York night aged thirty years was she.
In the year of 1850, Francis Jane believed!
And a vision caught the eyes that had never seen the light
For the echoings of mercy had come into her life!
And this is her story, this is her song!

Inspired, she went forth and she rose above the storm!
Soon Francis Jane was teaching at the local city school
Where she loved her poetry and the Bible by her side.
Now daily, she'd be writing about a different kind of sight!

For her eyes were eyes of faith and the Cross her only sight.
Soon God gave her a ministry, as a minister of light!
And she'd sing for the President for her music touched his soul,
From the White House to the farm yard, to the high and to the low!

And the writer wrote the songs that caused the crowds to see
The blessed assurance of a God who meets her needs!
And the songs became the prayers of the many who believed
That there upon the pages, Francis Jane could see!
And this is her story, this is her song!

On February eleventh, she wrote her final song.
For on the very next day, Francis Jane was gone!
In the final words she wrote; when the silver chord would break
And she would she His face and tell the story "saved by grace"!

For the ninety years she gave, nine thousand were her songs!
But countless is the blessing as her ministry lives on!
And to God went all the glory for she always looked above,
To a life full of assurance, for the whisperings of love.
And this is her story, this is her song!

Yes, the writer of the songs that still many sing tonight,
You can still hear God speaking through the music of her life!
From her trouble and despair, her story speaks to me
That trusting in her Saviour, Francis Jane could see!
Yes, there upon the pages blinded eyes could see!
Words and Music: Wes Davis / © New Music Enterprises 1999

Fanny lived a long and fruitful life and died in 1915, just before her ninety-fifth birthday. During her lifetime she wrote nine thousand hymns and songs. Many of Fanny's songs became part of the Blackwood Brothers' repertoire and remain worldwide favorites.

Ira David Sankey was born in 1840 in Western Pennsylvania. As the dignified superintendent of the local Sunday school and leader of the choir of the Methodist Episcopal Church, people would come from many miles around just to hear his rich baritone voice. A jovial, handsome individual, well known for his immaculate dress sense, he worked in the civil service as a taxman.

Serving in the American Civil War that tore communities apart and took the lives of tens of thousands, Ira Sankey said he owed his life to divine protection and to his popular singing voice. Perhaps his closest call with death was while on sentry duty. He came into the rifle sights of a Confederate sniper who would have fired if Ira's beautiful, baritone singing had not moved him. Instead, the gunman lowered his rifle and the vulnerable Union soldier's life was spared...Spared for a lifetime of gospel song.

In 1860, Ira's regiment was deployed to Maryland where Christian services were held among the tents of the camp. He was often called upon to lead the singing. Soon he found several other young men with fine voices and a sense of harmony. A choir, led by Ira, was formed that gained some renown in the neighborhood. In a short time, they all found themselves being invited out by the families in the community who had heard of the singing of "boys in blue".

At the end of his term as a soldier Ira chose not to re-enter the army but returned instead to Pennsylvania to assist his father. Abraham Lincoln appointed him as a tax collector for the Internal Revenue Service.

After the American Civil War, in 1870 Sankey was appointed a delegate to the International Convention of the YMCA in Indianapolis. Up and coming evangelist-preacher, Moody led morning prayer meetings but was not too impressed with the quality of singing at the convention. When he asked the unknown Sankey to vocally start something new, he immediately recognized Sankey's great vocal gift. A powerful partnership began that was to take Moody and Sankey all over the world.

From these humble beginnings Sankey would sing to thousands, dressed in his well renowned, plush, smart dress-suit. Then Moody, the stocky, no-nonsense preacher, would mount the platform and speak. Their vast influence ranged from the poor, to England's Queen Victoria and America's President U.S. Grant. Their fame spread even to the Mississippi homestead of the hard working Blackwoods.

Sankey's sixty-eight years of dedicated gospel music were brim full of achievements. He popularized a new concept of gospel song. He said the new concept was "designed to awaken the apathetic, melt the cold heart and guide the honest seeker". He sang these powerful revival songs himself and became as effective a gospel communicator as his preaching associate. In his heyday untold multitudes heard Sankey's rich, inspiring voice. Songs like *The Ninety And Nine, Under His Wings, Hiding In Thee, A Shelter in the Time of Storm,* and *God be with You 'til We Meet Again* have since become well-beloved evergreen classics of hymnology.

> *In history's rich vein of sacred singers*
> *Came a soloist, faithful and true.*
> *He sang of God's deliverance and mercy,*
> *And of a land beyond the blue!*
>
> *Born in 1840 was Ira.*
> *Early he learned to sing of God's love,*

And many a cold heart was melted,
Strangely warmed by the Heavenly Dove!

Raised on his parents' homestead',
He saw God's creation close around.
There were cows to milk, barns to clean,
Crops of vegetables in the ground.

When Unionists and Confederates divided
They fought a violent civil war.
Soldier, Ira marched for the North,
And sentry duty was his chore.

A Southern sniper aimed his rifle
To put the singing sentry down.
But was captured by Ira's psalm,
And surrendered to the sound!

Ira's life was spared that starry night
To sing to noble and low,
Destined to influence England's Queen,
And many presidents, that we know!
Yes, that we know!

Always looking smart and groomed,
In a tax office Ira earned his pay,
And after leaving the army,
Became a delegate for the YMCA.

At a prayer meeting God brought to Ira,
Preacher Moody, a partner so true.
Together, they sailed the oceans
Telling lost souls of life anew.

Many hymns co-penned by this tunesmith
Spanned the pages of history.
'There Were Ninety and Nine' safely 'Under His Wings',
Plus 'Faith Is the Victory!'

At the dawn of the twentieth century,
Still singing, the half has ne're been told!
Then 'Til We Meet Again!' filled chapel rafters,
God's balladeer was finally called home.
Yes, finally called home!
Words and Music: Roger Hill / © New Music Enterprises 1999

Vast audiences were melted and swayed by his simple, plaintive songs. Untold numbers of highly ranked recording artists during the last one hundred years recorded the folksy, sacred songs that Sankey made famous. The multi-faceted range of artistic expression of his material is truly panoramic.

Examples range from folkie Burl Ives, to syrupy Doris Day, to soulful Candi Staton, to yodeling Slim Whitman, to husky Nat King Cole, to Tex-Mex Marty Robbins, to crooning Pat Boone, to pop-charmer Cliff Richard, to the harmonious Browns, to stylish Ella Fitzgerald to Scottish folk -band-legend, Jimmy Shand...and on and on to almost infinity it seems! George Hamilton IV and Pat Boone in the nineties devoted entire albums to Sankey songs.

As Ira Sankey lay dying, Fanny Crosby wrote a final letter to her dear friend who by that time also suffered her affliction of blindness. Being his senior by several years, she said she never expected him to cross death's river before her.

" I will meet you in the morning just outside the Eastern Gate over there!" These words of hope in her beautiful, comforting letter touched the heart of the failing giant of sacred song. They were words of deep gospel music significance.

Fanny Crosby and Ira Sankey, both faithful pilgrims, were ready for the joy of that great hallelujah morning! The theme of her letter became the theme of one of the Blackwood Brothers' most memorable and beloved songs.

Sankey gave birth to many vocalizing-successors including the Blackwood Brothers. The subsequent decades saw many such performers successfully fulfil their gospel-singing or song-leading ministries usually in the evangelistic arena. This gospel music train included Charles Alexander, Homer Rodeheaver, Gypsy Smith, Cliff Barrows, and George Beverly Shea. The train was finally to usher in the arrival of the Blackwood Brothers who expanded the genre to daringly embrace the risky new concept of Christian music entertainment.

This relatively new phenomenon of white gospel music emerged essentially through the pious efforts of highly motivated, evangelistic singers of the early part of the century. This rich legacy enthused the Blackwood Brothers to sing message-music professionally.

The deeply spiritual and charismatic schoolteacher, James D. Vaughan, pioneered convention-style singing in the South. His groundbreaking quartet initially was composed of him and his three brothers. After music school, taught by E. T. Hildebrand, Vaughan practiced his songwriting to the full, going on to write hundreds of easy-on-the-ear ditties such as *I Feel Like Travelling On.*

Theologically, Vaughan was of Nazarene persuasion from a Holiness and Wesleyan background. *Gospel Chimes* was Vaughan's first published songbook embracing the shaped note techniques so users could recognize the fa-so-la or mi by reading the shape of the note on the stave.

Churches of every denomination prospered in number in the first quarter of the Twentieth Century as a result of the great revivals. With their steady growth came a hunger in lay people for new gospel songs. To meet common demand, Vaughan set up a publishing and marketing concern in Lawrenceburg, Tennessee with a network of enterprising quartets to promote the new sacred songs.

By 1912, they were selling eighty-five thousand songbooks per year and by the mid-twenties there were no less than sixteen quartets on the road.

Then Vaughan expanded into new, even more adventurous branches of activity such as radio stations, phonograph records and singing schools. Expansion came geographically too, as the organization extended into four other states including Texas.

Basically of Southern Baptist and Calvinistic theological persuasion, it was in Texas that the Stamps' gospel enterprise prospered most under the astute auspices of V.O. and Frank Stamps in the second quarter of the Twentieth Century. Later, their empire joined with the Baxter empire to form the renowned joint Stamps Baxter empire.

For many years, the Stamps Baxter quartet-style of music was slow in gaining acceptance in the South among mainstream, denominational churches. Serious-minded evangelicals were too distrustful of songs that had a beat. Some felt that the message was not deep enough, and the Pentecostal theology too emotional. Groups, who failed to sing in the strict tempo that the churches expected, were distrusted. They were also distrustful of songs when themes strayed from the well-trodden orthodox path.

The pentecostals were the first grouping to make widespread use of white Southern gospel music. Their emotional, enthusiasm-flavored worship was ideally suited to using songs with a beat. In the Twenties and Thirties, this type of music was commonly heard at All Day Sings and brush arbor meetings where enthusiastic Christians of several denominations would rally together. It was there that the young, impressionable Blackwood Brothers were introduced to this kind of engaging music.

The wholescale advent of the electronic media (including phonograph records and radio) was to explode, facilitating the expansion of gospel music. Within the time span of only one generation, gospel music eventually reached every corner of the world.

> *Come, let me sing of a wonderful love,*
> *Tender and true;*
> *Out of the heart of the Father above,*
> *Streaming to me and to you:*
> *Wonderful love*
> *Dwells in the heart of the Father above.*
>
> *Jesus, the Saviour, this gospel to tell,*
> *Joyfully came;*
> *Came with the helpless and hopeless to dwell,*
> *Sharing their sorrow and shame;*
> *Seeking the lost,*
> *Saving, redeeming at measureless cost.*
>
> *Jesus is seeking the wanderers yet;*
> *Why do they roam?*
> *Love only waits to forgive and forget;*
> *Home, weary wanderer, home!*
> *Wonderful love*
> *Dwells in the heart of the Father above.*
>
> *Come to my heart, O Thou wonderful love,*
> *Come and abide,*
> *Lifting my life, till it rises above*
> *Envy and falsehood and pride,*
> *Seeking to be*

Lowly and humble, a learner of Thee.
Robert Walmsley / Trad. arranged by Wes Davis / © New Music Enterprises 1999

Ace guitarist, Merle Travis, born in Rosewood, Kentucky, remembered how as a toddler he fell asleep in his mother's arms while the rafters rang to the sacred songs in the little country church in Ebenezer. As a child, he became enchanted with Southern Gospel music and as he told, "Many years later, I became associated with four young Southerners and their piano accompanist whose stirring renditions of many of the same gospel songs have echoed from the musical rafters of America. These young men made up the Blackwood Brothers Quartet."

Merle shared the Blackwood Brothers' admiration for the pioneer publishers who, between the World Wars, put in the hands of common folk, books with songs from James D. Vaughan, R. E. Winsett, Hartford Music, Stamps Baxter Music, and Gospel Quartet Music.

Merle observed that these prized publications contained three major types of sacred songs. "There were the sweet, solemn hymns, the beautifully repetitive spirituals, and the happy, rollicking gospel songs! The spirit of these numbers, as authentically performed by the Blackwood Brothers, inspired multitudes!"

5 CHILLING WINDS OF DEPRESSION!

The steps of a good man are ordered by the LORD:
and He delighteth in his way.
Though he fall, he shall not be utterly cast down:
for the LORD upholds him with His hand.
I have been young, and now am old;
yet have I not seen the righteous forsaken,
nor his seed begging bread.'
Psalm 37: 23-25

The seemingly lofty choice of music as a practical career was no novelty to the widespread Blackwood clan. It would appear that the twin rivers of musical ability and piety seemed to run deep in the family. As well as the three brothers and a son forming a quartet, their sister Lena also showed a promising gift of music. She had left her hometown to work in a cotton mill in Chattanooga, Tennessee where she met and married Ed Cain. They had two daughters who, together with their mother, formed a fine trio that sang in country churches all over the South.

Earlier still, just around the turn of the Twentieth Century, Mr. Blackwood Senior and Aunt Nola had played hillbilly fiddles in the Blackwood String Band. Tales of past family successes spurred on the adventurous exploits of the fledgling Blackwood Brothers Quartet.

"But I am poor... let thy salvation, O God, set me up on high. I will praise the name of God with a song, and will magnify him with thanksgiving" Psalm 69:29-30

The chilling winds of economic depression started to blow strongly across the continent. It forced every family to resourcefully adapt to the pragmatic realities of unemployment.

In 1934 Roy moved back to his impoverished hometown. Hopeful of success, the three brothers, along with Roy's son, R.W. (who was three years younger than James), banded together and decided to hit the road. They now proudly called themselves The Blackwood Brothers Quartet.

Carried along by their youthful enthusiasm and evangelistic fervor, they proudly had their first photograph taken as a music group in the front yard of their Aunt Nola Gladney's home in Eupora, Mississippi. Uncomfortably they stood in a line before the camera; Roy aged thirty-four, R.W. aged thirteen, James aged sixteen, and Doyle aged twenty.

"For heaven's sake, why don't you boys smile? This is a photo shoot not a firing squad!'" the frustrated photographer exclaimed cheerfully to the three excited, nervous boys who were unused to photography, or to so much attention. In contrast, Roy with seventeen years experience as an evangelist knew exactly what was expected of him.

Growing in confidence, one morning the Blackwood Brothers Quartet decided they would try and find out where their local radio station was!

"Hey, you guys let's track down our local radio station!" R.W. declared to the assembled group as they lounged around aimlessly on the front porch in the early morning sun. "Who knows they may be looking for a singing group just like us!"

The excitement in his eyes was contagious. The seemingly naive plan was to simply pay the station a visit with the exalted view of getting on the air. They found it all right! The grandiose radio station was in an old house! To their amazement, they discovered one lone person operating the whole thing: engineering, announcing, answering the telephones and emptying the trash!

With a high degree of nervousness, they boastfully told Mr. Radioman that they were a new quartet and wanted the opportunity to broadcast on the radio. They explained to the gentleman how they performed live singing and had their own instrumentation that was gaining great local support and acclaim.

"Please Sir, put us on air, and we'll tell all our friends, kin folks, and neighbours to tune in!" James pleaded with a great sense of nervous bravado. "That'll sure increase your audience, Sir...You just can't fail! We promise you!"

Their forwardness was surprisingly and immediately rewarded. Mr. Radioman pondered the proposal for a few seconds then announced, "Okay, boys...eh...well...You're on!"

He spoke hesitantly but with a helpful smile. Then, to their great delight, he readily agreed to give them fifteen minutes of prized airtime.

Audience feedback took no time at all! As soon as the boys started singing on the air, the station phone began to ring persistently with enthusiastic listeners requesting sacred songs and family dedications.

The public in the radio's listening area was clearly delighted and enthusiastically responded. They volunteered favorable comments on the Blackwood singing style, especially the harmonies and clear message.

Even after the first fifteen minutes of precious airtime were up, the overworked phone still rang and rang. Spontaneously, the old-man-in-charge motioned to the beaming boys to carry on with their singing. This went on for a full hour and fifteen minutes!

Mr. Radioman, the owner of the station, had taken a big chance but was naturally delighted at this unprecedented response. He asked the youthful group to return every Sunday morning and sing for thirty minutes. Happy to oblige, the Blackwood Brothers fulfilled that commitment for several months.

James replied on behalf of the group, "We sure are mighty grateful to you, Sir!" He was beaming from ear to ear. "We'll be here every week on time. We won't let you down!"

Thus indeed, the Blackwood Brothers' had their first radio broadcast on radio station WHEF in Kosciusko, Mississippi. Despite the overnight radio success, the ambitious boys knew that as a vocal team they had to further hone their talents to achieve greater impact. With their youthful minds focused and fixed on the discipline required to succeed, the harmony group developed a novel way of practicing their songs. Securing a weekday contract to cut timber for a local sawmill, they would practice their weekend concert skills while cutting timber! Like the comical seven dwarfs from Walt Disney's classic, movie-cartoon the Blackwood Brothers would sing as they toiled.

"We would saw a tree down," James laughingly recalled, "and while cutting the tree into logs, we would be rehearsing the songs for our concerts over and over again. Hi ho! Hi ho! And off to work we go."

Those far away, springtime years of long days and hard work were easy to bear, flavored with good-natured humor and camaraderie. Even the trials of life could be met with a smile.

Their humble mode of transport in those early days was Roy's '29 Chevrolet. It often would stubbornly refuse to start! Like a scene from a Laurel and Hardy silent-movie, they had to park it on a hill and push it off to start it! Then once it gained momentum, the difficulties were just beginning as the brakes did not work either! Roy would have to use the gears to slow the bumping vehicle to a halt.

One never-to-be-forgotten day, to the frightened passengers surprise and dismay, a wildly kicking mule bolted out into the narrow, dusty road in front of the smoking Chevrolet.

"Watch out! Watch out! Don't hit that critter!" The red-faced, wide-eyed James shouted in absolute panic!

Puffing out his cheeks, Roy broke into a fevered sweat, franticly shifted to second gear, then to first gear. It looked as if they were still going to hit the mule, foursquare!

Somehow, the impossible happened! He got the cranky old banger into reverse and they miraculously missed the bemused creature! As it scampered away, they gasped with relief as Roy wiped the perspiration away with the dirty hanky he pulled from his pocket.

In those young, carefree days every day was a joy and every new venture, it seemed, was fun!

The first talent competition that the ambitious Blackwood Brothers entered was a singing contest at the Union School near their country home. With high expectations, they entered both the quartet section and the duet section. To their absolute delight they surprisingly went on to win both of them!

Their unpretentious, though practical, prize turned out to be a twenty-four pound sack of flour, a bucket of lard, plus other groceries! After all, what use was a silver cup in the depths of economic depression?

In the exciting decades of hard work that followed, they gained more than their fair share of gold and silver awards!

Gaining in confidence, the always-ambitious boys began to think about radical new ways of launching their concerts in new communities. One such bright idea was the purchase of a public-address system. It was comical looking and passers-by stared in amused unbelief at the clumsy horns that were mounted on the roof of the car.

Driving around the community in their old banger during the afternoon of the concert, the boys rudely sounded their car horn and PA system as loudly as they could! Thus, they announced for all and sundry that they would be there for a concert in their community that night. It was a wake-up message that no one in the sleepy community could avoid!

This loud and disturbing method proved to be most effective. Indeed, on one memorable occasion, they scared a local farmer of great piety. He happened to be diligently ploughing his field, out of sight, as the Blackwood Brothers noisily drove past. Startled, he dropped his heavy plough, and dashed home to his dear, apron-clad wife, busying herself over the kitchen stove!

"Honey, honey! Come quick! Today must be the day!" He excitedly announced to her utter amazement the earth-shaking news awaited for twenty centuries! "Today must be the day! It must be the end of the world! I just heard the Archangel Gabriel blowing his horn for the last trump!"

In those carefree, youthful years most of the Blackwood Brothers' bookings were arranged through the radio announcements at WHEF. In surrounding churches they would be modestly paid with a love offering, and in schools they would charge the princely sum of five cents for children and ten cents for adults! Humble though the ministry may have appeared, their message in song gave an almost tangible hope and inspiration during the dark days of economic depression.

For a few months, the evangelistically inspired group decided to try a new door by moving to Jackson, the capital of the state of Mississippi. Coming up in the calendar, they knew was the prestigiously important Mississippi State Singing Convention held in the Armory building. Always keen to see new horizons, they applied, were accepted, and duly went there to sing. It was there that they had their first glimpse of a professional gospel quartet performing in concert. The Frank Stamps All-Star Quartet was at its proficient best and the wide-eyed boys were thrilled at actually being able to meet their famous hero-performers. Appreciation was mutual between the Stamps and Blackwoods Quartets.

Frank Stamps enjoyed what he heard of the Blackwood Brothers' performance that day. Indeed, he was so impressed that he astutely telephoned his brother V.O. Stamps. "Hey, there's a quartet of young men at the convention that is real good! You ought to contact them and get them to represent the Stamps-Baxter Music Company!" He did and there began an association with that company that was to last for many years.

Following their celebrated appearance at the convention, the Blackwood Brothers visited WJDX, the largest radio station in Jackson. They bravely announced that they would be willing to produce a daily fifteen-minute program on the station. The hardened management's response was cool, as they did not think there would be much of a public demand for a radio show that consisted entirely of all gospel songs.

On the station at that time was the colorful Country and Western singer, Tommy Gentry who hosted a program very early each morning. He heard about the Blackwood Brothers' growing fame and request for radio opportunities.

"If you will move to Jackson, you can sing a song on my program each morning!" Tommy Gentry grinned and spoke enthusiastically as he gestured invitingly to the boys with his hands. "Why not re-locate? I will also let you announce that you are open for engagements and you can promote any bookings you get!"

The grateful Blackwoods gladly took him up on his generous offer, getting up at the crack of dawn each morning to appear on the show. It was an early start and, as if to emphasize the point, Gentry had a bantam rooster that perched on his shoulder as he broadcast. Occasionally the rooster would loudly crow while on the air, a gimmick that earned him many early morning listeners.

It was not long before the well-disciplined, early-rising Blackwood Brothers were getting more mail from listeners than was the Gentry show. The observant management finally relented and decided to give the gospel boys fifteen minutes of airtime each morning following Tommy Gentry.

The station still was not happy with it being an all gospel show and insisted that they include secular songs in their repertoire as well. With some reluctance, the boys started to include such songs as Stout Hearted Men and Blue Hawaii.

The gospel songs proved, however, to be so popular with the growing band of dedicated listeners that the secular-minded management was forced to reconsider. After much deliberation they allowed them to do an all gospel show.

Life was fun but times were still hard! Lodgings while in Jackson were in a little, modest hotel on Capitol Street called The King Hotel. There was, however, nothing royal about it at the time. There they rented two rooms. Roy and his wife and young son, Cecil lived in one of them, Doyle, R.W., and James lived in the other. Rest was often difficult.

Beneath *the King* there was a little, well subscribed cafe located right under the Blackwood rooms. The eating facility also boasted a very loud jukebox! Customers munched their sandwiches to the deep, manly tones of Ernest TuBlackwood Brothers, Walking the Floor Over You. Day after day, the Texas Troubadours hit single blasted out its honky tonk lament and bass beat from the brightly-lit jukebox! As it was immensely popular at the time, it seemed to the-keen-to-rest, hotel guests that it was being played continuously day and night!

Money for even the barest of meals was sometimes hard to come by. The boys existed for a long time on five-cent hamburgers from a Krystal Hamburger place across the street from the King. Down the street from the radio station was the Echo Cafe. The helpful, sympathetic manager was a keen fan of their program.

"Boys! I never miss your great show!" He spoke with genuine warmth and pleasure. The assembled group had clearly made a favorable impression. "Your gospel songs early in the morning set me up real good! So, I wanna give you guys a special deal! Be sure to come down every morning, after your radio show.... I'll have the best breakfast you've ever had cookin' for you...and I'll only charge you fifteen cents each!"

What a blessing that offer proved to be! That welcome daily meal consisted of one egg, two strips of bacon, toast and coffee. The always-hungry quartet ate there, with great relish, whenever they could afford it!

By this time, their old '35 Ford had been driven into the ground until it would not run anymore! Furthermore, they could not keep up the payments so the finance company came and repossessed it.

They were now left without any visible means of transport to get them to their mounting engagements. As they were bemoaning this fact among themselves one morning at the radio station, one of the engineers overheard them.

The friendly, compassionate engineer spoke up with a helpful tone in his voice. "Say, guys...Do you need someone to co-sign with you at the bank to get another car?"

"We sure do," they replied almost in unison.

"Well, I have plenty of good credit and I will co-sign with you!"

It seemed to the boys as if their prayers had been answered. With the borrowed money, they bought a second hand '38 two door Ford that was thankfully reliable. They were back in business again!

6 COURTSHIPS AND BROADCASTS

My beloved spake, and said unto me,
Rise up, my love, my fair one, and come away.
For, lo, the winter is past, the rain is over and gone;
The flowers appear on the earth;
> *the time of the singing of birds is come,*
> *and the voice of the turtle is heard in our land;*
The fig tree puts forth her green figs,
> *and the vines with the tender grape give a good smell.*
> *Arise, my love, my fair one, and come away.*
Song of Solomon 2:10-13

The songbirds sang sweetly, the flowers bloomed colorfully amid lush, verdant greenery, and the warm sun shone brightly in the clear blue sky. About this time, in this carefree, idyllic setting, sweet romances began to beckon and blossom.

One sunshiny day, the Blackwood Brothers were booked to appear at an All Day Sing and Dinner On The Grounds. The beautiful setting was a little village called Weathersby that was about thirty-five miles from Jackson.

As the ever-vigilant James sat on the old timber platform during the event, enjoying the edifying program, he could not help noticing an attractive teenage girl sitting near the aisle.

The event concluded and the beautiful object of his attention rose from her fold-up seat and entered the aisle, chatting cheerfully to her friends. Failing to attract her attention from the platform, he slyly sneaked around to the front door, down the aisle and came up behind her.

The attractive girl was clasping a well-thumbed copy of the "Glory Dawn", a Stamps-Baxter songbook. James peeked over her shoulder and happened to catch a glimpse of the young lady's name written on the top of her songbook.

I know that name! The radio...The letters...Yes, I do know that name! He mused to himself in silence, as he smiled. He had immediately recognized the name of someone who had recently written to him in care of the radio station. Using this fact as an opener, he courageously, but hesitantly, started up a small-talk conversation.

"You sure...eh...have made good...eh...use of that songbook, eh...Miss!" The opening line came from an awkward, stammering, stuttering, red-faced James. His second line was almost as clumsy.

"My... eh...copy's been used...eh... so often it's got a few pages missin'!"

James' perspiring complexion was by now fully reddened, but he continued his courageous attempt at small talk. "Did you write to me at the radio station, Miss?"

The question asked by an ever more hopeful, confident James now put the conversation into her court as he surprised her with his observation. "I recognize that name on the top of your songbook from the letter you sent in! You must be Miriam!"

Eyes met eyes in enchanted attraction. Now it was the young lady's turn to be bashful as her complexion reddened! She smiled sweetly and lowered her gaze; surprised to be chatting with the handsome, young man she had just applauded on stage!

Yes, the slightly built, beautiful girl confirmed that her name was, indeed, Miriam. Nervously, she invited him to visit her parents' house later that day. "I don't live too far away! It sure would be right nice of you if you'd come home with me to meet my Ma and Pa, James! Ma bakes real well and I know she'll make you mighty welcome!"

James could not believe his good fortune. This first date started a long-lasting romance which culminated in marriage seven months later. This loving union was consolidated over time and endured to greet the Twenty-first Century.

Not to be outdone, the other Blackwood Brothers were also actively courting young ladies. Enthusiastically they took it in turns to have the jointly owned car on nights off to see their respective girl friends. James was generally more persistent than the others. When he could not have the car on the particular night that he wanted to see his young lady, Miriam (affectionately known as Mim), he rode the Greyhound bus to see her. Love always finds a way!

Resources were scarce. He only had enough pocket money for a one way ticket and was relying on Mim's mother to feed him! On one particular occasion, he was not met at the door by the welcome smell of country home cooking. The explanation given was that Mim's mother had a headache and would not be cooking that evening. Borrowing her father's car, Mim and James drove to the nearest drive-in cafe. On the way there, James was becoming more and more agitated in his mind.

There was one worrying question that kept going over and over in his brain! "How am I gonna be able to pay for both of our meals, and still have enough money left to pay for my fare back home?'"

When the cheery, gum-chewing waitress arrived for the order, James nervously pretended he was not hungry and needed nothing to eat! Mim, of course, had no idea of James' pressing monetary crisis. She ordered herself a substantial sandwich that he was forced to watch her eat! He had barely sufficient cash to pay for her sandwich, and he secretly knew he would have to hitchhike back to Jackson.

When the ever-cheerful waitress came for the money to pay the modest bill, wide-eyed, James was amazed to hear the smiling Mim announce that she would be paying! Her dear, thoughtful mother had given her daughter enough money to pay for them both! Proverbially, James could have kicked himself as he left the cafe that night with an empty stomach!

For many years afterwards, he would think it was funny to nostalgically recount this tale in front of Mim's friends. The ticklish tale was told in jest, not to embarrass his darling. She had not realized just how poor James was! His jesting would still often solicit a tear from her even decades later.

Who can find a virtuous woman?
For her price is far above rubies.
The heart of her husband doth safely trust in her,
so that he shall have no need of spoil.
She will do him good and not evil all the days of her life.
Proverbs 31:10-12

As he was so poor, James barely managed to afford three voice-coaching lessons. His competent teacher was the colorful, Harley Lester whom James admired so much that he tried to copy his singing. Still eager to vocally progress, from then on, he tried to copy how others sang by carefully listening to professional singing on the radio. After all, it was a cheaper musical education than singing lessons!

A great opportunity arose on the day that the Blackwood Brothers were asked to sing on V.O. Stamps' radio broadcast from Dallas called "Singing Convention of the Air." Listening-in attentively while in his car was Frank Stamps and his famous quartet. He was so genuinely impressed by the Blackwood Brothers' smooth, spirited sound that he later told them that they had the best harmony he had ever heard. The encouraging compliment was received gratefully by the Blackwoods.

After the performance, he showed them around the busy plant where his well-received songbooks were printed, and also where his radio programs were recorded onto sixteen-inch acetate discs.

"You see them big, ole, fragile discs?" V. O. Stamps spoke proudly as he expanded on his rhetorical question. "Well, we get 'em sent to the radio station in Del Rio, Texas and they transmit 'em to the whole of the North American continent! Impressive, eh?"

Once again, the Blackwoods were asked to sing a sacred song on this radio program. Opportunities were now coming in fast and furiously as the boys tried new door after new door.

A few months later, while the weary group members were peacefully asleep in their modest rooms in the King Hotel, their popular radio program was broadcast over the air from Del Rio, Texas, hundreds of miles away.

The startled owner of the hotel happened to tune in just when their songs were being played. Annoyed, he muttered and wondered to himself. *How can they be in two places at once?* He hurriedly charged upstairs to rudely check if the boys were truly asleep in their rooms and had not absconded to Del Rio overnight without paying their bill!

In the dead of night, there was a thunderous banging on their hotel bedroom doors! Jumping out of bed in their nightwear, the boys were in a panic, thinking the building was on fire! Hearts racing and adrenaline pumping, suddenly the door burst open!

The red-faced, angry hotel owner stopped abruptly in his tracks when he saw them all present in the dimmed bedrooms.

"Say...How can you be here?" He asked his stupid question in shocked embarrassment.

"What do you mean? We're all here asleep!"

"But I heard you on the radio!"

Initially, the bleary-eyed boys were somewhat agitated to have been rudely aroused from their deep sleep but eventually saw the funny side of the scene! Following stunned silence, they all burst out in hysterical laughter in front of the puzzled hotelier. They then explained to the ever increasingly embarrassed man about the miracle of acetate discs!

The Blackwood Brothers' first pianist was the talented Joe Roper who was astutely deployed to them by the farsighted V. O. Stamps. He also wisely appointed the proficient, John Daniel Quartet from Alabama to represent the Stamps-Baxter songbook product just as the Blackwood Brothers were asked to do. The enterprising firm had helpfully provided the Blackwoods with a 1939 Mercury car in return for selling Stamps-Baxter song books at their ever-busier concerts. The commercial deal was for the singing group to keep the first $18.50 per man, per week. Any income over that amount was sent to the firm.

"If we don't bring in that much, we just won't make the $18.50 that week!" The always-realistic James spoke with a frown as the boys nodded in mutual understanding.

The hardworking group was constantly on the move, traveling from town to town. Soon this began to take its emotional toll on the two courting couples of Doyle and Lavez, and James and Miriam. Both the loving couples decided, after much deliberation and prayer, to become married. Shyly, James had asked Mim's doting parents about tying the knot and her dad reluctantly gave his parental permission.

"Say, James! I don't understand why you want to marry my daughter. You know she can't cook!" Her dear mother grinned as she jokingly declared her criticism of her loving daughter's household skills. She knew that James would never be dissuaded.

"'You'll finish up, my boy, skinnier than you are already...ha...ha!"

"Well, Maam,' James responded laughingly, 'Ha...ha...ha...I guess I must be in love!"

Undeterred, the lovebirds decided to marry the week after Mim graduated from high school. Doyle and James then excitedly drove to Forest, Mississippi to bring back Lavez. The journey was lengthy and wearisome so the boys were late getting back. So late, indeed, that Mim's father thought James had cold feet and had stood her up!

Reassurances given, both loving couples then traveled to Jackson to the home of a friend of theirs who was a Methodist pastor. There, in his unpretentious front parlor, they had a double wedding and left with the pastor's amusing comment ringing in their ears

"I have never performed a double wedding before! I hope this one is legal!"

That honeymoon night, the newly-weds drove to Shreveport, Louisiana. James and Doyle had paid the one-month's rent of $32 in advance for the small, two-bedroom, furnished apartments. James had bought Mim, his seventeen years old bride, a bargain, a wedding ring for $32 at $5 down and $5 a month. Incidentally, Mim still wears that ring today!

A month later, R.W. married Elaine Whitehead. Now the entire singing group was married.

Louisiana's Governor Jimmie Davis fondly remembered the Blackwoods as the first gospel group to perform and operate out of Shreveport. As he recalled, he held them (and James in particular) in high esteem.

"James Blackwood was a great person full of personality. I'd describe him as a good salesman too! He knew how to give the public what they wanted when it came to good old gospel entertainment!"

Jimmie Davis after his politicking days became a powerful force in country-gospel music, borrowing richly from his memories of the Blackwoods' repertoire.

Much of the Davis career mirrors the mythical American dream with its rags to riches theme. He was the poor farm boy who rose to become the Governor of the State of Louisiana.

Jimmie Houston Davis was born on 9th November 1902 in a small, humble shotgun cabin nestled in the red clay hills of Beach Springs, Quitman, Louisiana.

Today the cabin is a monument, but once it was a bare roof over three rooms housing a sharecropper, his spouse, eleven children and assorted relatives.

Five years after the debut of the Blackwood Brothers Quartet, in 1939, Davis captured the imagination of the depression-ridden world with You Are My Sunshine. The sing-a-long soon became a standard, selling in its millions, making it one of the world's most popular melodies ever! Throughout WWII, it was popularized by, it seems, everyone from Bing Crosby to Gene Autry to Vera Lynn!

Studying at the Louisiana College in Pineville, he achieved a Bachelor's Degree despite, he claimed, having only one shirt that he wore every day, washed every night, and ironed every morning!

Singing became a passion for the hard-working Davis as he appeared on several local radio stations. His singing in the Thirties and Forties wonderfully blended country with a form of blues-tinged Dixieland. RCA Records signed him up, which impressed Decca Records who signed him up in the mid-Thirties to a contract that lasted some forty years.

At that time, he was lured to the bright lights of the movies. He made regular appearances in small parts but a big-time Hollywood career seemed not to be his destiny. Returning to Louisiana, he hit the big-time in country music.

In 1938, he was elected Police Commissioner of Shreveport. He served for four years and was then elected to a six-year term on the Louisiana Public Service Commission. He only served for two years, resigning to run for Governor. He had successful spells in the governor's office in the forties and sixties.

In mid life, Jimmy felt an inner call to write and sing gospel music, following the path pioneered by the Blackwood Brothers, which he continued until the close of the century! Switching from country to gospel he wrote many songs, the best known of which is Someone to Care, one of the Blackwood Brothers' most requested songs.

His spouse, Alvern Adams died in 1967. They lived with their son in Baton Rouge, kept busy with a public relations business, music publishing, and a cattle and horse farm managed by Jimmy Junior.

Davis had the rare honour of being elected to both the Country Music Hall of Fame and the Gospel Music Hall of Fame. Even at the age of seventy-three he was still actively singing, recording and running again for the governor's job for the third time. Assisting in his unsuccessful attempt was his new bride, Anna Gordon, one of the original members of the Chuck Wagon Gang, founded in 1936.

Amazingly, Davis continued to sing well into his late nineties, right up to the end of the millennium!

7 *STORMY WAR CLOUDS*

Our God our help in ages past,
Our hope for years to come,
Our shelter from the stormy blast,
And our eternal home.

Under the shadow of His throne
His saints have dwelt secure;
Sufficient was His arm alone,
So our defence was sure.

Before the hills in order stood,
Or earth received her frame,
From everlasting He was God,
To endless years the same.

A thousand ages in His sight
Are like an evening gone,
Short as the watch that ends the night
Before the rising sun.

Time, like an ever-rolling stream,
Bears all its sons away;
They fly forgotten, as a dream
Dies at the opening day.
Thou God, our help in ages past,
Our hope for years to come,
Be Thou our guard while troubles last,
And our eternal home.
  Isaac Watts / Trad. arranged by Wes Davis / © New Music Enterprises 1999

The troubled mid-Thirties saw the USA steadily climbing out of the economic depression that started in the mid-Twenties. Politically, the nation was hopefully clinging to its isolationist foreign policy. Meanwhile, fearful, storm clouds of war were unavoidably gathering in Europe and the Far East that threatened to rudely disturb the New World's peace and growing prosperity!

The Blackwood Brothers' public popularity continued to grow more and more as a result of their radio broadcasts. For eighteen months (from the spring of 1939 to the high summer of 1940), they beamed out twice daily on the 50,000 watt radio station KWKH of Shreveport, Louisiana. Yet they had only unadventurously ever traveled over their Southern homelands. Other beckoning parts of the USA were uncharted virgin territory to them and their exciting new brand of entertaining Christian music. Then in the summer of 1940, the V. O.

Stamps firm telephoned them and said that they wanted them to go to Iowa.

"Iowa? Iowa? You might as well ask us 'Will you go to China?'" James loudly declared in to the caller. "We've never been out of the South, Brother! We'll have to think it over and prayer about it!"

They eventually decided to take up the offer! But the controversial decision was not unanimously accepted, however, as James remembered!

"Our pianist at the time, Wallace Milligan definitely did not want to go to Iowa. So another pianist, called Hilton Griswold, was hired to take his place."

Years later, James, remembered the great vexed debates among the group that resulted from that telephone call. Their unity was severely challenged and shaken!

Soon, the always-enterprising Blackwood Brothers were re-united in purpose and back on the radio airways as they commenced live broadcasts in Shenandoah on KMA. Doing three taxing programs a day, many local farmers listened-in and sent in bagfulls of enthusiastic mail.

"Please could you sing *On the Jericho Road* more often! It seems my dairy cows give more milk when you sing that song!"

James laughingly remembered reading that one satisfied farmer's amusing letter out-loud to the Quartet assembled around the radio mike! It provoked hilarious laughter among the group. From that moment on, until the close of the show, it was impossible for them to retain their dignified composure. R.W.'s throwaway comment did not help!

"It seems, boys, although we're aiming supposedly at spiritual enlighten-ment, our music does have other purposes!"

With three daily radio broadcasts, their listening audience increased dra-matically. The Blackwood Brothers were soon outselling all of the other Stamps' quartets combined! Their basic salary at this time was forty dollars per week, per person plus a percentage from sales of merchandise.

Former President of the Gospel Music Association, Don Butler, remem-bered how early in his life he attended a concert of gospel music by the Blackwood Brothers, who were then based in Shenandoah, Iowa.

"Now for a lad who had never known anything but the purest church music in its normal, conservative atmosphere and never, no never, had heard anyone other than a lady play the piano, this was an emotional experience!

To hear four men sing not only perfect harmony, but also with enthusiasm and if I may use the phrase, 'a flair for showmanship', was, to say the least, exhilarating and exciting. Back then, I learned to appreciate and admire the Blackwood Brothers."

One hot day in August of 1940, some weeks after the group moved to Iowa, V.O. Stamps died suddenly. His sad yet triumphant, funeral service, held at the Bethel Temple, Dallas, was packed with mourners paying their last respects. Many more, unable to get into the building, were silently standing around in the crowded streets outside.

Always busy, the tired Blackwood Brothers had been wearily driving all night to get to the funeral service on time. Arriving at their Dallas destination, they found to their surprise that they were unable to get anywhere near the flower-jeweled church because of the crowds.

Fortunately, a vigilant usher had spotted them and led them through the pressing crowd into the church pews. The specially selected choir contained many members of the various Stamps' Quartets. James recalled that all the funeral songs sung were written by V.O. Stamps except for Precious Memories. Many of those beloved sacred songs dwelt on the subject the Christian's heavenly home, the end of the weary pilgrim's journey.

And God shall wipe away all tears from their eyes;
and there shall be no more death, neither sorrow, nor crying....
And the city had no need of the sun, neither of the moon, to shine in it:
for the glory of God did lighten it, and the Lamb is the light thereof.
And the nations of them which are saved shall walk in the light of it:
and the kings of the earth do bring their glory and honor into it.
And the gates of it shall not be shut at all by day: for there shall be no night there.
And they shall bring the glory and honor of the nations into it.
And there shall in no wise enter into it any thing that defileth,
neither whatsoever worketh abomination, or maketh a lie:
but they which are written in the Lamb's book of life.
Revelation 21: 4, 23-27

The influential V.O. Stamps was soon replaced in the busy office, by his just as influential, brother, Frank Stamps. Vocally, Harley Lester was hurriedly recruited to replace Frank in his quartet.

At the suggestion of the efficient-minded Frank, the Blackwood Brothers' photograph emblazoned the impactive front cover of the *Stamps Baxter News* as they had won the most recent book subscription contest. This bright, influential, monthly publication was also offered free to listeners on the Blackwoods' radio program for two weeks. To the boys' delight, no less than ten thousand cards and letters came pouring into the busy radio office requesting the prized booklet!

The pleased radio station bosses estimated from that mail response that a million people were regularly listening to the Blackwood Brothers' program every day in twenty-seven states and three Canadian provinces! Such a huge, written response reflected the boys' increased audiences at their concerts wherever they went. The evangelistic proclamation via the Blackwood Brothers was being broadcast far and wide!

At the end of a busy day, in a quiet moment, James leafed through his Bible and stumbled upon a familiar passage of scripture. It was in the last chapter of the book written by the tax collector, Matthew.

And Jesus came and spake unto them, saying,
'All power is given unto me in heaven and in earth.
Go ye therefore, and teach all nations, baptizing them
in the name of the Father, and of the Son, and of the Holy Ghost.
Teaching them to observe all things whatsoever I have commanded you:
and, lo, I am with you alway, even unto the end of the world!'

To some, it did seem that the end of the world was at hand! On the frightful world front, the thunder and lightning of global war had broken-out in Europe, rudely disturbing the calm of an otherwise peaceful Sunday morning.

That same fateful afternoon, as the tired group was wearily winding their way home from a well attended concert, they heard the dreadful announcement on the radio that Hawaii's Pearl Harbor was bombed that morning by Japanese airplanes. It was followed by President Roosevelt's declaration of war. It was an earth-shaking catastrophe that sent shock waves around the world. It was to affect every aspect of life, as the Blackwood Brothers were to soon to discover.

Humble yourselves therefore under the mighty hand of God,
that he may exalt you in due time:
Casting all your care upon him; for he careth for you.
1 Peter 5:7

Their increasingly popular, radio programs of gospel singing continued for a time but soon the full effects of the War and the unavoidable duties it imposed upon all citizens began to take its effect. R.W. and James nervously expected that they were most likely to be the first in the group to be drafted for military service.

With a heavy heart, they broadcast their final radio show. Their numbers were songs of hope and cheer designed to lift the worries of the many homes deprived of their husbands, fathers and sons.

Reluctantly, R.W. and James relocated to California on the West Coast to take work in the defense plants until the draft calls came. In equal reluctance, the difficult decision was initially made to break up the Quartet until after wartime hostilities ceased. Eventually, however, the whole of the singing group moved to California.

R.W. and James became certified Army and Navy journeyman welders and worked in the Rohr aircraft factory. Still, they ministered on weekends by singing in churches such as the San Diego Tabernacle. At the Service Men's Chapel in the San Diego Hotel, young servicemen in the surrounding area would come in off the lonely streets to listen. Many were converted to Christ in the Blackwoods' services before being shipped overseas to face the battle-fronts.

They sang the gospel message at every opportunity. That included their regular concert engagements and George Gaines's weekend God's Half Hour radio program in San Diego. They also appeared at a United Bond Rally in Pershing Square, Los Angeles, alongside an aspiring young actor by the name of Roddy McDowell and others such as Beryl Wallace, the entertainer at Earl Carroll's Hollywood nightclub. Group photos were taken with them and other movie stars alongside a beaming quartet of Roy, James, R.W., Don Smith, and pianist, Hilton Griswald.

R.W. was the first of the Blackwood Brothers to be drafted. Absent for two and a half years, he sailed east to join the Allies' fight against Japan. He saw dreadful, bloody scenes in active duty serving on the front line in Okinawa as a combat engineer.

Vocally, R. W. left a vast gap in the quartet. Doyle's health was poor in California, and he returned to Mississippi. Their places were filled on a temporary basis. Don Smith, from Texas, who was working in the local Lockheed factory, sang bass while Hilton Griswald, the pianist sang baritone.

The slightly built James received his draft papers next but was later rejected for military service. Pianist Hilton expected to be the next to be called and returned to Texas. The depleted group was now short a pianist and a baritone. God ensured that needs were met as Hilton was ably replaced by A.T. Humphries singing baritone, and A.T.'s wife, Lavera, became pianist. Cecil fondly recalled the couple.

"They were a wonderful team of husband and wife...Lavera was the first to pass away many years ago followed by her husband in the late eighties!"

World War II ensured that changes did not stop with the Humphries! Next, Roy, Susie (his wife) and their son, Cecil went back to their hometown for a few months. Roy was hurriedly replaced by Troy Chafin. Somehow, via great effort and skill throughout the duration of the War, James beavered away, managing to keep a full quartet going despite the disappointments and provocations.

Roy's replacement by Troy lasted only a few months because Roy's intention was to visit the grandparents' home in Mississippi. That done and missing the quartet, they all returned to California and Roy slipped back into the tenor role.

After the many initial defeats and the disappointments of the early years of World War II, the determined Allies steadily gained victories. The hope of peace that Christians prayed for started to dawn in people's hearts. First, a welcome victory was secured in North Africa, then in Europe, and finally, in the Far East.

After VJ Day, Roy and James, along with their immediate families (Susie and Cecil, and Mim and Jimmy), headed homeward to the sunny South, back to Mississippi. Years earlier, Hilton had already gone back home to Texas, expecting to be drafted. He eagerly awaited the quartet's peacetime reunion. James had been in touch with the station manager at KMA radio and had tentatively arranged to go back on the airways on the first day of October 1946. The line-up was Roy, James, Hilton and Don Smith.

Later, as the much missed normalities of peacetime returned, the re-united quartet thus joined together to resume gospel broadcasting in Shenandoah. When the excited singing team met up again in Iowa they began organizing gospel concerts again, firstly in Iowa, then Missouri, Nebraska, Dakota and Minnesota. The Blackwood Brothers' fame was gradually being re-established not least via the radio medium. Fortunately, R.W. was then discharged from the military service and joyfully rejoined the delighted group. Their large listening audiences on the radio continued to grow year after year.

Doyle Blackwood had at this time moved to Chattanooga, Tennessee to become the chief announcer at radio station WDOD and became music director at his lively church. He had reluctantly left the Blackwood Brothers due to his increasing physical difficulties made more acute by constant travel.

The pressures of constant work and travel took their toll. Retaining a viable team became increasingly difficult for organizer, James. After a year, with heavy hearts, Don Smith and his wife Peggy moved back home to California. That left the disheartened group without a bass singer.

Finally, however, the Blackwood Brothers secured the mellow, bass services of Bill Lyles, previously of the Swanee River Boys who were based in Atlanta. A tall, handsome individual with a shy, winsome smile, he was to remain an important part of the quartet until his untimely death in 1954.

Touring constantly in the vast Mid-West, the Blackwood Brothers enjoyed record numbers of crowds at all their evangelistic concerts. Bookings could barely keep pace with demand and, at one point, they were forced to have two quartets touring at the same time! Cat Freeman (Vestal Goodman's brother), R.W., Bill Lyles, Hilton Griswold and James Blackwood formed one group. Then Roy Blackwood, Doyle Blackwood, Johnny Dickson, Warren Holmes with Billy Gewin on piano formed the second group. Ken Apple later replaced Billy Gewin. Calvin Newton later also sang tenor with them but only stayed a short while. They drafted Cat Freeman in for a while but he became sickly so Roy substituted for several months followed by Alden Toney. Decades later, Cecil recalled why his father decided to call it a day as far as travel was concerned!

"Firstly, my Daddy (Roy) wanted to leave the quartet because he felt that he was getting too old. Secondly, he wanted to be involved with the record business in Tennessee. So, the quartet replaced him and acquired Aldon Toney from Detroit, Michigan. Dan Huskey later replaced Aldon."

Changes in vocal and instrumental personnel became an agonizing, ongoing issue to be unavoidably dealt with. Demand for more appearances, however, thankfully increased at this time. The boys were now being heard on no less than three programs every day on KMA radio. Based in Iowa, the Blackwood Brothers' success was riding on the crest of a wave and they were seeing great blessings from their ministry in song!

8 BACK TO THE BIBLE BELT

We are always looking for something that is genuine! No matter what the occasion or circumstance, we want something that's real! When it comes to gospel music, the Blackwood Brothers have always been, and still are, the standard for genuine Southern Gospel Music.
Phil Johnson

With dearly beloved, aging parents, all the boys felt the responsible call of love and duty imposing itself on the group's priorities.

For instance, with the Blackwood Brothers Quartet still based in Iowa, it was becoming increasingly difficult for James and Roy to visit their chronically sick father (Emmitt) and their concerned mother (Carrie) in far-off Mississippi. Added to that was the unavoidable fact that the long winters in Iowa were so extreme that daily travelling was regularly difficult.

> 'Honor thy father and thy mother:
> that thy days may be long upon the land
> which the LORD thy God giveth thee!'
> Exodus 20:12

After much prayer and great thought, the important decision was finally taken to move back down South in the warm spring of 1950.

"Where should we locate ourselves?...In Louisville, Kentucky or Memphis, Tennessee?" That was the question on the main agenda.

A respected individual in the group renowned for his keen spiritual insight, Hilton Griswold had felt the divine call to the pastoral ministry by this time. So, reluctantly, he did not join the Blackwood Brothers on this move down South. James was now faced with the unenviable task of finding a replacement pianist to fill Hilton's shoes!

"Hilton's sure gonna be a hard act to follow!" His expression was serious as he spoke to the boys around the supper table following the evening concert. They knew that quality pianists were few and far between. There was only one viable option which James knew.

"Let's pray for God's replacement!"

He then anxiously telephoned gospel music dignitaries, far and wide including Hovie Lister and Urias LeFevre and sought their advice. They both highly recommended the talented Jack Marshall who at that time was pianist for The Spivey's in Jacksonville, Florida. James, full of hope, telephoned him and after a satisfying conversation decided to hire him on the spot without even hearing him!

Little Jackie Marshall was known by everyone in the business for his flamboyant, Liberace-style piano playing. James remembered meeting him at the train station and the thoughts that went through his mind about his new recruit! *What have I got myself into? This Jackie Marshall sure does not look like much!*

His small stature and initially unimpressive demeanor was deceiving. Jackie Marshall quickly proved himself to be an outstanding pianist with an exciting, musical style. His confidence on the keyboard did not, however, transfer itself to his driving abilities! This proved to be a drawback for him, as sharing the driving with other group members for many hours at a time showed.

"I think Jackie started imagining that the Highway Patrol was after him!" James recalled with a grin, "It's true, we did drive cars pretty fast during the early morning hours, trying to meet our tight schedules! But Jackie thought the police were after him whether they were or not!"

Marshall's reluctance to speed-up slowed travel. It became a matter of joviality and well-stretched, tall stories. According to Cecil, the pianist's fear of the police lasted for seven years.

During that memorable, hot summer of 1950, the ever-busy Blackwood Brothers secured a prized, prime engagement in sunny Memphis. There, in that musical environment, the hard-working James met with the influential station director of radio station WMPS who promptly offered the boys a regular gospel spot on the High Noon Roundup. This specific invitation was the fleece that prompted the final decision to opt for Memphis as the home base.

It was time for the now famous group to again be based in the sunny South. The enterprising group was running a successful record shop and mail order business which they also moved to the new base city of Memphis. The music merchandising business was administered by Roy, Doyle and the diligent Carolyn Larson who was to work with them until her untimely death.

As the nation's mid-point, Memphis was already somewhat famous for its Christian music activity, located as it was in the buckle of the Bible Belt. The Blackwood Brothers were guaranteed adequate pay by the radio station. Milton Buhler, of *Buhler Mills* that produced *Dixie Lily Flour*, was their commercial sponsor throughout the early 1950's. *Dixie Lily's* mill was in Kansas but the helpful Buhler, who was the advertising executive for the company, conveniently lived in Memphis.

Before the arrival of the Blackwood Brothers, Memphis was renowned for many years for its cotton, its Mississippi River and its Beale Street. Since the group's relocation it has become a recognized cauldron of gospel music activity.

The quartet's already large radio audiences grew year after year. Even youngsters, like the poor eight years old, country boy from Arkansas named Johnny Cash, were becoming devoted fans of the Blackwood Brothers. Remembering back decades later, the aging country superstar was quick to point out how much spiritual direction he received via the musical radio messages of the Blackwoods in "those good old days when times were bad."

James holds the Man in Black in high esteem, as he observed with great conviction. "If any person could once be described as 'a diamond in the rough', my friend, Johnny Cash, would surely fit the bill! The years have honed him into a beautiful jewel of God's grace!"

Born on a cold, damp day at the end of February 1932 in Kingsland, Arkansas, Cash knew severe hardship from the start!

The Blackwoods hit the road in 1934 as the Great Depression was sweeping across America, taking its dreadful toll from people in all walks of life. Yet, from the depths of despair faith arose in the hearts of those who looked heavenward!

Ray and Carrie Cash, Johnny's poor, sharecropper-parents, found themselves in dire, economic plight. So Ray adventurously decided in that bitter winter of 1935 to take up President Roosevelt's New Deal offer. Twenty acres of scrubland, a house, a barn, and a mule were on offer. Thus the family set off for the Dyess Colony of Arkansas. There young Johnny learned the real meaning of hard work and family tragedy! The sad and painful loss of his dear, older brother, Jack, shook his security to the core!

In the midst of his family struggle, at the young age of twelve, Johnny opened his tender heart to Christ, came to personal faith, and experienced a deep-seated inner power and conviction. That faith was to be his abiding refuge and strength throughout his life!

Life was still tough! He picked cotton, sometimes picking as much as three hundred and fifty pounds a day that he dragged along behind him in a nine-foot sack. He made extra money by hauling five-gallon water jugs to the prisoners of the work gangs deployed on the banks of the Tyronza River.

They kept him running as fast as he could! While he was getting the water, he would slip in the workers' cars, turn on the radios and listen to the country songs! Music was the joy of his rough life! He thrilled to the country sounds of the Grand Ole Opry but nothing touched his heart as much as gospel music. He surrounded himself with the sound of the music of the Blackwood Brothers and others. Without doubt, gospel became his favourite kind of music, his inspiration and his encouragement. Its message slowly refined the diamond in the rough into a jewel.

At the age of eighteen and at the height of the tensions of the Cold War, Johnny was drafted away from his beloved Southland into the United States Air Force. Always a leader, he rose to the rank of staff sergeant. Cold War service-life broadened his horizons as he saw the harsh life of Europe recovering from war-weary years of conflict.

Leaving the Air Force in 1955, his deep desire was to fulfil his musical talents in a professional career in show business. Motivated by the Blackwoods' pattern, he auditioned for a person in Memphis telling him that he was a gospel singer! That did not go down too well, and he was asked to sing some country songs as well as his self-penned gospel song, *Belshazzar*!

Eventually, he secured a prized record-contract on the now legendary Sun Records label along with other all time greats from the same era. Elvis Presley, Roy Orbison, Jerry Lee Lewis, Charlie Rich, Conway Twitty, and Carl Perkins became life-long buddies. All in some way had been inspired by the gospel music of the Blackwood Brothers.

Cash's stage attire was to be predominantly black. He said his dark clothing was indicative of the sad, social causes that his songs would be crusading for!

His exciting first release, the plaintive, *Cry, Cry, Cry,* initially sold one hundred thousand copies and set the Man In Black on his way! He had a million seller with his third release, in 1956, called *I Walk the Line,* followed by *Ballad of A Teenage Queen* that finally bought him international recognition.

The public loved his songs because there was realism in them. His ballads mirrored true human emotions. Johnny's road in life was not always an easy road, and his songs often reflected his own personal battles with the temptations of the world. Songs about blood, sweat, tears...cars and trains... cowboys and Indians...booze...prison!

In summary, his songs were songs of life!

Each battle won helped fashion this diamond in the rough into a jewel. Life in the sometimes tough crucible of human emotions and experience became a growing discovery of how Christ's grace can transform trials into triumphs!

Cash's boyhood conversion, despite the meandering roads he followed, was always a spiritual rock! His faith in God inspired him to pen many great gospel songs such as *When He Comes,* often sung by his friend George Beverly Shea in the memorable Billy Graham mission meetings.

Johnny Cash was always a beloved folk-singer of the highest order. When he wrapped his tortured voice around the lyrics of any song, one knew that every last syllable was steeped in sincerity. He once stated emphatically that he did not hold any strong political views and was never called to be a preacher. But James testified that the Man in Black did the job he was cut out to do!

Yes, Johnny Cash saw (and heard) the Light via the Blackwoods Brothers' witness. As the years rolled on, the diamond in the rough was refined and transformed steadily into a translucent diamond of God's grace!

Frequent visitors in the Blackwood Brothers' WMPS studio audience were the unknown Tammy Wynette (then a fifth grader, and later a telephone company employee), and a young truck driver from Tupelo Mississippi, with the strange name of Elvis Presley!

The knock-on impact that the Blackwoods' style and showmanship un-doubtedly would have on the future course of popular and country music is often underrated. Both Wynette and Presley, of course, rose to dazzling heights of achievements in their respective fields. By 1998, both were deceased and yet the Blackwood name continued in great esteem via James, the family's long surviving patriarch, and Cecil with his on-going group. Incredibly, as the Third Millennium dawned, Cecil was fast heading for his fifty years Golden Jubilee.

Changes in the Blackwood Brothers' personnel still persisted, no matter how hard James tried to maintain the status quo. The likable Alden Toney went back north to Detroit. Dan Huskey who served the quartet faithfully until 1952 hurriedly replaced him. He was to be on the first historic recordings that the Blackwood Brothers were to wax for RCA *Victor* after they signed that prized recording contract in 1951. Bill Shaw then replaced Dan and served twenty-one years with the quartet. Pat Hoffmaster followed him when the group was James, Cecil and Ken Turner.

After twenty years (1934 to 1954), in the forefront of the gospel music media, despite the passage of time and changes of personnel the Blackwood Brothers endeared themselves to the hearts of millions of Americans. Their popularity was demonstrated by an experience that James had during a severe winter.

Lost and caught in a snowstorm in a very sparsely populated, rural area, he struggled through the snowdrifts to a lonely farmhouse. Knocking at the door, the stranger from out of the night patiently waited for ten minutes for the door to be answered. But there was no response.

"Is anyone in there! Our car has broken down! Please can I use ya phone!" he shouted out as loudly as he dared, knowing the lateness of the hour. By this time, he was very cold, wet and discouraged. In a matter of seconds, the door was widely swung-open by the farmer's wife who greeted him warmly.

"Why I recognize that voice!" her booming exclamation echoed around the deserted farmhouse courtyard. "You must be one of them Blackwood Brothers! We listen to you guys every week on the radio! You're mighty welcome! Come on in!"

Clearly, to James' delight, the group's fame had proceeded them on this occasion.

9   THE GOSPEL TRAIN

Be strong in the grace that is in Christ Jesus
and the things that thou hast heard of me...
the same commit thou to faithful men,
who shall be able to teach others also.
Thou therefore endure hardness,
as a good soldier of Jesus Christ
II Timothy 2:1-3

The now legendary RCA producer, Steve Sholes was responsible for bringing an impressive, diverse range of talent to his label during the forties and fifties. The much loved and long lasting talent ranged from Hank Snow to Eddy Arnold to George Beverly Shea to Chet Atkins to Elvis Presley, among others.

In 1951, aware of the Blackwood Brothers' fame and potential, he contacted James Blackwood saying that he would like to sign up the Blackwood Brothers. Never had Christian performers been offered such an inviting opportunity from secular origins.

Since peace was re-established in 1946, the boys had been modestly minting custom recordings for their own labels, a practice then almost unique in the gospel music field. A few gospel groups were producing their own records but none of them were on secular labels. The Blackwoods' enterprises on vinyl 78's were very successful as they advertised in the nationally published *Christian Herald* and *Sunday School Times* to attract mail order sales. This built up a valuable mail order list of gospel music enthusiasts from across North America.

Consequently, James refused an exclusive contract with RCA; he wanted to keep the right to retain the group's own custom recordings. To everyone's amazement, even James', RCA conceded accordingly! It was a unique pact likely never to be repeated again in history.

James had surprisingly been able to retain the Blackwood Brothers' evangelistic vision and ministerial objectivity while at the same time being able to maximize the group's potential in the secular marketplace! The specific deal was that no duplication of songs should occur on the custom material and the RCA material. Song repertoires for the two sets of releases were to be carefully segregated.

But seek ye first the kingdom of God, and His righteousness;
and all these things shall added unto you.
Take therefore no thought for the morrow:
for the morrow shall take thought for be the things of itself.
Sufficient unto the day is the evil thereof.
Matthew 6:33-34

The RCA Victor pact was not only a major boost to the Blackwood Brothers' career but also for Christian music as a whole! It gave positive, evangelistic exposure to the whole of the American nation and beyond via the RCA marketing network. An astute businessman, James kept a cool head in discussions with the legendary, RCA Victor kingpin, Steve Sholes who wanted to sign-up the Blackwood Brothers.

Not overwhelmed, James did more than secure a prestigious recording contract. He also signed a distributor deal with Sholes for an RCA gospel product while amazingly retaining the right to continue the Blackwood Brothers' custom record label.

The non-exclusive, initial, five-year recording contract in 1951 with RCA Victor soon produced the world's first-ever, full-length, gospel album (12 inch long-play) which was also the Blackwood Brothers' second album. Their first album was a ten-inch release.

It was a dream come true for the boys! In the early days the RCA gospel train followed Bev Shea, the Statesmen, the Speers, Stuart Hamblen, Tony Fontane, Jack Holcomb, Cliff Barrows, the Billy Graham Choirs plus Eddy Arnold, Hank Snow, Connie Smith, Skeeter Davis, Hank Locklin, the Browns, Porter Wagoner, Floyd Cramer, Jerome Hines, Kate Smith, Dottie West, Bobby Bare, Wendy Bagwell, Perry Como, Elvis Presley, Jake Hess, and many, many more. But the Blackwood Brothers were the first!

The Blackwoods first ten-inch LP album entitled *Favorite Gospel Songs and Spirituals* was recorded in Atlanta in 1952 on the bright, crispy morning of the fourth day of January.

These first historic RCA waxings were laid down with the personnel line up for the group as Dan Huskey (first tenor), James Blackwood (second tenor), R.W. Blackwood (baritone), Bill Lyles (bass), and Jackie Marshall (piano). They recorded with the best equipment of the day, yet compared to modern day equipment, it was basic.

Steve Sholes presided in the little studio that was backstage and upstairs in the Fox Theatre in Atlanta, Georgia. The ten-inch album boasted eight songs, the arrangements of which were perfected before the session. The producer, Sholes was merely there, James remembered, to monitor the accuracy of pitch and tempo. It was the Blackwood Brothers who drew up the song-agenda. In 1999, the ten-inch classic album was favored with a placement on the wall of the Grammy Hall of Fame.

In 1955 came the revolutionary introduction of twelve-inch LPs. The Blackwood Brothers' *Hymn Sing* was the world's very first LP gospel album. It featured James, Cecil, J.D., Bill and Jackie. This twelve-inch release preceded the ten-inch LP entitled *Favorite Gospel Songs and Spirituals*. With the introduction of twelve-inch LPs, that first ten-inch LP was re-issued in 1955 on twelve-inch with an additional four tracks from single releases featuring Bill Shaw in lieu of Dan Huskey.

Cecil recalled the confusion its twelve-inch sleeve caused, "The twelve-inch cover photograph displayed the latter-1954, after-the-crash line-up that was somewhat misleading. It showed Bill, J.D., James and me but most of the recordings actually featured the pre-crash line-up that included my brother, R.W.!"

Throughout the lengthy recording career of the Blackwood Brothers, James was to remain firmly in charge of song selection. But he said he was open to suggestions on a democratic basis from the rest of the group or from RCA officials, always retaining the power of veto.

Down the years, the Christian influences that were brought to bear on RCA bossman, Steve Sholes were considerable in view of the line-up of Christian artists that he signed up. The tough-talking businessman was a fine musician in his own right. Initially, he merely saw the sanctified talent as a "good meal ticket"!

Sholes prime task was to ensure that RCA made acceptable profits after paying musicians, vocalists, arrangers, and songwriters! Many years after signing the Blackwood Brothers, George Beverly Shea enjoyed recounting the event when, at a Billy Graham meeting in Pittsburgh, he was informed that Sholes had responded to the evangelist's call. It had taken many years for the gospel seeds to germinate.

Later in New York, Bev attended a celebration in honor of Steve's twenty-five years in the industry, that the National Association Of Recording Arts And Sciences organized. Next day in Steve's office, Steve commented favorably on Bev's soulful version of Fanny Crosby's *Safe in the Arms of Jesus,* just produced. Radiantly smiling, Steve indicated to his pleased friend that the lyrics reminded him that he personally was now safe in the fold!

Bev remembers well his mixed feelings when he heard of the death of Steve Sholes. "I received the cable in Sydney, during the Australian Crusade, which told me of Steve's passing. Surely, I thought, remembering the day in his office, Steve Sholes is indeed, safe in the arms of Jesus!"

The Blackwoods' astute, repertoire choice (on that fourth day of the New Year, 1952) was diverse and challenging. Without doubt, the ditty, *Rock A Soul* was early rock and roll. Despite the rhythm, bounce and sellability of the commercial sound, there was no conscious effort in those days, according to James, for the Blackwoods to attempt to impact what was then known as the hit parade. With hindsight that now seems surprising!

They recorded a plaintive, death-song that was destined to become a classic. *I Won't Have to Cross Jordan Alone.* Thomas Ramsey and Charles Durham for the **Stamps Baxter** Company originally copyrighted it in 1934. The Blackwoods had initially, during the forties, featured Hilton Griswald, their pianist, doing a vocal solo but this RCA version was recorded in moving quartet harmony.

Their hauntingly beautiful, sacred song, *The Love of God* was different from the same title that George Beverly Shea was popularizing into an evergreen. The Blackwoods' item was written by relative newcomer, Vep Ellis, a Church of God minister who also wrote *Everywhere He Went He Was Doing Good* for the Atlanta session.

Alabama-born, singing-evangelist, Vep Ellis was based in Cleveland Tennessee. Starting off at the age of fifteen, he wrote hundreds of inspired gospel songs of timeless quality.

"*The Love of God* and *Do You Know My Jesus?* were always favorites of mine!" James recalled. "It was a great joy when we sang them again on the top selling Gaither music videos in the latter Nineties!"

While attending the Lee College Bible School in Tennessee, Vep Ellis met and later married, fellow student, Pat. They parented four boys and one girl. At the height of his career, Vep Ellis wrote for the Stamps Quartet and their associates. Every year in his heyday, his church publishing company issued a new songbook which was enthusiastically well received.

In 1962 Ellis became the song leader and soloist for the renowned revival-preacher, Oral Roberts.

Roberts said of Ellis, "His songs have real spiritual depth and meaning with a direct approach to the individual , directing him to find help and hope in Christ!"

Ellis remained a close friend of James Blackwood throughout his life. They first met when James was seven years old. His family had moved from Mississippi to Chattanooga, Tennessee and Ellis' father pastored the church that the Blackwood family attended. Two years his elder Ellis took James under his protective wing.

Later in life, Ellis planted and pastored a new church in Clearwater, Florida. Sadly, his health deteriorated and after several heart attacks, he was forced to move to Tulsa. There he spent his final years under the care of his son, the minister of a local church.

Four month's after the 1952 Atlanta debut recording sessions, came another set of RCA sessions on the ninth and tenth days of May. *Take My Hand Precious Lord,* according to James, was a spiritual, primarily chosen that day for the message of the song and because it was his dear father's favorite.

Take My Hand Precious Lord was penned by Thomas Dorsey, the pastor of a lively church in Chicago. He also wrote *Peace in the Valley* that was originally published by Ben Speer who in error thought that it was in the public domain. Years later, Speer gave *Peace in the Valley* to the Blackwoods to record and it has since become a classic. The Blackwood version was loved by the impressionable, young Elvis Presley. Since the limelight that Elvis' version gave the song, it has traversed the globe!

Author of *Peace In the Valley,* Thomas M. Dorsey was born on July 1, 1899. He was raised in the poverty of rural Georgia that resented and begrudged the freedom from slavery granted to his parents following the Civil War.

When he left his deprived boyhood home he rubbed musical shoulders with some of the legendary blues and jazz artists of his day such as Bessie Smith. Morally, he struggled between such unwholesome influences and the pull of the Holy Spirit! Finally he surrendered to heaven's claim on his wayward life.

Later, as the pastor of a Chicago church, he penned *Take My Hand Precious Lord* and *Peace in the Valley,* the former song came from his heart-rending, personal experience of tragedy. Booked for a St. Louis church meeting, upon his arrival, after his long journey, he was given devastating news. Slowly and sensitively, he was told of the death of his dear wife in childbirth.

Heartbroken, he immediately drove homeward arriving only to receive another blow, the new-born baby too had died. Greatly distressed he drove aimlessly around the streets of the big city as he conceived, under divine inspiration, the now renowned prayer-in-song, *Take My Hand Precious Lord.* The composition is accepted today as standard fare with plentiful recordings available in both black and white traditions.

There were other great songs recorded that day.

The writer of *My Journey to The Sky* was the black gospel singer/songwriter, Dorothy Austin. *Wanta Rest* also came from the black gospel field although James cannot exactly recall from where.

"Back in those days," James recalled with great satisfaction, "we got many of our songs from the black gospel field. This crossover from black to white was somewhat revolutionary in a South still segregated. The Blackwoods use of this material in the late Forties was definitely something new!"

The Golden Gate Quartet, well known throughout the USA and Europe, contributed *Swing Down Chariot* to the Blackwoods' repertoire. They had a weekly radio broadcast on the CBS network that was well beloved by the Blackwoods.

"At the time, we, the Blackwoods, were living in Shenandoah doing three radio broadcasts daily plus our nightly gospel concerts. Returning from evening concerts, we always tried to tune into the Golden Gate to see what the other guys were doing. Later in 1951, we had the privilege of doing joint-concerts. They had a unique wonderful style of working the microphone. Sometimes they would be ten feet back and other times right up close. They moved back and forth as volume increased and decreased giving light and shade. They were masterful showmen and wonderful singers. We were the first white act to record *Swing Down Chariot.* Clearly, Elvis Presley borrowed considerably from the Blackwoods for his version of the song years later!"

Extremely popular since the conversion of cowboy songwriter, Stuart Hamblen, *It is No Secret, Until Then,* and *He Bought my Soul at Calvary* have been recorded hundreds of times. The RCA versions by the Blackwood Brothers were some of the first recordings ever. *It is No Secret* was first heard on a Decca 78-rpm solo recording by Bill Kenny of the Inkspots.

Born on the twentieth of October 1908 in Kellyville, Texas, Stuart Hamblen became very popular on the West Coast. He came to national fame in the golden age of the Hollywood cowboy. Movie stars such as Gene Autry, Roy Rogers, Tex Ritter, Rex Allen and the like were his close buddies. Songs such as *Remember Me, I'm the One Who Loves You, Texas Plains,* and *My Mary* penned by Hamblen became established standards.

Convicted of a life of waywardness, Hamblen responded to the young evangelist, Billy Graham at his first major city crusade in 1949, in Los Angeles.

"William Randolph Hearst, the famed newspaper publisher in Los Angeles", James recalled, "was so impressed by the Billy Graham phenomenon that he gave the instruction to all his newspapers to 'puff Graham!' That meant provide positive publicity!"

The wayward Hamblen's lifestyle was changed dramatically for the better. In latter years, he also penned evergreen, sacred songs such as *These Things Shall Pass, Known Only To Him,* and *My Religion's not Old Fashioned.* His best known composition was the toe tapping *This Old House.* It had enough bounce in it to be a big hit, decades later, via Hollywood's Rosemary Clooney and Shakin' Stevens from Wales.

The famed, western movie star, John Wayne gave Hamblen the idea for *It is No Secret* after hearing of the fuss the Hamblen conversion had caused.

Top class acts in great abundance have recorded from the Hamblen songbook ranging from Sir Cliff Richard to Mahalia Jackson. High ranking gospel songwriters in their own right, Bill and Gloria Gaither, devoted an entire album to Hamblen material. Seldom does one find song-writing legends of Gaither status saluting another song-writing legend. Cliff Barrows and George Hamilton IV have each recorded Paul Davis' biographical tribute to Hamblen entitled *The Open Secret.*

Mansion Over the Hilltop was written by the soon to be successful, Ira Stanphill. It was yet another song by the Blackwoods to impress a young Elvis who took the song to even greater heights!

Recorded initially as a single, *Keys to the Kingdom* was a Blackwood Brothers' all time gem conceived by country music's Jenny Lou Carson. It remains as one of the few songs the Blackwoods have recorded more than once through the years. She jointly composed the seasonal hit *C-H-R-I-S-T-M-A-S* with Eddy Arnold and it was a big hit at the time.

Angels Watching Over Me had its roots firmly embedded in the black spiritual tradition. Dorothy Austin was a fine, black writer/performer who made the original recording of *My Journey To The Sky.*

Recording success prompted yet another Blackwood Brother's recording session, again in Atlanta Georgia, on the thirteenth day of October. The year of 1952 was to be a prolific year for the boys' recordings.

Pop songwriters, Sylvia Dee and Sid Lippman composed *The Hand of God* that James Blackwood described as one his top favorites.

"Bill Shaw did an inspired solo part on that. Behind the solo there's R.W. and me doing some ooh's and aah's, R.W. was in tremendous voice! Every time I hear the song, I get cold chills...It is so inspired!"

Oh What A Time, penned by Lucy Matthews, was a song the boys heard first on an album by the original Gospel Harmonettes. They were a black ladies group from Birmingham, Alabama who were headed up by the highly talented, Dorothy Love Coates.

C.C. Boddie fronted a black group from Rochester, New York and wrote *Joy, Joy, Joy* that was a regular concert number for the Blackwood Brothers in the early Fifties.

The evergreen *,My God Is Real* was written by Kenneth Morris. It was popular at the time especially because of Wally Fowler's promotion of the song at his Nashville All-Night Sing at the Ryman Auditorium. It was successfully recorded later by Pat Boone.

"The song's appeal is to those who have a testimony to tell!" James exclaimed his position with great emotion. "My God truly is real! I hope we never lose the testimony songs. There was a movement towards the end of the Century towards only praise and worship songs. But testimony songs still speak to the unsaved. We should remain missionaries for the gospel!"

I waited patiently for the LORD; and he inclined unto me, and heard my cry.
He brought me up also out of an horrible pit, out of the miry clay,
and set my feet upon a rock, and established my goings.
And he hath put a new song in my mouth, even praise unto our God:
many shall see it, and fear, and shall trust in the LORD!
Psalm 40:1-3

After Dan Husky left the Blackwoods, they were joined by the qualified, voice-trained tenor, Bill Shaw from Anderson, South Carolina. He had until then been singing with the All-American Quartet in Illinois. Reflecting back over the years, James considered Bill to be his all-time favorite tenor, serving the group faithfully for twenty-one years! His versatility ranged from the classical standard, *The Holy City* to the peppy spiritual, *The Devil Can't Harm A Praying Man.*

The fifties opened with the Blackwood Brothers' diary getting more and more in demand. Constant bookings meant continuous traveling. The primitive road systems of the day were yet to see the wholescale innovation of high-speed highways. Even the city-to-city and state-to-state roads often meandered slowly mile after mile. From their home, based in Memphis, the prospect of air travel seemed a more and more a desirable solution to the vexing travel problems.

In their successful year of 1952 came the major decision that the Blackwood Brothers Quartet would fly to their future engagements. Flying would enable the boys to fulfil their busy concert schedule and their live program commitments on WMPS radio. It also promised to release them to spend more time with their growing families in their beloved Memphis, Tennessee.

Their first, modest purchase of an airplane was an aging twin Cessna. It was to be the first of three planes that they would buy. Their second plane was a smaller, five-seater Cessna 195. The Blackwood Brothers were the very first gospel quartet to use air travel as a means of getting to engagements. R.W. took flying lessons and gained his prized pilot's license in 1952. He became the group's pilot with Bill Lyles serving as navigator and co-pilot.

10 SUNSHINE STUDIO MEMORIES

His name shall endure forever:
His name shall be continued as long as the sun:
and men shall be blessed in Him: all nations shall call Him blessed.
Blessed be the LORD God, the God of Israel,
who only doeth wondrous things.
Psalm 72:17

The next couple of years were to be made up of eventful memories for the now very popular Blackwood Brothers Quartet. As a group they were approaching their twentieth year on the road.

The sun shone brightly on that fresh, summer day in Music City. As the excited Blackwood Brothers crossed the dusty sidewalk and entered the dimmed, RCA studios in Nashville Tennessee, the well-marked calendar on the wall read May, twenty-fifth, 1953. It took very little time for them to focus on the projected recordings, laid out on the typed running-order, to be achieved that day!

Recognizing the first song, they all erupted into carefree mimicry and fun.

"Okay pardners, saddle up!" James jokingly declared with a John Wayne stance, "leave your six guns and Stetsons at the door! We sure don't want no shootin' in here today!"

Top on the list was a dreamy cowboy ditty, *At the End of the Trail*, a popular single to be released by the Blackwood Brothers. It was written by the versatile Vep Ellis in western style and was a fun take for the vocal group.

Changing musical direction, *How Many Times* was another Thomas Dorsey song. Not as familiar as some, this composition was more rhythmic in style. From similar roots, *He Knows Just How Much You Can Bear* (by black writer, Phyllis Hall) was re-mastered in the late nineties by Bill Gaither for his welcome RCA re-release of the Blackwood Brothers. The harmony on the final verse was somewhat special. James sang the melody above the first tenor Bill Shaw. Bill Shaw, R.W. and James blended for the really high parts of the last verse.

Governor Jimmie Davis of Louisiana wrote *Someone to Care*. Originally a gutsy, country singer with a country band, he first met James in 1939 when the latter moved from Jackson, Mississippi to Shreveport, Louisiana for radio opportunities. At the time, James recalled that Davis was Commissioner of Public Utilities and his classic gem, *You Are My Sunshine,* was beginning to break. It became a wartime favorite when popularized by Bing Crosby, Gene Autry, Vera Lynn and many others.

Davis served as governor for three terms. In his latter decades, he switched entirely to gospel music but is probably unique by being in both the Country and Gospel Halls of Fame. In 1999, then nearing his one hundredth birthday, he still held some selected singing dates such as his annual Jimmy Davis Homecoming at a church in Louisiana. Then, on September tenth, 1999, James Blackwood attended Jimmy's one hundredth birthday party.

Back in Nashville's RCA studios, the summer nights of the twenty-second to the twenty-fifth of September 1953 were beginning to get shorter. Disciplined as ever, the Blackwoods settled down to the familiar studio routine.

"Let's sing it through a couple of times! Then if it sounds okay, let's have a take!" Speaking of the first song of the day, the breezy voice of Steve Sholes came from behind the studio's glass partition with an air of authority.

Sure enough, after a little tweaking and slight adjustments of microphones, the quartet settled down and waxed another set of classic sacred songs.

Peace Like A River originated from the father and son team of W.B. and James Walbert. W.B. served in the James Vaughan Quartet of the early twenties. His son, James, played the piano. In 1939, the Vaughan Quartet was in Shreveport where the Blackwood Brothers made their initial contact. James Walbert in 1998 lived in Birmingham, Alabama, and according to James was still a fine pianist. The recording featured a deep bass part from Bill Lyles after a high trio by the others.

Everyday Will Be Sunday By and By was very radical with its rock 'n roll beat. James recalled how some churches did not readily accept the Blackwood Brothers because of that sound!

"We would watch as stern eyebrows were raised and disapproving glances would be exchanged between married couples especially when the concerts were in churches!" James recounted the scenes of times gone by with a seasoned smile.

"The kids loved the rock 'n roll songs! Sitting between the serious looking parents, the grinning children would clap along and tap their feet!"

Widespread acceptance of songs with a beat did not come about until the late sixties and the introduction of contemporary Christian music.

Buford Abner, the author of the get-up-and-go *Gloryland Jubilee,* was a member of the Swanee River Boys prior to World War II. The group was featured on Atlanta's fifty thousand watts WSB radio station. Buford's brother, Merle was drafted into the military of World War II and Bill Lyles was hired to replace him. Lyles joined the Blackwood Brothers in 1947.

Jack Hoffman and Jimmy Macdonald wrote *One Step.* Macdonald was also a soloist for various well-known American evangelists.

The afternoon session that day in September 1953 was extra special because it saw the Blackwood Brothers vocally backing the legendary Singing Ranger, Hank Snow. A well-deserved Country Hall of Famer, the Canadian was then at the height of his lengthy career. Short in stature perhaps, but mighty with a country lyric, this was Hank Snow at his deep treacle-voice best!

The trio of outstanding sacred songs consisted of *God's Little Candles* composed by British tunesmith, Jimmy Kennedy; the uptempo *I'm Glad I'm on the Inside*, co-written by Snow and Rusty Gabbard; as was the intriguing *Invisible Hands*. Sessioners in attendance, some from Snow's Rainbow Ranch Boys, were Jack Shook (guitar), Joe Talbot (steel), Tommy Vaden (fiddle), and Marvin Hughes (organ).

With his high-healed western boots and sequinned cowboy suits, The Singing Ranger, Hank Snow was an imposing personality. He became a major star in country music before the hostilities of World War II.

Born Clarence Eugene Snow on the ninth of May 1914 in Brooklyn, Nova Scotia, his parents bitterly divorced when he was only eight years old. Four unhappy years later, while living with his elderly, stifling grandmother, he ran away from home at the tender age of twelve. The sea life beckoned and he spent four years on the wild Atlantic doing exhausting dirty work in the fishing fleet. During these years, he developed a love of and a talent for country music. Later, during the tough days of economic depression, he somehow managed to scrape a living out of his fledgling musical career.

Hank's great Canadian ballad *My Nova Scotia Home*, poetically and sentimentally painted a wonderful, accurate, romantic musical canvas of the life of the fishermen of Nova Scotia.

Hank joined the Opry on the seventh of January 1950 and recorded more than eighty albums, more than two thousand songs and instrumentals. In 1978, he started the Hank Snow Child Abuse Foundation. He died ten days before the dawn of the third millennium. His wonderfully rich voice, gaudy rhinestone suits and million-selling hit songs such as *I'm Movin' On* made him a country music legend for more than fifty years. He was 85 when he died at his home north of downtown Nashville.

Hank's son, Jimmy Rodgers Snow, for many years pastored the Evangel Temple Church in Nashville, hosting the *Grand Ole Gospel Time* radio show that followed the *Grand Ole Opry* broadcast each week.

Jimmy's choir, the Evangel Temple Choir, provided the back-up vocals to the well beloved, Johnny Cash, million-selling, Jerry Reed song, *A Thing Called Love*.

After the musically adventurous Jackie Marshall came to the Blackwoods' reconstituted group, replacing Hilton Griswald, the practice of singing parts in Southern gospel quartets changed somewhat. He introduced the novel idea of swapping vocal parts frequently to achieve better harmony-technique and variety. This novel practice became a gospel music hallmark. Jackie remained with the group until 1958.

The Blackwood Brothers varied repertoire was culled from many quarters and cultures, but particularly, not least, from the black gospel circuit. It was a time of regressive human rights legislation in the South, but nevertheless black gospel was generally well received in the white market place.

James, contemplating the issue decades later, pondered over what remains a mystery. "Black gospel was always generally well received in the white market place. That has always been a puzzle to me! I never understood the reason why black gospel was so well received by the whites and yet, generally speaking, white gospel was not well received by the blacks!"

This puzzling reality was the main reason why the Blackwood Brothers were never to cross over in any major way into the black gospel music domain. Nevertheless, the quartet was always very active in extending the horizon of black gospel songwriters by utilizing their material so freely.

Now therefore ye are no more strangers and foreigners,
but fellow citizens with the saints, and of the household of God;
And are built upon the foundation of the apostles and prophets,
Jesus Christ himself being the chief corner stone;
In whom all the building fitly framed together groweth unto an holy temple in the Lord:
In whom ye also are builded together for an habitation of God through the Spirit.
Ephesians 2:19-22

11 FLYING HIGH AND CAREFREE

Even the youths shall faint and be weary,
and the young men shall utterly fall:
But they that wait upon the LORD shall renew their strength;
they shall mount up with wings as eagles;
they shall run, and not be weary;
and they shall walk, and not faint.
Isaiah 40:30-31

Spring was in the air with all its refreshing promise.

The prized venue was the Thomas Street Studio of RCA Victor in Nashville, Tennessee. The dates were the fifth and sixth days of March 1954, just a couple of months before tragedy was to strike...

The Blackwood Brothers' energetic first ditty captured their carefree spirit and the sense of springtime! *I'm Feelin' Fine* was a lively, Mosie Lister, testimony song in the key of C. James recalled both Jackie Marshall (piano) and Chet Atkins (guitar) taking instrumental breaks. Bill Shaw (the tenor) did not hit an accurately high note that day so R.W. (the baritone) had a try. He managed to gain the high note of high C on the final lyric of the word 'fine'.

Mosie Lister remains one of the greatest and most enduring of the Southern gospel singers. Born in 1921 in Cochran, Georgia where his father was a singing teacher and choir director, his first song was published at the age of eighteen years. Soon after, he gained considerable radio experience.

Originally part of an early Statesmen Quartet line up, he decided, after great prayer and deliberation, to quit and concentrate on song writing. Following military duty, Lister was encouraged by his dear wife to compose more seriously.

"Looking back," he declared, "I have written so many songs that even I have lost count!"

Outstanding, quality songs of Lister vintage include *How Long Has It Been, Where No-one Stands Alone, Then I Met The Master,* and *'Til The Storm Passes By. His Hand In Mine* is perhaps Mosie Lister's greatest.

When this worthy songwriter was proudly inducted into the rare honor of the Gospel Music Hall of Fame in 1998, the playing of the recorded version by the Blackwood Brothers' of *His Hand In Mine* formed part of the induction ceremony. It became the classic, title-song of Elvis Presley's first gospel album for RCA recorded at the height of his career. Artists who have recorded Lister materials through the years are legion, but include BJ Thomas, Jim Reeves, Elvis Presley, Faron Young, Jan Howard, Jimmie Davis, Jimmy Dean, Webb Pierce, and Bev Shea. In the late nineties, he resided in Tampa, Florida. Even in old age, he still produced quality material. He was a frequent guest on the Gaither videos.

Black writer, Sammy Lewis composed the bouncy *Jesus is the Way Maker* for the Blackwoods' exciting, jolly and carefree session in March, 1954.

"Okay you guys, listen up! Let's do this one in hand-clapping style!" James suggested, taking control as he glanced through the glass at Steve Sholes for a nod of reassurance that he was not usurping Steve's role.

"That's a good idea, James!" The reassuring, laughing voice of the experienced producer came warmly through the earphones decked unceremoniously around the quartet members' necks.

"I've noticed your audiences love your hand-clapping, spiritual songs! They even stir the most conservative folk...ha...ha! They eventually melt the coldest of em...and if they don't clap their hands they secretly tap their toes...ha...ha!"

At that time, there were several Tin Pan Alley songs being bandied about on the subject of the Holy Bible including *Take A Look In The Book* (recorded by the Blackwood Brothers on the nineteenth of January 1955) but James could not remember where *Brush The Dust Off The Bible* specifically came from. His memory told him that the writers, Johnny Hicks, Jack Gwyn, and Jim Leisy were studio musicians. But he was not definite! Of one thing he was sure! It was the importance of what he described as God's written revelation. How well he recalled one of his dear old mother's favorite texts in scripture.

> But continue thou in the things which thou hast learned
> and hast been assured of, knowing of whom thou hast learned them;
> from a child thou hast known the holy scriptures,
> which are able to make thee wise unto salvation through faith which is in Christ Jesus.
> All scripture is given by inspiration of God,
> and is profitable for doctrine, for reproof, for correction, for instruction in righteousness:
> That the man of God may be perfect, throughly furnished unto all good works.
> 2 Timothy 3:15-17

In the early fifties, the most popular show on the increasingly popular medium of American TV was the *Arthur Godfrey Talent Show*. Through their RCA contacts the Blackwood Brothers auditioned for the influential show. They commendably passed the stiff audition, and finally flew excitedly into New York and made their historic appearance in the warm, hazy days of early June, 1954.

Being on a national television show, the Blackwood Brothers were naturally nervous. They had lost count of the numbers of times they had performed before crowds of thousands. But this was altogether different!

"Should we tone down our Southern accents for the Northern audience?" R.W. enquired as he furrowed his brow in thoughtfulness.

"No, Sir!" the kindly but stern reply came from James. "Let's be ourselves, guys, no false airs and graces! Let's just let our little lights shine real natural-like!"

Back stage, they apprehensively went through their routines, going over who should stand where and when to look at cameras!

As their time drew closer and they listened to the other acts, the Blackwood Brothers were both impatient to get on stage, and dreading their coming moments in America's front parlor!

At last the stage hand ushered them into position and the boys, with eyes fully alert, looked to Mr. Godfrey for their cue. When the lofty introduction was given, the blinding beam of the lights and the glare of the audience flashed onto these Southern men in anticipation.

Forgetting their nerves, the boys erupted into the energetic melody! As they had rehearsed, they sang their harmony-parts to perfection and moved around with precision. Before they knew it, they were singing their final, protracted chord.

As the last long note silenced, the Blackwood Brothers awaited the audience response.

They took the glitzy show by proverbial storm, winning with their vocally-acrobatic rendition of the question song, *Have You Talked To the Man Upstairs?.*

James recalled with some humor that his extrovert Southern Gospel quartet wore eye-catching, matching, shiny-maroon suits and shoes that evening. Their startling attire had the Northern audience gasping in wide-eyed surprise! Apparently, maroon suits were not cool fashion attire in that up-town vicinity among the sophisticated at that particular time! Indeed, they were positively loud and gaudy!

As successful winners, they were then booked to sing on Arthur Godfrey's morning show all that following week on CBS TV and radio. One of the regular groups on the show was the McGuire Sisters.

Back in 1949, a star-girl-trio had been in the audience as fans when the aspiring male-quartet had sung in Dayton, Ohio. They were now regulars on Arthur Godfrey's Show. They contacted James and invited the Blackwood Brothers over to their home to have dinner and to sing. That enjoyable evening, around the piano, both vocal groups practiced a sacred song to sing on the next morning's radio show.

Thus it was that the next morning, the Blackwood Brothers and the McGuire Sisters duetted on the gospel song, *Lead Me to That Rock* on the radio show. The two groups remained friends throughout the ensuing years although following differing career paths.

> *Hear my cry, O God; attend unto my prayer.*
> *From the end of the earth will I cry unto thee,*
> *when my heart is overwhelmed:*
> *lead me to the rock that is higher than I.*
> *For thou hast been a shelter for me, and a strong tower from the enemy.*
> *I will abide in thy tabernacle forever:*
> *I will trust in the covert of thy wings.*
> *Psalm 61:1-4*

Despite their national success, the Blackwood Brothers were determined not to sell their souls to the world of show business by becoming mercenary and going secular. They resolved to remain true to the Great Commission, to what they saw as their gospel music calling. It soon seemed that these successful boys had the entertainment world at their feet.

Their brief appearance on the *Arthur Godfrey Show* had ensured huge audiences wherever they performed particularly in their home territory of the South. It seemed that everyone had seen them on the TV show! Indeed, they were heralded by the community as the first Christian group ever to appear on national TV. This fame, in turn Christian, favorably affected their record sales. Incredibly, their recordings were now hitting the lofty heights of RCA's label top ten. Soon, the well-deserved success was to come unexpectedly, tragically crashing down over their heads.

The third day of June 1954 was steamy and uncomfortably warm on the dusty streets of New York City. The thrill of sweet success was pumping through the veins of the now highly successful boys from below the Mason Dixon Line.

Following the Blackwood Brothers' unprecedented success on the *Arthur Godfrey Show*, the next morning they taped the winning song *The Man Upstairs* and *How About your Heart?* for single release on RCA Victor.

How About your Heart? was a challenging and questioning song that they received at a country hotel in West Texas where they met the young evangelist, Bennie Tripplett. He was in town for revival services and auditioned the song on the hotel piano. James purchased the song there and then and it remained in the BB repertoire ever since. In 1998, backstage at a University concert, James met the writer again, by then a minister of the gospel in Ohio, and hugged him in nostalgic embrace.

The Man Upstairs was the ditty that won the *Arthur Godfrey Talent TV Show* for the Blackwood Brothers. They first heard it from a Kay Starr record. She, like the Blackwood Brothers, based her career in Memphis. Arthur Godfrey was so intrigued with the song that he interspersed the rest of his prized show to its catchy rhythm.

12 THEN TRAGEDY STRUCK

Although affliction cometh not forth of the dust,
neither doth trouble spring out of the ground;
Yet man is born unto trouble, as the sparks fly upward.
I would seek unto God, and unto God would I commit my cause:
Which doeth great things and unsearchable;
marvelous things without number.
Job 5: 6-9

As with, it seems, every great success in life, triumphs are often tainted with tragedies.

By 1954, the Blackwood Brothers were now at the pinnacle of their profession. They were not only the first gospel artists to perform on nation-wide television but they were also enjoying massive success with their recordings.

All the indicators pointed towards even greater heights. The boys were eagerly being swept up in the wash of radio and concert appreciation...soon they would be amazed how suddenly one event could extinguish their joy!

On that fateful day of June 30, 1954, the now nationally renowned group flew into Clanton, Alabama to sing at the Chilton County Peach Festival sponsored by the local Lions Club.

Flying into the small, local airport in their twin engine Beechcraft, R.W. was at the controls. He carefully maneuvered it onto the very end of the airport's short runway. Spirits were high and expectations great as the young group disembarked, and then meandered across the green turf to perform at the noon Lions Club luncheon.

That eventful, summer evening, the Blackwood Brothers, along with the Statesmen Quartet from Atlanta, had been booked to sing at a gospel concert being held in the airport hanger.

Earlier in the day, R.W. decided that it would be safer if he took the plane up on an afternoon test flight. It would be dark after the concert when they would eventually make the return journey back to Memphis. As it was just a small airport and it had no runway lights, it was the custom to line up cars on either side of the runway. The general idea was to shine their headlights onto the runway thus floodlighting the runway for the pilot to be able to see where he had to go.

Bill Lyles (the co-pilot) and a local fan eighteen year old, Johnny Ogburn also went along for the afternoon practice ride. This was Johnny's first plane ride. After gaining his parents permission he was ready to climb aboard.

"Okay, you guys, let's go! Let's get this bird in the air!" R.W. shouted cheerfully to Bill and Johnny as he clambered aboard with them in tow.

R.W. and Bill ran through their usual instrument checks while the widely-grinning Johnny waved out of the window at those faces with whom he was familiar. With the safety checks completed, the fragile plane took-off without any fuss. They were now in the air. The three guys playfully chatted about the joys of flying and the forthcoming evening concert. Johnny, gazing at the ground, looked forward to telling his buddies back in town how he had flown with the famous Blackwood Brothers!

However, on coming in to land, the wind direction had ominously shifted.

On the ground, the gazing crowd of people were surprised to see that R.W. was coming in to land at the opposite end of where they were planning to take off that night.

On the approach was a hill just before the runway began. To avoid this, R.W. had to pick up sufficient airspeed to adequately clear it before coming in to land. On the first attempt, he never touched the ground as the fragile plane was going too fast after clearing the hill. After several attempts in which the plane was still unable to land safely on the short runway, R.W. went up again.

During all this time, more and more concert-goers had been gathering for the forthcoming, evening performance and were watching the plane's increasingly desperate attempts to land. The anxious performers were watching opened mouthed and with bated breath too as R.W. battled furiously to get the maverick plane onto the runway, but to no avail. On his final attempt, the plane's engine stalled as R.W. fought in vain to ascend up in the air again.

The fragile plane came hurtling down and hit the runway midway with a heart-stopping force and sound.

In dramatic panic, James Blackwood, Jackie Marshall, and Bill Shaw immediately ran impulsively towards the crashed, flaming plane. James reached the disaster first and through the fearful flames could see R.W. still strapped into his pilot's seat. Desperately, he started to run into the flaming wreckage to try and free him.

"Get 'em out!...get 'em out!" The wild, anguished cry echoed across the shocked airfield from dry mouths.

Out of his mind with shock, James' well meaning but vain attempts at rescue put his own life at risk. Fighting, kicking, and screaming, somebody picked him up bodily and unceremoniously carried him off the green field to safety. Not until years later did James find out that it was Jake Hess of the Statesmen Quartet who had violently pulled him out of the dreadful tongues of flame. Jake's reward for saving the life of his long-time friend that fateful day, was a body-bruised and sore from the struggle.

The awful disaster took its dreadful toll that day as the three young men aboard the plane perished in unspeakable circumstances. Autopsies showed that their necks had been broken immediately on impact, sparing them the pain of the explosive flames. The bodies were burned beyond recognition. Bill Lyles was found under the instrument panel, his safety straps broken. R.W. was still strapped in the pilot's seat.

Initially, the exact cause of the crash was professionally undetermined, but there was the possibility that R.W. had suffered a mental blackout of some sort.

Vainly looking back, James Blackwood felt that it might have been wise if R.W. had flown on to the Montgomery Airport when he found that it was too dangerous to land at the Clanton airstrip.

The tragic crash became national news. *United Press International* and *Associated Press* immediately carried reports as did CBS radio and television. It was mentioned on the *Arthur Godfrey Show* and by Walter Winchell on his Sunday night news broadcast. America was in shock!

Trembling with emotion, Jake, at the request of James, telephoned Memphis. He broke the tragic news to James' brother, Doyle, and then to the local pastor, Reverend James Hamill so that he could give urgent support to the families of the deceased.

Grace be to you and peace from God our Father, and from the Lord Jesus Christ.
Blessed be God, even the Father of our Lord Jesus Christ,
the Father of mercies, and the God of all comfort;
Who comforteth us in all our tribulation,
that we may be able to comfort them which are in any trouble,
by the comfort wherewith we ourselves are comforted of God.
2 Corinthians 1:3-4

Tragic scenes of grief were repeated throughout the USA, particularly in the South, as people carried the bereavement as if it were a personal, family loss!

In the heart of the Lone Star State of Texas, Larry, the six year old son of Mr. And Mrs Gatlin broke down in seemingly uncontrollable grief at the tragic news. Years later, he remembered that he sobbed uncontrollably for three long days.

Along with his younger Gatlin brothers, Steve and Rudy, the family trio later started to exercise their wings in family harmony inspired by Blackwood Brothers' example.

13 DEEP SHOCK

The Blackwood Brothers Quartet is indeed a credit to 'Musical Americana'!
I am sure their songs bring to others, as they do to me,
a happier heart and many precious memories!
Merle Travis

One of the many people to be deeply affected emotionally by the crash was a young Blackwood Brothers enthusiast, a truck driver named Elvis Presley. At the time, he was dating a pretty, young woman by the name of Dixie Locke. On dates, he took her to many gospel concerts and all day sings.

Hearing the dreadful news of the tragic crash, he hurriedly drove Dixie to a nearby park where heartbroken, he grieved and reminisced about R.W. and Bill. His deep admiration for the Blackwood Brothers was shown clearly when Gladys, his mother, died several years later. Elvis paid to fly the famed Quartet from Anderson, South Carolina to sing at her funeral service. He then flew the boys straight back again for their concert engagement.

Buddies of the same age, Cecil recalled his friend, Elvis with great affection, "The Blackwood Brothers were Elvis' mother's favorite gospel quartet. Elvis also loved the Blackwoods as he did gospel music in general. He particularly enjoyed the livelier songs that the Blackwood Brothers and their partners, the Statesmen Quartet sang! His love affair with the Blackwoods and gospel music never waned. He will always be remembered as a special friend!"

At the time of the tragedy, Dixie Locke attended the First Assembly of God church in McLemore Avenue, Memphis. Ruth Lyles, Bill's wife, had been her Sunday School teacher at the church. The tragic crash hit the church family hard.

Be kindly affectionate one to another with brotherly love...
fervent in spirit; serving the Lord;
Rejoicing in hope; patient in tribulation;
continuing instant in prayer;
Distributing to the necessity of saints;
given to hospitality....
and weep with them that weep.
Romans 12:10-15

Panic stricken and deeply shocked the Statesmen put the distraught and emotional James Blackwood into their overcrowded, eight-seater, black-limo car and took him home to Memphis. By this time, he was out of his mind in deep shock and vowed that he would never sing again. James was adamant that his singing career was over!

"How can I go on, Hovie?" James tearfully asked Hovie Lister, the leader of the Statesmen Quartet. Words of comfort seemed so inadequate. All the Statesmen tried to remain upbeat and positive as James sobbed out his deep grief.

"How could...somethin' like this happen? It's a nightmare! I'll never...never sing...again! Never!"

"We can never say never, James! Don't give Satan any room in all of this!" Mustering as much courage as he could, Hovie spoke calmly and maturely with heartfelt compassion through tear-blinded eyes.

"Life must go on for the living! You are greatly loved, James! Never forget it! We want to stand by you and pray for you to get through!"

The words dried-up! A comforting hug from a friend was now more appropriate.

Life had dealt a tragic blow!

The Blackwood Brothers had just won the *Godfrey Show* favor; they were the most popular group in gospel music; and they were now top ten sellers with RCA.

What was that worth in the light of this tragedy?

At the end of the Twentieth Century, almost fifty years later, the still vivid memory precipitates heart-felt tears. The trauma left deep emotional scars that only eternity will heal.

"The supportive prayers of many Christian people all over America brought us tangible comfort and strength. Amid the grief there was the light of hope!" James movingly testified of his conviction as he thoughtfully pondered this tragic episode. "Renewed in hope, we were determined to hold on! I changed my mind about giving up!"

Before long, the call of duty came. With the still traumatized team of Jack and Bill, James courageously got into a car and drove to Fort Worth, Texas to fulfil a long standing engagement, booked with the Statesmen before the plane crash. As well as having to bear his own pain, he had to be strong for the sake of Jackie Marshall and Bill Shaw.

"Come on, Jack! Come on, Bill! God's called us to help fulfil the Great Commission! We can count on His strength even in this deep valley!"

James softly spoke through a pained expression. His eyes were misty, his brow furrowed and his voice cracked as he spoke.

"Let's remember... that He has promised... that His grace will always be sufficient!"

No doubt, still numbed by the shock, the remnant of the group bravely mounted the stage in Fort Worth and sang of the mercies of the Lord!

Decades later, with a lump in his throat, James still painfully recalled through salty tears, "I do not remember whether I sang a note or not on that first time I went up back on stage!"

The funeral, held at Ellis Auditorium, Memphis on the second day of July 1954, was the first funeral ever held at the vast auditorium. The weather was hot, the crowds were deep. It seemed as if the whole of the shocked Southern city wanted to pay its respects! It was the largest funeral that Memphis had witnessed to that date. The south hall of the auditorium was packed with two and a half thousand, emotional mourners There were many more in the overflow in the north hall. Overall, it is estimated that there were more than five thousand mourners at the funeral.

The funeral caskets and the beautiful flowers faced the south hall but the stage was between the north and south auditoriums. As the stage straddled both auditoriums, separated only by a curtain, with the curtain drawn, one could stand on the stage and be seen both ways.

Officiating at the sad event were James E. Hamill, who was then pastor of the Blackwoods' church, First Assembly of God, Dr. R.G. Lee, the pastor of the Bellevue Baptist Church in Memphis, and Jimmy Stroud, head of the Memphis Union Mission. The State Governor, Frank Clement attended, canceling a political trip to do so. He delivered the eulogy.

The deep trauma affected the entire gospel singing public, but more so the immediate family.

R.W.'s dear, distraught mother, Susan Hall Blackwood, of course, experienced deep anguish of spirit. Nevertheless, she was able to come to terms with her heartbreak to declare a testimony with courage and faith. In the midst of her grief, her words were seeped in conviction.

"The reason why R.W. and Bill were taken is known only to God. I do not question His will."

Nearly fifty years later, Cecil sadly recalled how the tragedy adversely affected his dear mother for the rest of her life.

"It was a deep loss from which my darling mother would never fully recover. One can come to terms with it but never lose the emotional scars."

There were long, tearful eulogies in sacred song from the deceased's friends that included the Statesmen Quartet and the Speer Family. Also in the weeping congregation, although separated from the whites, were a number of black people who had asked to attend the funeral.

It is to their credit that the crossover music and non-racist attitudes of the Blackwood Brothers had cut across racial lines during what was a sensitive time of strictly enforced segregation.

It was reported that the funeral procession stretched out for about five miles to the burial at Memorial Park in Memphis.

I will not leave you comfortless:
I will come to you...
the Comforter, which is the Holy Spirit,
whom the Father will send in my name,
he shall teach you all things,
and bring all things to your remembrance,
whatsoever I have said unto you.
Peace I leave with you, my peace I give unto you:
not as the world giveth, give I unto you.
Let not your heart be troubled, neither let it be afraid.
John 14:18,26-27

No one can over estimate the shattering impact made on the remaining group and their families. No one could emerge from such a tragedy unaffected. James said that it did not ultimately shatter his faith but the emotional scars still remained years later.

Speaking in March of 1998, he said, "Yesterday, my wife and I received a letter from Bill Lyles' wife. In it she said she has yet to see any good come from the tragedy! She was left with three little boys to raise and R.W. left two little boys. They all needed their daddies. There must be a reason and we'll know it when we get to heaven! I thank God for the truth of my theme song I Will Meet You In The Morning, *written by Albert Brumley, and I get comfort from God's word!"*

> *Thou wilt keep him in perfect peace,*
> *whose mind is stayed on Thee:*
> *because he trusteth in Thee.*
> *Trust ye in the LORD for ever:*
> *for in the LORD JEHOVAH is everlasting strength.*
> *Isaiah 26:3-4*

Looking back nearly fifty years later James praised God for the strength, courage, hope and peace that He supplied in abundance through those days of severe tribulation.

Misty-eyed, James spoke with deep conviction.

"Down here, I don't expect to know the reason for such a tragedy. Down here, we know only in part. But up there, in heaven's glory, all will be revealed. We will then know the whole story."

> *Like a river glorious is Christ's perfect peace,*
> *Over all victorious, in its' bright increase:*
> *Perfect, yet it flows fuller every day;*
> *Perfect, yet it grows deeper all the way.*
>
> *Stayed upon Jehovah, hearts are fully blessed*
> *Finding as He promised, perfect peace and rest.*
>
> *Hidden in the hollow of His blessed hand,*
> *Never foe can follow, never traitor stand;*
> *Not a surge of worry, not a shade of care,*
> *Not a blast of hurry touched the Spirit there.*
>
> *Every joy or trial falleth from above,*
> *Traced upon our dial by the sun of love.*
> *We may trust Him fully, all for us to do;*
> *They who trust Him wholly find Him wholly true.*
> *Frances Ridley Havargal/ Trad. Arranged by Wes Davis/*
> © *New Music Enterprises 1999*

14 OUT OF DESPAIR

Many groups have been called to sing for Jesus but no calling has been so significant as that of the Blackwood Brothers who have touched lives with their beautiful ministry.
Barbara Miller

The tragic images of those days remain colorfully vivid and emotionally painful nearly fifty years later. With heavy heart, Cecil Blackwood remembered the frantic efforts the quartet made as they sought to regroup.

"After the plane crash came the funeral. Then the reformed Blackwood Brothers did quite a few television shows in our hometown, letting people know what was happening. Roy, my father sang the tenor, James the lead, I sang baritone and Kent Higgenbotham sang bass. Kent was the bass for the Songfellows...When we went back on the road to Little Rock and to various places in Tennessee, the group was 'Big Chief' Weatherington, James Blackwood, Bill Shaw, and, of course me, Cecil Blackwood!"

Prior to the unforeseen tragedy, the Statesmen and the Blackwood Brothers had formed a mutually supportive, team-pact and were doing most of their gospel concerts together. In a desperate attempt to help and fill the gaping void created by the crash, "Big Chief" Jim Weatherington, the Statesmen bass, stepped in.

Cecil Blackwood also helped by singing baritone for two weeks. It gave sufficient time to allow the two acts to re-group and take stock as their welcome vacation period was imminently upon them.

It was the previously agreed practice for the two Christian groups to take a two-week break together in July. No holiday was ever so providentially timely, necessary, or relevant. It was during this recuperative vacation period that James asked Cecil Blackwood, R.W.'s younger brother to continue to sing baritone. J.D. Sumner who was singing with the Sunshine Boys at that time was invited to sing bass.

To his credit, through thick and thin, Cecil was to faithfully remain in the Blackwood saddle for fifty years and oversee the group's entry into the third millennium as their leader.

The re-formed quartet returned to give their first, emotion-packed performance in Clanton, Alabama on the warm, clammy evening of the fifth day of August 1954.

Therefore seeing we have this ministry,
as we have received mercy, we faint not;
But if our gospel be hid, it is hid to them that are lost:
For we preach not ourselves, but Christ Jesus the Lord;
and ourselves your servants for Jesus' sake.

For God, who commanded the light to shine out of darkness,
hath shined in our hearts, to give the light of the knowledge
of the glory of God in the face of Jesus Christ.
But we have this treasure in earthen vessels,
that the excellency of the power may be of God, and not of us.
We are troubled on every side, yet not distressed;
we are perplexed, but not in despair;
cast down, but not destroyed;
Knowing that he which raised up the Lord Jesus
shall raise up us also by Jesus, and shall present us with you.
For which cause we faint not;
but though our outward man perish,
yet the inward man is renewed day by day.
For our light affliction, which is but for a moment,
worketh for us a far more exceeding and eternal weight of glory;
While we look not at the things which are seen,
*   but at the things which are not seen:*
for the things which are seen are temporal;
but the things which are not seen are eternal.
2 Corinthians 4

Born in Lakeland, Florida in 1924, J.D. Sumner was a most prolific writer for the Blackwood Brothers Quartet during his term as bass singer. Incredibly he wrote five hundred songs during that time and is credited with hundreds of songs recorded mainly by quartets.

The Blackwood Brothers mainly published their own songs under the *Gospel Quartet Music* banner. They jointly owned and published the Sumner titles. Although James Blackwood usually fed him the ideas and concepts and Sumner would come up with songs, James never pushed for shared creditation.

Earlier, Sumner spent several years singing bass with the Sunny South Quartet and then the Sunshine Boys, gaining valuable experience. After the plane crash that killed two of the Blackwood Brothers group, James invited him to replace the deceased Bill Lyles. Other basses were considered but James was impressed with Sumner's recorded version of the old English hymn *Oh Happy Day* that featured a unique bass solo. Initially undecided, Sumner asked for time to think and pray over the invitation as he had recently re-dedicated his life to the Lord at a pastor-friend's church in Atlanta.

While with the Sunshine Boys, J.D. was not encouraged as a songwriter. Indeed, surprisingly, they had not recorded anything he had written! His new pact with the Blackwoods considerably boosted his songwriting. They encouraged him, particularly James, who was an ever-flowing source that fed him with ideas and titles.

Many of the songs the Blackwoods recorded for RCA were written by Sumner in transit on the tourbus. Indeed, RCA was so impressed with the Sumner Hawaiian ditties on the album *Paradise Island* that they commissioned him to write enough material for a full Hawaiian gospel album entitled *Beautiful Isle of Somewhere.* He subsequently obliged, completing all the songs on a bus ride between Indiana and Ohio.

As most of Sumner's compositions featured him as bass, it became a source of friendly banter! James would often joke from the stage when introducing one of the Sumner songs.

"Ladies and gentlemen," with a broad smile on his face, James would make the tongue in cheek declaration. "Here's yet another fine song that J.D. wrote and features him...and...ha...ha...of course, most of his own songs do feature him...ha...ha!"

Perhaps, Sumner's most popular written work was the sing-a-long marathon entitled *The Old Country Church* featured so successfully on the high-selling video by Bill and Gloria Gaither entitled *Down at the Tabernacle*. The song draws together the choruses of well-known, Ira Sankey style hymns. It was inspired in Montgomery, Alabama after an old gentleman asked Sumner a challenging question!

"Tell me Mr. Sumner, why don't the Blackwoods sing more church hymns?"

In response, the following week, Sumner wrote *The Old Country Church* on the bus on tour in Illinois.

After eleven productive years with the Blackwood Brothers, Sumner successfully transferred to the famed Stamps Quartet. He went on to became world famous as a result of his group's association with Elvis Presley from 1972 to 1977. This fame was extended further when he was even honored by the *Guinness Book of Records* as the lowest bass.

In later years, J.D. served with the Master's V Quartet alongside fellow, legendary veterans James Blackwood, Jake Hess, Rosie Rozell, and Hovie Lister. During his last five years, he was a familiar participant *world's* in the *Gaither Homecoming* videos.

James joined the Master's V on a part-time basis in 1979. He would alternate between the Master's V and the Blackwoods until going full time with the Master's V in 1981.

Sumner died from a heart attack on the fifteenth of November, 1998, aged 73.

Like the proverbial cowboy he was to die in the saddle. With him was the Stamps Quartet that he had led for eleven and a half years, since he left the Blackwood Brothers in 1965. He was performing to the end, in Myrtle Beach, South Carolina.

15 MISSION RESTART

Restore unto me the joy of thy salvation;
and uphold me with thy free spirit.
Then will I teach transgressors thy ways;
and sinners shall be converted unto thee.
Psalm 51:12-13

Time moved painfully but onward at tremendous speed for the new team. For those who had experienced the trauma, the flaming memories were still a nightly nightmare to be endured!

It was time to return to the weary task of minting another session for the RCA people pressing for fresh Blackwood material. So it was back, not to a sunny Tennessee this time but rather to the dull, overcast, Nashville studios on November 5, 1954

Brighter feelings started to pick up and smiles returned as pianist, Jackie Marshall was featured, so engagingly on Stuart Hamblen's *Workshop of The Lord* backed up by Marvin Hughes (organ), Ernie Newton (bass), and Jack Shook (guitar).

Refreshed in spirit, James recalled that the Blackwood Brothers were willing to record almost anything cowboy Hamblen sent them at that time!

Strutting around like a bow-legged, rodeo cowboy, Cecil playfully announced the song-plan in John Wayne mimicry mood. His faked western accent and comic antics produced smiles around the famed studio.

"Okay, pardners, let's show our tough humbre friend, Big Stu how this song should be sung!"

"Yee, ha! Ride em, cowboy!"

The high-pitched, cowboy yell came from the usually soft-spoken Chet Atkins as he busied himself setting up the microphones in the optimum positions.

The ice was broken. The boys were now warming up in spirited mood.

Next came *I Don't Care What The World May Do*, a ditty from Alex E. Bradford Jr., a big name in black gospel.

Years later, James recalled that the Artist and Repertoire man (A&R) Chet Atkins' guitar was becoming a regular feature by that time, although he is not credited as an instrumentalist in the paperwork held in the archives of RCA. Four decades later, Cecil was convinced he knew the reason.

"Chet Atkins was our A&R in charge of the session. He didn't feel he should be paid double. He was enjoying playing the guitar but didn't put it on paper because he was being paid from A&R and was just playing the guitar because he wanted to. We're sure glad he did!"

In 1955, the re-organized Blackwood Brothers were nervously paraded before the waiting nation via a special concert in Montgomery, Alabama hosted by NBC television and radio host, Dave Garroway.

And let us not be weary in well doing:
for in due season we shall reap, if we faint not.
As we have therefore opportunity,
let us do good unto all men,
especially unto them who are of the household of faith
Galatians 6:9-10

The Blackwood Brothers' new team was now back, up and running in mission restart mode. Next, it was back for a second appearance on the Arthur Godfrey show, *Talent Scouts* in September 1956.

Singing Kay Starr's song, *The Good Book,* they won the prized competition against stiff opposition. This unique achievement was to earn them the distinction of being the only gospel group to achieve a clear-cut win twice on the program.

In the previous year, one year after the plane disaster, J.D. Sumner made the bold, revolutionary suggestion to buy and customize a big bus for concert travel. Earlier, Cecil had observed the usefulness and efficiency of the airport passenger transportation with the convenient five-door design.

"That's the kinda thing we need."

The initially intrigued group agreed with Cecil's general idea.

"Fellas, we can each have our own door, our own seat, our own bunk and our own space to store our baggage. Let's go for it!'

Many other ideas were also discussed. Eventually, they sold their Cadillac and bought themselves a 1947 Arrowcoach from Continental Trailways in Memphis. Next, they had it comfortably customized to their own design.

The newly-purchased bus was initially parked outside the Sumner home while Cecil masterminded the re-structuring of the interior. With the help of Cecil's carpenter friend, J.D. and Cecil himself, the bus was gutted then refitted. Carpets, curtains, recliner seats, air conditioning, partitions and bunks were installed accordingly.

When the smart customized bus hit the road, Cecil and J.D. shared the driving with great pride.

This innovation set a precedent that thousands of acts in show business were to follow. At the time, many people thought that it was too costly and impracticable. The boys wondered whether they did the right thing when the repair costs for the first three months totaled $3,300! Nowadays, such expenses are accepted as part and parcel of budget expenses.

Many other buses were later purchased as the older ones gave up the ghost! Each were progressively updated and refined with every comfort imaginable by Cecil and J.D.

The first big white Arrowcoach from Continental Trailways now holds pride of place in Dolly Parton's Theme Park, Dollywood. There in the Hall of Fame section it can be publicly viewed.

Times spent on those buses were long and wearisome but in nostalgic memory even the bad times were good and sometimes fun, as Cecil recalls with some humor.

"Years later, we had driven from Pennsylvania all the way to Broken Bow, Nebraska for a fair date. Unfortunately for us, the air conditioning had broken down on the bus. That meant that when we arrived at the venue we were in need of a shower! But, having arrived at the town by the skin of our teeth there was nothing for it but to just comb our hair and get out on stage and sing."

On the return journey back East, the weary group members were still in their unwashed state as the bus was without a shower. Cecil could barely contain his laughter as he continued the tale.

"Sitting there in the bus we were feeling pretty uncomfortable and, I suspect, were beginning to smell! Outside the rain was pouring down. As I watched the rain, I suddenly had the thought that the rain looked just like a heaven-sent shower! As we were in a pretty lonely location in Nebraska, I commented to the others that it would be great to get out into that rain and take a shower. The thought of being out there in the sweet smelling air, and the opportunity of the cool rain washing off all the perspiration from our long journey was just too good to pass up. So we did!

"We backed the bus up on a side road, leaving the bus lights on so nobody would run into it on the lonely dirt road. Some cars were going by so we waited until they went and took off all our dirty clothes and stepped out into the rain! All, that is except me. I hastily put on my blue tennis shoes as I didn't want to tread on anything sharp with my feet! Nobody else had anything on! When a car would come, we'd run behind the bus, away from the road, and hide until the cars went by. Then we would continue our shower.

"We soaped ourselves all over and just let the rain do its work. Unfortunately for us though, the rain suddenly stopped, leaving us covered with soap suds! So, we just had to towel ourselves dry and get back on the bus, and as James later said, 'We smelled like Palmolive all the way back to Memphis!'

But there was just one little bitty problem. As I removed my blue tennis shoes, I was horrified to discover that the blue dye had run out from them and completely covered my feet. Believe me, it took several days to get that blue dye off my feet! But it was worth it all to feel clean again!"

The New Year of 1955 brought with it the promise of fresh pastures and new opportunities as the Blackwood Brothers again traveled across country to the Nashville studios on the nineteenth day of January 1955. The Tennessee air was fresh and invigorating that morning, a contrast to the staleness of the studio environs.

Two catchy numbers, *Take A Look In The Book* and *Dear Lord, Remember Me* shared single record release that year. The latter was penned by black singer-songwriter, Myrtle Jackson. It is nowadays often featured by church choirs or Christian chorales, such as Cliff Barrows' Victory Voices. In 1955, it was rarely recorded.

Country singer, Faron Young had a major, country honky-tonk hit with a reckless ditty that was just about the opposite of *Live Right, Die Right*. The

Blackwoods' ditty was a pounding number from the black field and a hit for them at the time. Backing was by Jack Marshall (piano), Chet Atkins (guitar), Ernie Newton (bass), and Murray Harmon (drums). Finishing up the session was *Led By The Master's Hand,* one of Mosie Lister's early masterpieces, made famous later by Jack Holcomb, the sacred music tenor with a tear in his voice.

Trips to the Nashville studios became pleasantly recurrent that year. It seemed the public was gaining a definite appetite for the Blackwood sound. Thus it was on March 4,1955 they waxed Tim Spencer's best known sacred song.

Cowboy group, Sons of The Pioneers' member Tim Spencer, wrote *Christ is A Wonderful Savior* in response to his conversion to Christ. Using the melodic tune of his hit number, *Room Full Of Roses* (recorded by Jim Reeves, Mickey Gilley, Eddy Arnold, Slim Whitman and others), he substituted gospel lyrics to celebrate his born again experience. George Beverly Shea and Jack Holcomb also recorded the popular new lyrics at the time.

The Blackwood Brothers' version that day used the country-style fiddles of Tommy Jackson and Dale Potter plus Floyd 'Lightning' Chance on stand-up bass.

In contrast, Bennie Tripplett wrote *Will Heaven Be Heaven Without You?* a moving song where violins were utilized. It was a musical question to ponder as the clear spring evening's studio session concluded.

Six weeks later, in between busy concert dates, the RCA management persuaded the quartet to return to their Nashville studios for the April, twenty-first waxings. Entering the studio, the international news on the radio announced that day was the birthday of England's Queen Elizabeth. The news item caught Cecil's imagination. He turned around abruptly and faced the Blackwood Brothers squarely.

"'kay, boys! Let's turn in a royal performance today for the King of Kings!"

Cecil made the serious declaration emphasizing the royal while he smiled and playfully came to attention, saluting his grinning colleagues. They then busied themselves to address the running order of the day.

Jazz styled, pop singer, Dinah Shore had a big hit with *Church Twice On Sunday* and the RCA folk had great plans for the Blackwoods' harmony version. This peppy ditty did do well for the Blackwood Brothers. Written by Korky Robbins, they received the sheet music from the New York pop publisher and learned it from the Shore recording.

What A Morning was decided for the flip side of *Church Twice On Sunday*. The song was penned by, and featured their bass, Sumner. In the decades since, many other quartets have utilized the song to great effect including the Florida Boys.

Seven months later, winter was beginning to settle in. On the fourth of November 1955 the Quartet returned to Nashville, Tennessee for yet another inspiring set of recordings.

"Let's see boys, whether we can give this first song on our list some real soul!" A breezy, smiling James exclaimed how the first song should be approached as he glanced over the running order before him. Then recognizing the theme of the song, he added further comments in a more serious tone.

"*Just Can't Make it By Myself....* This one, guys, has a truth we can all identify with!" Heads nodded in agreement around the famous studio.

Just Can't Make it By Myself was written by the well-known black-gospel celebrity, Clara Ward. When the BB quartet was singing in the heart of the gambling world (in a church in Las Vegas, Nevada) they saw a local newspaper advertisement for the Clara Ward Singers. Clara Ward and her Singers were engaged to sing in the lounge of one of the Vegas hotels on the Strip.

Eager to see Clara and her group, the Blackwood Brothers were keen to attend her concert after their own church concert had concluded.

The Strip's show lounge was dark and atmospheric. Gazing at the surroundings, the boys settled down in their plush seats. A few yards away from their table, a young man rose from his seat and slowly sauntered towards them. It was Elvis Presley, one of the Blackwoods' long standing admirers! He was also there to listen to Clara Ward. Both he and the Blackwoods were true-blue enthusiasts when it came to music of the gospel, black or white!

"James Blackwood in Las Vegas! I've seen it all! Ha...ha!" Elvis laughingly made his declaration before going over to the surprised James Blackwood and casually sitting down. He enthusiastically shook hands with all his Blackwood buddies.

Elvis, James, Cecil, Bill, J.D. and Jackie were all far away from their Memphis homes but they were hometown friends. Mutually warmed by their renewed acquaintance, they embraced each other in brotherly fashion, and then engaged themselves in deep animated conversation.

The best selling recording artist of his day... the highest paid entertainer of his day.... Elvis Presley began his rise to stardom as a country blues singer and became one of the most vital forces in American pop culture.

Elvis once made the comment that he must know the words to every hymn ever written! Certainly, he had been singing hymns and gospel songs all of his life as he had been taken along to his parents' Tupelo church when he was almost too young to even say the words! Elvis never forgot those roots and his sacred recordings were always among his most successful and personally rewarding.

Coming from the Deep South, Elvis, like countless many country music singers, was influenced by the musical sounds around him. Country, blues, and gospel were the musical influences that the young Elvis grew up with.

Church music and hymns made up the first music Elvis Presley ever heard. Church music was also the first kind of music Elvis ever sung. It was as natural to him as nursery rhymes and Mother Goose stories are to other children.

Elvis started his life in Tupelo, Mississippi, a small quiet town where families grew together in harmony and mutual kindness and where heartfelt religious belief was at the center of the community.

In Tupelo at this time, every day would have begun with a religious devotion both at school and in the home, and in this the Presley household was no exception. One of Elvis' most enduring memories was of his mother, father and himself singing together at Tupelo's First Assembly Church of God.

Some years before his beloved mother, Gladys, died, she delighted in recalling that time.

"When Elvis was just a little fellow, he would slide off my lap, run down the aisle, scramble up to the platform of the church, and try to sing with the choir. He was too little to know the words, of course, but he could carry the tune!"

Years later, the Presley family could be found singing hymns at camp meetings, revivals and church conventions as a trio.

Thus, Southern Gospel music was deep in Elvis' memory and persona. It was bound up tightly with his birthplace and his vivid memories of his mother and the wonderful life she helped create for him. His deep admiration for the Blackwood Brothers was such that when Gladys, his mother, died Elvis flew the famed quartet from South Carolina to sing at her funeral service. The Blackwood Brothers were his mother's favorite gospel quartet. Elvis also loved the Blackwoods but was known to also enjoy the lively musical style of the Statesmen Quartet.

Elvis' first gospel music album was an EP (four tracks) entitled *Peace in The Valley*. Released in April 1957, tracks included Thomas Dorsey's *Take My Hand Precious Lord*, the title track *Peace in the Valley*, *I Believe* (which was a popular hit of day), and the Stuart Hamblen classic *It Is No Secret What God Can Do*.

One of the great all-time Presley best sellers, it confirmed the feeling of Presley fans that Elvis could sing almost anything with an astonishing sincerity and feeling. It also made countless new fans of his music.

After the success of *Peace In The Valley*, a follow up LP was released entitled *His Hand In Mine*. This album was pure southern country-gospel with tracks such as, Ira Stanphill's *Mansion Over The Hilltop*, Albert Brumley's *If We Never Meet Again*, Stuart Hamblen's *Known Only to Him* and Mosie Lister's *He Knows Just What I Need*. Rumor has it that Elvis played piano on some of the tracks. Backing Elvis on this project was by the southern gospel quartet, The Jordanaires.

The choice of a southern gospel quartet to back him on his gospel albums stemmed from Elvis' great love affair with this genre of music. Elvis' favorite gospel groups were the Blackwood Brothers Quartet and the Statesmen Quartet. Perhaps, his favourite songs tended to be the faster 'rock 'n roll' style of gospel songs that Elvis could sing along to. Indeed, Elvis was pictured singing on stage with them on several occasions at gospel music conventions.

Elvis once auditioned for The Song Fellows Quartet, headed by his buddy Cecil Blackwood, later of the Blackwood Brothers. They turned him down, as his voice was too individualistic for singing in a quartet group! History was to prove them totally correct in this, summing up of his unique abilities. Nonetheless, Elvis' love affair with quartet music was to continue for the rest of his musical life, as his use of quartets illustrates. These included J.D. Sumner and the Stamps, the Imperials and the Jordanaires on most of his recordings and stage appearances.

After his stage performances, it was not unusual to find Elvis seated at the piano in the early hours of the morning, singing southern gospel songs with whatever quartet was accompanying him at the time. It almost seemed that these sessions filled a spiritual need in Elvis's life that fame and fortune could not fulfil.

In 1965, Elvis topped the British Charts, ousting the Beatles for the first time in three years, with an Easter single of the song *Crying In The Chapel*, with *I Believe in the Man in the Sky* on the flip side. This religious hit single caused America's *Daily Variety* newspaper to comment that "Presley's Swivel, Rock to Religioso, Waxes Him Hotter!"

In March 1967 *How Great Thou Art*, another gospel album was released. The album went Gold and earned Elvis a Grammy Award. The album was also featured across America on a special radio program of sacred music from the LP. The concept of the program was both created and sponsored by Elvis, with all proceeds going to the International Red Cross.

Following on the good reception that the album received, Elvis recorded the *He Touched Me* LP, featuring songs written by the likes of Andrae Crouch *(I've Got Confidence)* and Bill Gaither *(He Touched Me)*.

In 1978 he released a compilation album entitled *He Walks Beside Me - Favourite Songs of Faith and Inspiration*. As far as Elvis was concerned all these albums were a labour of love. He chose the southern gospel songs as a tribute to those Tupelo and Memphis memories. They remain a true and fitting memorial to his mother and to the great vocalist himself. They also met a response to the ever-insistent demands of his countless fans for gospel music albums.

In 1994, under the appropriate title of *Amazing Grace*, BMG re-issued all Elvis' RCA Victor sacred song repertoire on a double album. Included were a number of previously unreleased recordings to delight the fans such as *Turn Your Eyes upon Jesus*.

Down through the years, one of the favorite subject matters in the Blackwood Brothers' songs was the anticipation of heaven.

Inside The Gate came from J.D. Sumner for the recording session of the fourth of November 1955. Then came *Heavenly Love* that was one of Vep Ellis' most popular ditties. When the song ended, a sudden exclamation was heard.

"Praise God! Hallelujah!"

All eyes turned to James who had made the sound. Peering over his specs with a furrowed brow, he said he was pondering the prospect of heaven in the light of the plane crash that took two of his dear pals.

"Soon, we'll all be citizens of the New Jerusalem. Down here we're all just aliens and strangers passin' through. Heaven seems that much closer knowing we got kinfolk and buddies over there." The comments set the tone of their next song.

I Bowed On My Knees and Cried Holy received renewed interest in the nineties via the Gaither Vocal Band but probably the first version heard by Gaither was the Blackwoods! Credited to Bea Packer (a pen name for Wally Fowler), James ardently attested that Fowler did not write it! At the time of the recording, the Blackwood Brothers thought he did as he claimed it. Later, it was discovered that it was from the black gospel field.

I Saw A Man originated from the colorful, Arthur 'Guitar Boogie' Smith from North Carolina. It has been recorded by the likes of Johnny Cash, Connie Smith, George Hamilton IV, George Beverly Shea, Paul Wheater and countless others.

Arthur Smith was famous for his Guitar Boogie that was a multi-million dollar seller for MGM and *Feudin' Banjos* (otherwise known as *Dueling Banjos*). He successfully proved ownership of the latter tune in a bitter litigation dispute with the Hollywood makers of the movie *Deliverance*.

A hugely, successful businessman in the North Carolina community with TV and radio interests, he also sponsored his Crossroads Quartet and Crackerjack Band for many years. A close friend of Dr. Billy Graham, many country and gospel artists have utilized the Smith repertoire consistently.

Born on April 1, 1921 in Clinton, South Carolina and raised in nearby Kershaw, Smith is a multi-instrumentalist and album producer with many key country and Christian artists to his name. Among his best known compositions are *Acres Of Diamonds, The Shadow Of A Cross, You Are The Finger Of God, The Fourth Man, and I Saw A Man.* As well as the Blackwood Brothers, big-time artists who have recorded Smith's tunes include the Statler Brothers, Pat Boone, Johnny Cash, Paul Wheater, George Hamilton IV (who did an entire Arthur Smith album) and George Beverly Shea. By 1998, Shea had recorded no less than twenty-two Smith titles.

Billy Graham always recognised something special about his lifetime friend George Beverly Shea.

"Music speaks to hearts frequently where sermons fail. Over the years Bev's voice has ministered to people everywhere and will continue to do so until our Lord returns. For 'when He comes', in the words of the song and as someone has said, preaching will be no longer be needed, but music and singing will be enjoyed in heaven throughout eternity."

Bev Shea can be accurately described as the most influential and most popular gospel singer of the twentieth century. His name and rich, baritone voice were known world-wide as a result of his fifty- years-plus association with evangelist, Dr. Billy Graham that took them to every continent on earth. Together with song- leader Cliff Barrows they forged a powerfully effective partnership in evangelism.

Humble in nature, he was to rise from an obscure clerk in a little insurance office to the world's best known gospel singer. This phenomenal change of career Bev would excitedly describe as a divine call.

He found the Lord in his early boyhood years as he carefully observed the simple, sincere faith of his Christian parents. Their godly prayers for their son played their part too. Bev Shea was to dedicate his life as a living testimony of service to the Lord he came to love.

Born on the first day of February 1909, he was the son of a Methodist preacher the fourth of eight brothers and sisters. His mother played the organ in church. Bev, as he is affectionately called, was raised in Winchester, near

Ontario, Canada and his first public singing was in his father's church.

He progressed into radio work, and then the opportunity came in 1944 to share in a popular hymn program *Songs in the Night*, also featuring an unknown pastor from Western Springs, Illinois, named Billy Graham. So began a lifetime's association of fruitful service.

Later the duo became a trio of dedicated co-workers as song-leader Cliff Barrows joined them. He recalled with great affection, "God gave Bev Shea a wonderful gift. My memory overflows with the numerous occasions that his rich and vibrant singing brought inspiration and strength. It was as though Bev offered a personal plea in song to the Holy Spirit to visit every soul with His saving grace. Mr. Graham always wanted Bev to sing before he spoke, for few singers prepared the hearts of an audience like Bev. People were moved to reverence and praise our Lord when he sang!"

Added to that, Bev had the great joy of recording about a hundred albums of hymns and gospel songs that have reached the hearts and homes of so many millions more. Remembered well, with great affection, was the milestone album entitled *Surely Goodness and Mercy* for RCA Victor that featured him with the Blackwood Brothers Quartet.

The Lord Is A Busy Man was a strange title but a strong number for the Blackwood Brothers from the pop field. Penned by Ray Allen and Jerry Joyce, it was submitted to James by New York's Hill and Range publishers.

A play on the words of the national anthem *The Soul Spangled Soul* comes from Memphis-based, Byron Faust who had some early hits in the gospel field. His best known song was *Echoes from the Burning Bush* that was successful for the Chuck Wagon Gang. He worked for the Keithley Bakery and sang in a local male quartet that was called the Keithley Harmony Boys. The song featured the low bass of Sumner on solo.

J.D. Sumner, the long serving bass, also wrote *I Don't Mind* as the final song in a tiring session.

With the Thanksgiving of 1955 over and Christmas fast approaching, the boys found time amid their busy personal appearances to head back to Nashville, Tennessee for their December 6th recording session.

"I gotta feelin' guys, that this is gonna be an important session," James spoke in his clear inimitable way with a smile. "We've picked out some mighty good material here...So, let's see if we can do it justice! Otherwise, we'll have old men, Sumner, Davis, and Stanphill at our backs chasin' us!"

Grins were shared around the studio as eyes looked toward J.D. Sumner as he pulled a funny face at James. "Remember, James," he responded in truthful jest, "there's many a beautiful, classic tune played on an old violin!"

Swiftly, the always-talkative Cecil chirped in with his laughing retort that he directed to J.D.

"Yea! There's also some wheezin' 'n whinin' that comes from old fiddles too! Ha...ha!"

The good humored session kicked off with one of Sumner's early compositions entitled Wonderful Savior, *a worshipful song of praise.* I Wanta Go There *was a Golden Gate Quartet original. That was followed by Ira Stanphill's story-telling* Suppertime *that was a big hit for Jimmie Davis. After* You Are My Sunshine *and* Nobody's Darling But Mine, *it was perhaps the Louisiana Governor's most popular song!*

Ira Stanphill wrote several beloved classics including *Mansion Over the Hilltop* (later recorded by Elvis Presley), *Room At The Cross* (recorded by Tennessee Ernie Ford, the Statesmen, and Bev Shea), *Suppertime* (recorded by Ricky Van Shelton, Johnny Cash, Jimmie Davis, Faron Young, Vernon Oxford, and Jim Reeves) and *He Washed My Eyes With Tears* (recorded by Bev Shea). It is likely that these artists learned many of their Stanphill songs from Blackwood Brothers' recordings.

"I knew Ira well!" James recalled his dear, white-haired friend with heart-warming nostalgia.

"I had the wonderful privilege of doing some joint concerts with him. Hilton Griswold, our pianist from 1940-50, worked with his son, Larry, a pastor of a large church in Juliet, Illinois. Hilton syndicated a TV show to about twenty-five stations, taping the show in Chicago in Channel 38's Christian studio and later in Milwaukee. I guested several times with Ira. We also did some Sunday evening services.

"Ira and Gloria, his wife, were also with me on a Gaither video taping and we were booked for more. Sadly, he suffered a heart attack and died! But Gloria sang a song with me on the next video as a dear tribute to my brother in Christ!

"Several of Ira's songs were performed on that video taping day including, at my suggestion to Bill Gaither, *Unworthy* by John McDuff of the McDuff Brothers. It was so moving. I had previously recorded the song on an RCA solo album."

In the latter fifties, the public was still heavily buying singles while LP's were slowly gaining acceptance. For a time, RCA issued the same singles on both '78 and '45 speeds. It took a while for the public to switch. *Something Old, Something New,* a Sumner song, was made for single release.

The other side of the single was Charles Matthews' *My Saving King.* Charles Matthews, a young man based in Atlanta, Georgia, had a rather tragic life. He penned *Stop and Pray* in the midst of emotional problems. He was, sadly, to die young.

The King and I Walk Hand In Hand was one of Mosie Lister's greatest compositions. Jack Holcomb had a popular recording of the song in the late sixties and used it as a title track on an RCA Victor release. James Blackwood re-recorded the song in the nineties for the Nazarene Publishing House of Kansas City. They issued two CDs of Mosie Lister songs featuring various artists, each contributing a song, such as Bill Gaither, the Stamps, the Statesmen, the Kingsmen and others.

16 CONVENTION BIRTHPANGS

I thank my God upon every remembrance of you,
Always in every prayer of mine for you all making request with joy,
For your fellowship in the gospel from the first day until now!
Being confident of this very thing,
that he which hath begun a good work in you
will perform it until the day of Jesus Christ.
Philippians 1: 3-6

During the Cold War years of the fifties and Sixties, the Blackwood Brothers took many a community hostage with their engaging, entertaining and unashamedly evangelistic message. Old and young became deeply challenged! One such youngster, named B.J. Thomas, growing up in Houston, Texas, years later remembered the life-changing experience.

"The music of the Blackwood Brothers," reminisced B.J. Thomas, "more than their message, held me spellbound at the Music Hall. You can still hear their musical influences on my music today!"

Since his born-again experience, B.J. Thomas declared, "I have a new appreciation of their lyrics today! I feel that I have come full circle. The Blackwoods' lyrics now have great meaning in my life!"

In 1956, the ever-enterprising Blackwoods went on to organize the first National Quartet Convention in Memphis. Little did they realize that it would become an annual event. The National Quartet Convention continues to this day, an on-going reminder of their innovative enterprise.

The Annual Convention, initially in Memphis contributed greatly to the revitalization and continuation of gospel music into a new generation. It continued to meet at the turn of the millennium in Louisville, Kentucky.

Originally, it was a two-day and one night event in duration. It eventually expanded to five days and five nights in the sixties, such was its popularity. It presented a unique opportunity for the gathering of the gospel groups, singers and promoters. The event enabled them to swap ideas, share good-practice, and have fellowship.

The National Quartet Convention also enabled gospel music enthusiasts the golden opportunity to see and to meet face to face with their favorite groups or singers. Memphis seemed the ideal place initially to hold the convention given its central position and excellent convention facilities. Other cities such as Birmingham, Atlanta, and Nashville were later used but by the end of the century the convention seemed happily settled in Lousville.

As usual, Chet Atkins presided as the A & R director of the session held in Nashville, Tennessee, on the sixth of January 1956. There was a nip in the air as he gazed up and down the street.

The usually punctual Blackwoods were late in appearing at the studio that day. Eventually, somewhat ruffled and irritated, the boys arrived with Chet Atkins waiting patiently at the door.

"Sorry, Chet! You know I hate to be late! But we got stopped by a speed cop!"

"That's okay, James! We've bin usin' the time usefully! Did ya git a ticket?"

"No, Chet but we did git a mighty-long lecture we could've avoided!"

James and the anguished group mutely, looked daggers at Jackie Marshall who sheepishly was setting himself up behind the piano.

"Okay, James what happened?" Chet smiled quizzically at the Blackwoods' leader and driver for the day.

"Well, Chet," James vexed expression turned into a smile as the ludicrously, humorous nature of the event he was bringing back to mind dawned on him. "We got stopped by this big ole cop who accused me of doin' eighty miles an hour...He was gonna let me off the hook with just a quick telling-off...Then, Chet, from the back seat the voice of Mister Marshall piped up and spoke to the lawman!"

"I'm gonna pray for you!"

"Why pray for me, boy?"

"The cop addressed the question to where it came from, Chet...And before we could stop him, stupid Mister Marshall replied, 'B'cause ya lied...We was only doin' seventy!"

"That's why we're late, Chet! Ha...ha...That ole cop read us the first five books of his traffic bible before he let us go!"

"Ha...ha...okay! Let's git to task of the day!"

As boss, Chet spoke with authority as he persuaded the high-flying quartet to calm down and mentally return to their musical roots with some nostalgic, revival favorites.

Sure enough, memories flooded back as the melodies soared!

James Rowe and M. L. Yandell originated *Wonderful* in the early Twenties. Rowe also wrote the well beloved, standard hymn, *Love Lifted Me* (recorded by Red Foley, B.J. Thomas, Kenny Rogers, Bev Shea and many others). Yandell was in the original Stamps Quartet.

Two years had now passed since that tragic plane crash. In some ways, things were easier and back to normal but in other ways the scars of painful memory were legacies which even the most strong-minded and determined of men could not shake off.

Six months later, the quartet was back in the famed Nashville studio on July 6.

"You know, Bill," a thoughtful James chatted to his tenor partner, Bill Shaw as they sauntered up to the familiar studio mikes awaiting the tape to roll, "ever since the plane crash, heaven seems so much more real. I can't help but think of Bill and R.W. when we sing these songs about heaven!"

"Sure James, I know what you mean," Bill responded seriously. "Heaven does seem closer and these lives of ours seem so fragile, do you agree?"

With head bowed, James nodded in silent agreement as the talented, session musicians commenced their rehearsal of the first songs introduction.

The quartet commenced their short session with *I've Heard About A City*, an Arthur Smith jewel. It featured Sumner as the deep bass. After that, *If I Pray*, the flip side of *I Heard About A City*, written especially for the Blackwood Brothers by Bennie Tripplett, was waxed with some enthusiasm.

Ten weeks later, RCA's New York studio was the rallying point for the nineteenth of September 1956 session. It followed the boys *Arthur Godfrey TV Show* success. This up north arrangement allowed the Southern gospel quartet to radically experiment somewhat with exciting new sounds to augment their vocal acrobatics!

Donald Douglas, author of *I Will Lift Up Mine Eyes unto The Hills* hailed from Birmingham, Alabama.

"As far as I know," declared James as they intently practiced, "this is the only song Donald Douglas ever wrote that was ever recorded, although he has written others."

Looking seriously at his colleagues, Cecil jokingly added a telling comment.

"Looking at the title now...*I Will Lift Up Mine Eyes Unto The Hills*...it looks as if he should have shared publishing with the Psalmist David.'

The boys all burst out in uncontrollable, irrational laughter at his sharp remark!

When it was time to serious-up, they could not retain their composure because of their hysteria. This irritated the sound engineer, concerned about so many aborted takes. After an untold number of false starts, they did get down to the business at hand.

The Good Book was penned by Hal Stanley and Irving Taylor for their *NBC* production entitled *The Lord Don't Play Favourites*. The Blackwood Brothers got the song from one of their well-worn Kay Starr records.

Some discerning music experts say that the beautiful *Give Us This Day* recorded that day was the Blackwood Brothers highest audio achievement in close, sophisticated harmony. It featured unusual chords for a gospel song. It originated from the pop field, Bobby Day and Buddy Kaye being the writers. Receiving the song from the New York publisher, it was fitting that the Blackwood Brothers recorded the song the morning after their second time on the *Arthur Godfrey Show*.

Joining Jack Marshall, were instrumentalists, Jack Lessberg (bass) and Bunny Shawker (drums). James recalled the harmony being so difficult and sophisticated that it required more re-takes than any other recording the

Blackwood Brothers ever did! The classic lyrics came from *The Lord's Prayer* and knowledgeable music buffs have praised the special harmony.

Cecil remembered the frustrations of doing take after take.

"We had to keep starting over and over again. It was the first time we could punch-in on the recording tape, which was better than starting each time again from scratch. I recall it took forty-six takes to get it right! It was the hardest thing we'd ever recorded!"

The taxing session done, it was time to do some quick shopping before heading back south.

"New York City sure is a fine place to visit," Cecil jokingly made his remark to the quartet as they busily packed their bags ready for the taxi arrival. Then Jackie chimed in with a cutting comment.

"But I sure would hate to live here...Give me the sunny South every time!"

James responded with a knowing grin, "Well, Jack, I guess most people up here don't have too much of a choice. We're kinda lucky that we was born in the land of Dixie."

"Yea!" Cecil chirped up, "I'll be glad to get home to some fine country cookin'."

The Blackwood Brothers had enjoyed their excursion up north to New York City but it was even better to return to the familiar recording environment of Music City (Nashville, Tennessee) on the second of November, 1956. The warming, country-gospel sounds of the South were again the menu of the day!

"Here's a great new song, guys. Arthur Smith from North Carolina sent it to me in the mail." James announced his value judgement to the assembled studio team.

"It sure made me think!" He spoke as he busily handed out the lyrics and music.

You are the Finger of God was a challenging message from Arthur Smith that George Hamilton IV and Bev Shea also recorded later. They most likely heard it first by the Blackwood Brothers.

The Touch Of His Hand and *Then I Met The Master* were Mosie Lister gems later to attain a standard status. The latter was destined to be sung by James in almost every concert he ever did!

Next in line was *I Was There When It Happened,* a toe tapping, gospel classic. Since, many classy artists have usefully performed it including Johnny Cash, Walt Mills, the Speers, and Jimmie Davis. The latter is credited with co-writing the song of Christian testimony with Mrs. R.L. Jones. Originally, the Blackwood Brothers issued the song on the small EP form. Due to their rarity, such extended-play discs with their colorfully printed jackets are highly prized today by ardent collectors

The shorter days and cold nights were a reminder that the year of 1956 was fast drawing to a close. The quartet had packed the year brimful of concerts and recording sessions. Life was getting faster and faster.

New Year resolutions were still being struggled with in the Nashville studios as January 23, 1957 were close enough to the *Auld Lang Syne* celebrations to be easily called to mind.

Arranged on their music stands was a bumper-bundle of sacred songs, all desperately crying out for the Blackwoods' special touch to bring them alive! By now, the quartet was so skilled at its trade, little rehearsal was necessary before they documented their talent into audio wax.

The Blackwood Brothers recorded several Buford Abner numbers in their early RCA days including He Lifted Me From Sin, Peace Of Mind, *and* There's One. *The former was his biggest, popularized by Horace Parish of the Rebels Quartet of Tampa, Florida.*

Born in 1905, songwriter and publisher, Robert S. Arnold composed No Tears In Heaven *and* Jesus Lifted Me *and enterprisingly printed them in his self-published book. Later in 1997, James sang with him at the annual Albert Brumley Sing and later at a Gaither video taping.*

"He still sang like a bird even in his nineties," remarked James. "It's amazing how God continues to give us a song throughout all our days....even in old age!"

Give Me Strength to Stand *was a Sumner original while Vep Ellis and Bill Lakey combined on* Jesus Holds the Keys. *First done as a Blackwood Brothers single, it later followed in LP form.*

Never, I Wouldn't Trade, His Love, *and* Jesus Is Mine *was a quartet of Sumner products.* Never *had a catchy chorus repeating the title rapidly and drawing a smile from the listener. James, in the late nineties, unearthed an old movie clip of the ditty which he made available to the public on video. Several other acts recorded the trade song.* Jesus Is Mine *featured James and was penned in response to another song.*

Farther Along *was a true standard in Southern Gospel. Printed by V.O. Stamps of the* Stamps Baxter *company before WWII, it was merely credited as being sung by the Burnett Sisters, a ladies act from Texas. In 1940, after the Blackwood Brothers sang in a high school in Greentop, Missouri, James was introduced to the elusive writer. He was Rev. W. B. Stevens, an elderly Methodist minister. James informed Frank Stamps and rightly, forthcoming prints became writer specific.*

I'm Bound For That City *was an Albert Brumley jewel. Albert Edward Brumley was country-born on October 29, 1905 in Le Flore County, Oklahoma. His enterprising farming parents raised corn and cotton on their rural property. Always keen on music, in his teens he enthusiastically attended a community singing school in Rock Island, Oklahoma, his hometown.*

In 1931, he married the love of his life, Goldie Edith Schell and they parented five sons and one daughter. One son, Tom Brumley became a famed West Coast steel guitarist. He spent many successful years with country-hitmaker, Buck Owens as a member of his band, the Buckaroos.

Speaking of Albert E. Brumley, James remarked, "I think one of the marks of a truly great man is humility and this is clearly evident when you met Albert E. Brumley. He was completely unassuming, always reluctant to be in the limelight to receive the honors he so richly deserved! Mr. Brumley was the second living man to be voted into the Gospel Music Hall of Fame, an honor he richly deserved!"

Several true classics have come from Albert E. Brumley's pen including I'll Fly
Away, River Of Memories, Turn Your Radio On, Jesus Hold My Hand *and
many more. High-selling recordings of Brumley songs are plentiful from the likes of
Ray Stevens, the Statler Brothers, Pat Boone, Jim Reeves, Tennessee Ernie Ford, and
such. The Chuck Wagon Gang and the Statesmen devoted entire albums to Brumley.*

"Let's pray before we leave the studio,"James suggested to the already tired
quartet at the close of their busy two day session. "I sense that we've recorded
some timeless classics today. Let's thank the Good Lord for the truths of what
we sing!"

With heads bowed around him, James offered a prayer of thanks with a final
benediction. The prayer concluded, the vocalists and musicians 'amens' resounded as one voice from the acoustics of the famous studio.

By May 3,1957, the boys were very familiar faces in the RCA studios in
down-town Nashville, Tennessee. The regular waxings that the gospel boys did
were welcome respites in the heavy touring schedule! The change of pace,
though still busy, was refreshingly different and uplifted the spirits of the
quartet.

That day several of the quartet came into the studio with individual high
hopes. Several of the group were trying their hand at songwriting! Long serving,
trained tenor, Bill Shaw wrote and featured himself on *I'm Thankful.* He completed the final take with a deep sigh of relief and satisfaction.

On The Other Side Of Jordan was written by Sumner after James challenged
Sumner, Shaw and Varner to come up with a new song on the subject. The
challenge had taken place in transit, on the bus in the vast expanse of West Texas
to relieve the boredom of travel! James had judged J.D.'s ditty to be the best so
he made a loud, lofty, and measured announcement.

"Ladies and gentlemen! Lend me your ears! Here we have, at great expense
another great song written by your friend and mine, J.D. Sumner! Like all his
others, this one too is destined to be a classic and like all his others it features
him too!'

Laughter broke out spontaneously throughout the studio as daggers were
drawn in jest at James by the half-smiling, half-scowling J.D.

Next was *Without A Prayer* that was credited to Cecil Blackwood although
according to James, Sumner was the sole author. Cecil, however, was strongly
featured vocally on the ditty so they added his name!

Sumner's tongue in cheek, *Pay As You Go* was inspired in somewhat cheeky
response to a sermon entitled *Pay Someday* by Dr. Robert G. Lee, pastor of the
Bellevue Baptist Church in Memphis for many years.

17 NIGHT AND DAY

It is a good thing to give thanks unto the LORD,
and to sing praises unto thy name, O most High:
To show forth thy loving kindness in the morning,
and thy faithfulness every night,
Upon an instrument of ten strings, and upon the psaltery;
upon the harp with a solemn sound.
For thou, LORD, hast made me glad through thy work:
I will triumph in the works of thy hands.
Psalm 92:1-4

Merely a month later, the sun shone brightly on the seventh day of June 1957. It was uncomfortably hot. The Blackwood Brothers Quartet was back in the studio and the members were relieved to feel the cool air of the air conditioner.

At the start of the session, RCA insisted on a change of title for Sumner's *Night And Day* to avoid confusion with Cole Porter's standard of the same name.

The rather lengthy, *Night And Day I'll Follow Where He Leads* was the newly chosen title. *Wonderful Love* also came from Sumner while Bob Prather (who wrote *Roll Jordan Roll*) penned the yearning *Take Me Home* and plaintive *Though I'm Unworthy* for the session.

Western close-harmony singing was popularized greatly between the thirties and the fifties by the singing cowboys of Hollywood such as Gene Autry, Roy Rogers, Tex Ritter and Rex Allen. The music genre was, however, pioneered, in a very real sense, by a harmony group (who often sang with 'the singing cowboys') called the Sons Of The Pioneers. By 1957, the Sons Of The Pioneers member, Tim Spencer was being thanked by many for publishing and publicizing *How Great Thou Art* via his Manna Music.

The Blackwoods version of *How Great Thou Art* was recorded in Nashville on September 6,1957. This classic hymn was already a major world-wide hit for George Beverly Shea. Shea received the song in London in 1954 from Mr. Gray of the Pickering and Inglis firm.

Originally, its melody roots were in Sweden and Russia, and English missionary Stuart K. Hine provided the translation. James recalled the experience of singing the majestic song one Sunday morning in Moscow's Baptist Church at the height of the Cold War.

"A thousand people packed the sanctuary of Moscow's Baptist Church. The pastor introduced me. My first words to the congregation were 'Greetings from fellow believers in the United States!' The pastor interpreted and the congregation jumped to their feet and responded in a greeting to me in Russian. I then introduced Billy, my son, and together we sang *How Great Thou Art*.

We sang the verse through first. Then, when we got to the chorus, the thousand people again rose to their feet, and at the top of their voices joined in the chorus. That will always be a moving, special memory for me!'

Still fairly new in the late fifties, *Do You Know My Jesus* is today a classic co-written by Vep Ellis and F. Lakey, popularized by versions by Skeeter Davis and Bev Shea among others. It was also re-recorded by the Blackwood Brothers on the twenty-third of April 1959.

Sumner's *He's All That I Need* featured tenor, Bill Shaw. At the end of the Century, the number still gets a Blackwood Brothers annual airing at the Grand Ole Gospel Reunion in Greenville, South Carolina where old quartet members of various groups get together for three days of nostalgia.

Sumner also originated *He's My King* that focuses on Christ's kingship. It was a fitting conclusion to the session's hard toil, at the close of the day.

Winter shadows were beginning to deepen on November's 22, 1957. Thanksgiving Day fast approaching gave an urgency to the proceedings at the session.

James recalled that, on that day, bossman Chet Atkins was the kind provider of the *I'm Free* song to the Blackwood Brothers although it was written be Joe and Taty Rogers.

Ex-lead singer of the Swanee River Boys and good friend of the Blackwood Brothers, Buford Abner, who originated from Wedowee, Alabama but resided in the late nineties in Indianapolis, contributed *Do You Go To Church, and Inside Your Heart*. The session was closed on a happy note with *I Get Happy,* another cheery ditty from Buford Abner.

Thanksgiving was soon over and the Christmas season was in the air on the bright, crisp morning of December 16, 1957. Colorful, twinkling lights bedecked the stores but there seemed little time left for the quartet to find opportunities to do their Christmas shopping. Their first duty was to complete their concert schedule and recording commitments. Christmas shopping, however, was the topic of their small talk before getting down to the business of the day.

That morning, the Music City waxworks of RCA resounded to a classic trio of recordings on the concept of God's hands. Recorded that day was 'His Hands' that originated from Stuart Hamblen and had high sales by Tennessee Ernie Ford.

Invisible Hands was recorded by the Blackwood Brothers as a vocal back-up originally for the Hank Snow solo on September 23, 1953. Written by Buddy Kaye, Bill Harrington, and Frank Stanton, Kaye was also the co-author of *Give Us This Day*.

Grossly underrated, the blind, Texas-born, country songsmith, Leon Payne (1917-1969) penned the superb *Gentle Hands*. Several years earlier he wrote *Lost Highway* and *They'll Never Take Her Love From Me*, massive sellers for Hank Williams. Biggest of all was, of course, *I Love You Because* and *The Blue Side of*

Lonesome by Jim Reeves. George Jones devoted an entire album of Payne songs to his memory.

I'm Happy and Free and *God Made a Way* from J.D. Sumner bounced along that day with a happy lilt backed up by Chet Atkins (guitar), Bob Moore (bass) and, of course, Jack Marshall (piano) in the little, hit-making RCA studio.

James Blackwood doubted the accuracy of the later, hastily completed paperwork kept by RCA. He is convinced the bass-player was Lightning Chance! Cecil, however, was convinced that the Bob Moore documentation is correct.

"I know it was Bob Moore because, after the recording session, when we went downtown to eat at a place down an alley behind the Noel Hotel, Bob was there. He came up behind me and grabbed me in jest...He made a big deal, laughing and remarking how glad he was to see us at that restaurant...Yet we'd just been recording together a few hours earlier in the studio. I remember him playing up-right bass that day on *God Made A Way*."

Shortly after the founding of the Gospel Music Association, J. D. Sumner, who by then was managing the Stamps Quartet for the Blackwood Brothers' organization, began singing bass for the Stamps Quartet. 'Big' John Hall then joined the Blackwood Brothers from the Stamps Quartet. The astute swap had far reaching effects on the revitalized career of the Stamps. Reconstituted, the Stamps appeared for six years on stage with superstar, Elvis Presley, as his classy backing singers on many of his million-selling recordings.

Elvis' background and aspirations had clearly been deeply influenced by the Blackwood Brothers. His home church, as a young boy, was the First Assembly of God in Memphis, the same church the Blackwood Brothers attended at that time. He regularly attended the teen Sunday school where a fellow classmate was Cecil Blackwood.

Cecil remembered with great affection his initial meeting with Elvis, his new sixteen years old buddy.

It was time to start, and the chattering was dwindling away as the Sunday School teacher took her position, Bible in hand. The attention of the teenage boys and girls was focusing on the lesson of the morning. Just as the teacher was about to commence, the classroom door opened with a disturbing squeak turning all eyes in its direction. It was a moody-looking, sixteen years old newcomer with dark, deep-set eyes.

"Good mornin' Maam...eh...I'm sorry to be late. Eh, can I join ya class, please Maam?"

"Why of course! Come on in! You're most welcome. You ain't late 'cause we're just gonna start. Take a seat next to Cecil Blackwood. . By the way, what's ya name, Son?"

"Eh... Ma name's Elvis...Elvis Presley!"

Elvis, coming into that class of teenagers late that morning created a stir because of his striking appearance! Every eye was upon him as he sauntered in and took his seat.

His dark, sleek, raven hair with long sideburns set the girls glancing at each other and then to giggling. Meanwhile, Cecil noted that his loud dress-sense was somewhat different from the norm! His clothes looked second-hand but were nonetheless impressive. His bright red jacket and white shoes were raising eyebrows that morning.

"Hi, Elvis! I'm Cecil Blackwood! Just make yurself at home!"

When the class was over Cecil and Elvis turned to each other and smiled, "Say, Elvis did ya enjoy class this mornin'?"

"I sure did, Cecil! It was good! I'd like to come ev'ry week. Say, did ya say your name is Blackwood?"

Cecil nodded with some satisfaction that his distinctive surname had been recognized. A wide grin beamed across Elvis' face.

"Tell me, are you related to them Blackwood Brothers? I love gospel music and that quartet's ma favorite."

"Well, I sure am related 'cause my brother's R.W. Blackwood."

From that moment on, a rapport developed resulting in a great friendship.

Cecil and Elvis were never short of pals because of their gregarious natures and also because they were the only two in the teen class who drove cars! Elvis had a 1941 Lincoln and Cecil had a 1948 Studebaker.

Elvis loved cheeseburgers! One night, while heading for Leonard's Barbecue, Cecil recalled that Elvis packed thirteen of the class into his car, weighing the springs down so far that on corners the chassis touched the tires! To continue the journey, Elvis had to unload his passengers accordingly.

As they journeyed, it was the custom to sing and to harmonize. The teenage friends gained a deep appreciation of gospel songs during these times of fun! Cecil remembered his friend with great affection.

"There is a story going around that Elvis was once asked to quit singing with the Songfellows Quartet because he could not sing well enough to harmonize with the group! Well, as I recall that simply is not true!

"Elvis and his folks lived across the street from me on Alabama Street, in an old house that had been turned into a duplex. His family lived on one side and a black family, the Kings, lived on the other side. The King's daughter Sally King, became my children's nursemaid and our house keeper for fifteen years."

Cecil, along with Jim Hamill, their pastor's son, was starting a church gospel quartet called the Songfellows. Already it had received radio exposure. Members included Jim himself, Bobby Ball, another pastor's son from Riply, Tennessee, Kemp Higgenbotham, a sixteen year old bass, piano-player Eddie Reese and Cecil singing lead and baritone.

Elvis desperately wanted to join the group but initially no opening was available. That did not curtail getting together with Cecil and the others for carefree sing along times, as Cecil recounted.

"There was no room for young Elvis in the group but we hot rod around in our cars, sang together and went to sings together. We were close buddies.... When Jimmy Hamill went off to the Assemblies of God College in Springfield, Missouri, Elvis was excited about taking his place. But it was short-lived cause ole Jimmy got kicked out of college for setting an alarm clock off in the organ during chapel. He was sent home after just a couple of months!"

"One day Elvis, all hot and sweaty, sporting his guitar across his back, came over to see me. He then went on to ask me to tell Jimmy Hamill that he wouldn't be able to sing with the Songfellows any more because, as he put it, 'I have signed a contract to sing the blues!' I later told Hamill, the new leader and he said that was okay and hired another singer to replace him.

"Unfortunately later on, *Photo Play* magazine ran an article in which they said they had interviewed Hamill's father, Rev. James E. Hamill, and he told the interviewer that Elvis was fired because he could not sing. That simply was not true... he quit because the group had trouble with the fact that Elvis at that time was sporting long sideburns, and he had trouble with the harmonies. But he was definitely not fired!"

It seems likely that the Blackwood Brothers were probably his first specific contact in the performing arts. The influence that the boys had on the growing Elvis was greater than any other professional performers. No one could imagine back then, the heights of stardom he would achieve. He never lost his enthusiasm for the quartet even amid the excesses of his latter years.

In his impressionable youth, Elvis idolized the Blackwood Brothers.

Eager to perform, Elvis was a painfully shy, unknown kid from Tupelo. He had a day job driving a pick-up truck but his deepest longing was to sing and perform. His persona seemed so unsuited for the stage, at that time.

The Songfellows invited him to attend, what turned out to be a stiff audition for the church's quartet group. Jim Hamill concluded that Elvis could sing well enough as a lead vocal. But he was rejected because it was thought that he would have trouble singing in team harmony! His long sideburns were also an issue of contention.

Thus, the Songfellows turned the King of Rock 'n' Roll down. Later, however, the still young Elvis was asked to join several other leading quartets. These included the Songfellows after Cecil left to replace R.W. in the Blackwood Brothers Quartet. By then, however, Elvis himself was showing great innovation in other areas. The King of Rock 'n' Roll was destined to reach the highest stars in the show business galaxy.

It is a reasonable conjecture to assume that Elvis always revered and highly cherished the gospel quartet scene. He seriously aspired, on several occasions, to join a major professional gospel group before other forces swept him up. Clearly, gospel music figured highly in his musical priorities at the time and throughout his years.

This love of Christian quartet music never left him. This is evidenced in the clear fact that throughout his immensely successful career, Elvis used gospel quartets as back-up singers for both his recording and stage work. Christian groups that worked with him included The Imperials, with Terry Blackwood, son of Doyle Blackwood as lead vocalist, J.D. Sumner and the Stamps Quartet, the Jordanaires, and the Sweet Inspirations.

It seems strange, looking back over his uniquely successful career, to contemplate the outstanding fact that the only Grammy Awards that Elvis would ever receive would be for his gospel recordings! Those prized recordings were echoings, indeed, of his Blackwood Brothers memories.

The wintery day of February 4, 1958 showed signs of the promise of spring in the fresh Music City air. Multi-colored flowers were just beginning to peek through the soil and birds whistled their sweet songs amid the trees of Music Row.

Yielded afresh to their evangelistic task, the Blackwood Brothers appropriately waxed *Not My Will* that came from the Arthur Smith stable. Time and time again, James felt that it was his duty and responsibility to draw the quartet back to spiritual basics.

"Oh, my brothers, what a great joy it is for us to serve the King of Kings and to be involved in telling the world about Him!" It seemed to him to be an appropriate declaration to announce at the outset of the session. "Let's not forget that He is a wonderful Saviour who we serve!"

The legendary, Leroy Abernathy, a writer that James rated as an innovator, penned *A Wonderful Time up There*. Also titled *Gospel Boogie*, it was one of the few gospel songs ever to impact the pop charts. Controversial for its day, it was the tenth million seller for the evergreen, crooning rock 'n roller, Pat Boone. It remained in the chart for nineteen weeks peaking at number four.

Boone's great, hugely successful version of the ditty was recorded in March of 1959, a full thirteen weeks after the Blackwoods' version. Therefore, it is likely that Boone first heard the song by the Blackwoods.

The album title track, *Stranger Of Galilee* (a familiar Bev Shea ballad), was penned by Mrs. C. H. Morris. Like the whole album the ace guitarist, Chet Atkins skillfully produced it in Nashville on May 22, 1958.

RCA Victor gave the Blackwoods a striking sleeve with a unique Sunday school flavor for their Silver Anniversary year project. It was nostalgically conceived as a keepsake album of established church-favorites, not necessarily of Southern gospel origin. It was the opportunity to delve into the best of hymnody.

Written by the renowned English, eighteenth century reformer, Augustus Toplady, *Rock of Ages* was truly inspired and inspiring. It was written after he was caught in a fearful thunderstorm. His rugged shelter was in a cleft of a huge rock in Cheddar Gorge near Bristol, England.

Often called America's favorite hymn, *The Old Rugged Cross* was written in 1913 by Reverend George Bennard of Albion, Michigan.

When I'm Alone was written by Sumner just prior to or just after joining the Blackwood Brothers. *Sweet Peace* was a common hymn-theme and title but this one too came from Sumner. The pieces blended well with the hymn classics.

> *Amazing grace! How sweet the sound*
> *That saved a wretch like me;*
> *I once was lost, but now am found,*
> *Was blind, but now I see.*
>
> *'Twas grace that taught my heart to fear,*
> *And grace my fears relieved;*
> *How precious did that grace appear,*
> *The hour I first believed.*
> *Through many dangers, toils and snares*

I have already come;
'Tis grace that brought me safe thus far,
And grace will lead me home.

The Lord has promised good to me,
His word my hope secures;
He will my shield and portion be
As long as life endures.

Yes, when this heart and flesh shall fail,
And mortal life shall cease,
I shall possess within the veil
A life of joy and peace.

When we've been there a thousand years,
Bright shining as the sun,
We've no less days to sing God's praise
Than when we first begun.
John Newton / Trad. arranged by Wes Davis / © *New Music Enterprises 1999*

Writer of *Amazing Grace,* John Newton was born in 1725 and wrote the hymn in 1779 as an autobiography. He entered the Royal Navy at the age of eleven, eventually deserting and becoming a slave trader. After his dramatic conversion he became the faithful minister of the Anglican church in the small town of Olney, Buckinghamshire, England.

Also British in origin *What a Friend We Have in Jesus* was written in 1857 by Northern Ireland's Joseph Scriven. It followed the tragic death of his fiancée on the eve of their wedding and later, his mother. Written specifically for his mother, it was discovered, almost by accident, years later and printed and circulated accordingly.

What a friend we have in Jesus,
All our sins and griefs to bear!
What a privilege to carry
Everything to Him in prayer!
O what peace we often forfeit!
O what needless pain we bear!
All because we do not carry
Everything to Him in prayer.
Have we trials and temptations?
Is there trouble anywhere?
We should never be discouraged;
Take it to the Lord in prayer.
Can we find a friend so faithful
Who will all our sorrows share?
Jesus knows our every weakness;
Take it to the Lord in prayer.

Are we weak and heavy-laden,
Cumbered with a load of care?
Precious Saviour, still our refuge,

Take it to the Lord in prayer.
Do thy friends despise, forsake thee?
Take it to the Lord in prayer;
In His arms He'll take and shield thee,
Thou wilt find a solace there.
Joseph M. Scriven / Trad. arranged by Wes Davis /
© New Music Enterprises 1999

A contemporary of James Blackwood's early life was the great, gospel song-writer of Billy Sunday days, Charles W Gabriel. He wrote *Tell Someone About Jesus*. It was typical of the songs James heard in his youth.

The Blackwoods three-song medley of *The Last Mile of the Way, When I Make My Last Move* and *When I Take My Vacation In Heaven* followed the same concept of earth's final farewell. The boys harmonized with moving emotion and engaging sentiment as the recording machines turned silently behind the glass of the studio partition.

Whispering Hope was written by Septimus Winner under his pseudonym name Alice Hawthorn. Despite the name, Alice was a male, a Philadelphia music publisher and music teacher who wrote many music instruction books and songs like the well-loved *Listen To The Mockingbird*.

The Blackwoods' lyrical question *Who Is That?* was penned by E. M. Bartlett, author of the popular *Victory In Jesus* recorded by Billy Walker, Burl Ives, Bev Shea and many others. *Who Is That?* was considered by James to be a fine invitation hymn. The boys gave it a respectful interpretation that day.

The last song of the heavy day was a great challenge to the boys priorities. The plaintive title of *Shall I Crucify Him?* came from the combined efforts of Mrs. Frank Breck and G. C. Tuller. It was a serious musical consideration. The repertoire of the Blackwoods ranged from the very serious to the happy-go-lucky, almost-flippant, fun songs. Theirs was a musical journey through the ups and downs of life. This great diversity in life was clearly obvious when they started recording their next session, five weeks later.

I've Got It, You Can Have It, a Buford Abner original, was an unusually catchy number to kickoff with in Nashville on June 25, 1958. The Blackwood Brothers changed keys much in the fashion of *Dry Bones,* the spiritual of great renown. The fun song sparked off some gentle, playful miming in the studio by the quartet.

They returned to more sober attitudes as they completed the session with three challenging songs. Lucy Campbell was the author of *Footprints Of Jesus* while *One By One* was jointly credited to Marshall Pack and Jimmie Davis. The very productive Buford Abner of the Swanee River Boys was probably inspired by the Psalmist when he provided *There Is A God*. It was a strong affirmation of God's existence.

The fool hath said in his heart, There is no God! ....
The LORD looked down from heaven upon the children of men,
to see if there were any that did understand, and seek God.
Psalm 14:1-2

18 THE NASHVILLE SOUND

There are many symbols of class in the fields of music.
If you think of instrumentalists, you think of Chet Atkins!
Thinking of country singers, you think of Johnny Cash!
When you think of gospel groups, you think of the Blackwood Brothers!
They have proven, through the years, that they are class!
Eddie Miller

Between Thanksgiving and Christmas, on December 4, 1958 the meeting point for the Blackwoods was again Music City's highly successful, hit-making studios.

By this time, the Nashville Sound was gaining worldwide attention. Coming to international fame was such great talent as Eddy Arnold, Jim Reeves, George Hamilton IV, Connie Smith, Bobby Bare, Porter Wagoner, Skeeter Davis, the Browns, and many others. In the thick of the excitement were the world's most successful Christian music performers -the Blackwood Brothers! All were part of a select team of Nashville-based, RCA Victor artists known as the Chet Atkins' clan.

The essential part played by these gospel quartets in the formation of what became termed as the Nashville Sound should not be underestimated. Like their celebrated peers, the Jordanaires, the Imperials, the Statesmen, and the Stamps, the Blackwoods were most proficient at quality back-up vocals. Their masterful album recordings with Hank Snow, Porter Wagoner, Barbara Mandrell, and George Beverly Shea display this ability to the full.

A good name is rather to be chosen than great riches, and loving favor rather than silver and gold.
Proverbs 22:1

Truly the Blackwoods achieved the kind of reputation, following, and fame from which legends arise. The Blackwood Brothers' panoramic vocal-vistas, complicated harmony-techniques, and ear-catching arrangements gave the quartet a distinctive quality that stands out from among other groups of this genre.

The first week of December had a sense of urgency as the Blackwood Brothers buckled down to the hectic recording schedule. Soon the Christmas rush would be upon them.

The Blackwood Brothers first heard *For My Good Fortune* by a black pop singer whose name they could not recall. It was published by the Blackwood Music company of New York which was actually unrelated to the boys. The heavy seller of the day, Pat Boone utilized the same song as a love-lyric song in the late fifties. This was new information to James in the late nineties and also a puzzle to him! Boone's first secular recording of the song had taken place on the eleventh of August but the tape was duly lost. So, it was re-recorded ten days later. It was penned by Otis Blackwell and Bobby Stevenson.

Sumner wrote *Walkin' And Talkin' With My Lord*. James considers it one of the boys' finest recordings because of the clever arrangement and unusual harmony.

Kentucky-born, Martha Carson, a principal personality in early fifties' country-gospel, wrote *I Can't Stand Up Alone*. The Blackwood Brothers were often to dip into the song repertoire of country performers.

Behind Your Tears and *Walking In The Light* were Sumner originals for the Nashville session on the fourth of February 1959, the latter of which was somewhat unusual. It featured James in what he described as an unusual interlude. Back up on instrumental bass was by Ben Speer who did a few RCA recordings with the Blackwood Brothers. With his brother Brock he was heavily involved in the Skylight label of the sixties most of which were waxed in the RCA studios in Nashville.

Memories came flooding back to James as they focused on *Beyond God's Horizon*. Months earlier, James was at home, casually listening to a newscast by the famous newscaster, Paul Harvey, interviewing the grieving parents of a young man. Sadly, their son had been killed in a tragic road accident after returning from armed service duty. The parents movingly expressed their faith in God's promises and in the belief of an after-life beyond God's horizon. This gave the idea to James who asked Sumner to come up with *Beyond God's Horizon* and *He Will See You Through*. Other Sumner originals for the session that day were *Each Step I Take* and *My All I Give*.

That day, J.D. felt greatly favored as a song-writer by his colleagues as they recorded so many of the bass's compositions. He expressed his gratitude with some good humored advice to the boys as they huddled around the studio mikes.

"You know, guys," growled J.D. , "I've heard it said that every quartet is convinced that their own bass singer is the best in the world. But I just wanted to assure you this morning, on my authority, that ya' all really do have the best. I hope you appreciate that!"

J. D. 's jesting, over-confidence, and playful banter drew moans from his colleagues as they wryly raised their eye-brows and made faces at the smiling bass.

Despite the playful boasting of their bass buddy, he was quickly reminded that the next song *A Land Called Heaven* was authored by James Wetherington (known as The Big Chief) , bass of the Statesmen Quartet. Sumner and Wetherington were often to be found bantering with each other jokingly over the subject of who was the world's greatest bass singer.

Nashville did not boast any palm trees, or indeed, much sunshine on February 19, 1959 yet the soothing, musical theme of the Blackwoods' outstanding session that day was firmly centered on the Hawaiian Islands' artistic genre.

Paradise Island, the title track of the Hawaiian project, was written by Oakley

Sharp of the old Stamps Quartet Music Company. The original thought behind a Hawaiian album came simply. It occurred at an after-concert, suppertime discussion in a Hawaiian restaurant in California.

While a Hawaiian trio played, James birthed the idea that he later put to RCA. Initially, they consented to half an album only to test reaction. It was an immediate hit and opened the door for a whole album of South Sea styling. Ace guitarists, Jerry Byrd guested on steel and Chet Atkins guested on ukulele. Extrovert pianist, Wally Varner composed the fanciful *Dreams Of Tomorrow* and tenor, Bill Shaw provided *My Lord Goes Before Me*.

Such was his love for the genre, in later years, James Blackwood was to tie up with Bud Tutmarc (the ace steel-guitarist of Hawaiian fame) for yet another expedition into Hawaiian-styled, sacred songs. The joint album was entitled *Aloha Time* and released on the Skylite label.

By April 23, 1959, the RCA hierarchy in Music City had changed just before the Blackwoods' returned for their session. After years with Chet Atkins at the helm, now Brad McCuen became A & R director for this session. In other words, McCuen was now the man in charge.

Musicians for the day were Chet Atkins (producer/guitarist), Wally Varner (piano), and Joe Zinkin (bass). The Blackwood Brothers surprisingly re-cut Abner's *Do You Go To Church ?* and Sumner's *Pay As You Go* before they turned their attention to a Vep Ellis favorite.

Still fairly new in the late fifties, *Do You know My Jesus?* is today a classic co-written by Vep Ellis and F. Lakey. It was popularized by versions by Bill Gaither, Skeeter Davis and Bev Shea among others, and was previously recorded by the Blackwood Brothers on September 6, 1957.

There was great excitement in the air when the southern gospel singers traversed the long miles to sunny Los Angeles, California for their July 18, 1959 concert. RCA Victor wanted to capture the exuberant Blackwoods live in full flight for album release.

Recorded live, and produced by Neely Plumb, this concert album session re-cut many familiar songs already featured in this book. But the boys added other gems to their growing recording credits.

The Devil Can't Harm The Praying Man originated from the Dixie Hummingbirds of Houston, Texas. Ira Tucker, their manager, was the credited writer. James offered to buy the song and paid the required sum accordingly. Later, James said that he discovered that the song had been sold two or three times previously.

Hide Me Rock Of Ages was an old-time quartet evergreen written by B.C. George from Georgia. It was a re-working of the *Rock Of Ages* hymn theme to great effect. As the boys sang in harmony on this newer song, their minds drifted back inevitably to the lyrics of the old, familiar favorite they knew so well.

Rock of Ages, cleft for me,
Let me hide myself in Thee;
Let the water and the blood,
From Thy riven side which flowed,
Be of sin the double cure,
Cleanse me from its guilt and power.

Not the labour of our hands
Can fulfil Thy law's demands;
Could our zeal no respite know,
Could our tears forever flow,
All for sin could not atone:
Thou must save, and Thou alone.

Nothing in our hands we bring,
Simply to Thy cross we cling;
Naked, come to Thee for dress;
Helpless, look to Thee for grace;
Foul, we to the fountain fly:
Wash us, Saviour, or we die.

While I draw this fleeting breath,
When mine eyes shall close in death,
When I soar to worlds unknown,
See Thee on Thy judgement throne,
Rock of ages, cleft for me,
Let me hide myself in Thee.
Augustus Montague Toplady / Trad. arranged by Wes Davis /
© *New Music Enterprises 1999*

Control of the Blackwoods' recordings were fated to change again that year! By the time of the sessions in Nashville on the fifteenth and sixteenth of May 1960, Hollywood's Daryl Rice was now firmly in the Blackwood Brothers production seat. A talented musician in his own right, Daryl was to put his individualistic stamp on the quartet's repertoire

Hawaiian guitarist, Jerry Byrd was the ideal choice for the South Seas recording. He was then living in Hawaii, a contact of Bud Tutmarc, thus he provided Hawaiian guitar. Other sessioners included Roy Huskey, Jr. and Ray Edenton.

Sumner's brother-in-law, John Matthews, manager of The Rebels quartet, wrote *When I Stand With God*. The Blackwood Brothers received their musical numbers from near and far but not least from family and friends. This South Seas' concept album would be largely taken up with song compositions of their popular bass, J.D.

Crossing Chilly Jordan featured Bill Shaw and was one of J. D. Sumner's better known crowd-pleasing originations. Sumner also wrote *Heaven For Me* and *Paradise Valley. Jesus Fills My Every Need* and *I'll Be True* were provided by Vep Ellis. All lent themselves well to the Hawaiian style. The latter had a falsetto yodel break in it.

I Want To Meet you Up In Heaven , On That Happy Golden Shore, What A Glorious Morning, A Land Where Milk And Honey Flows, I Found God and *Eternal Paradise* were written by Sumner when commissioned especially for the Hawaiian album project. The latter melody featured James on a falsetto yodel. He re-recorded the song along with *Aloha Time,* also penned by Sumner, for his duet album with Hawaiian guitarist Bud Tutmarc in 1987 on the Skylite label.

The Hawaiian journey ended with the classic, *Beautiful Isle Of Somewhere* which was written by Jessie Brown Pounds in 1867 in the aftermath of the American Civil War. Her husband was the pastor of the Central Christian Church of Indianapolis.

Such was the great success of the live recording, Long Beach, California was chosen for another live recording venue on the twelfth of July 1960. Later the tapes were tidied up in Hollywood California, on the last day of August. This remote, live, tour-concert recording from Long Beach was to be the Blackwood Brothers most successful RCA album to date. Many of the songs were to remain favorites for years to come and the album became a unique, souvenir keepsake of the quartet's concert skills.

The Old Country Church was a most popular Sumner sing-a-long marathon. In 1997 it was resurrected and featured on the popular Gaither video *Down By The Tabernacle* recorded on an old Methodist camp ground in Indiana.

Other ditties given typical, Blackwood Brothers on stage treatment in Long Beach that day included *When I Stand With God* written by John Matthews, *Crossing Chilly Jordan* written by J.D. Sumner, *The Prodigal Son* written by D.D. McCool, *Happy People*(written by Bob Prather, *Bells Of Joy Keep Ringing* written by Wally Varner, *Because Of The Love Of The Lord For Me* written by Bill Shaw, *Some Wonderful Day* written by J.D. Sumner, and *Only Believe Him* written by Wally Varner.

What A Homecoming Day was a common Southern gospel theme but the Blackwood Brothers live cut was a Sumner original. Jimmie Taylor, pianist for the Rebels Quartet of Tampa, Florida, wrote *Dear Jesus Abide With Me* that featured the tenor, Bill Shaw.

J.D. Sumner wrote *Because Of Him* in response to Albert Brumley's *If Anyone Makes It, I Surely Will* that was often sung by the Speer Family and Rosie Rozell. Sumner considered the Brumley song to be presumptuous and self-righteous. He reasoned that the saved were saved solely by grace.

Bill Shaw sang solo on and composed *Pablo* as a tribute to a missionary to Mexico of the same name that he met.

The session of the last day of August 1961 was booked to enhance the live July 12, 1960 recordings of the songs *Pablo* and *Because Of The Love Of The Lord For Me.*

Socially, a radical, new decade was dawning. Many traditions and conventions would be brought tumbling down on many fronts. The sixties came when the Blackwood Brothers were receiving unprecedented acclaim for a Christian group from the general public, the recording industry, and their peers involved in the world of gospel music.

The keynote to the continuation of the quartet's success was unity within variety. It was a rule that applied to the personnel as well as to their wide gospel singing repertoire. Although members of the group frequently changed, the quartet never lost its ability to blend perfectly in harmony and expression.

Still eager to make gospel singing even bigger, and to expand it to every possible corner of the USA, the Blackwood Brothers scheduled a concert in Anchorage, Alaska. It was renowned to be the first appearance of a gospel quartet in the forty-ninth state! The audience was large and highly receptive to the Blackwoods. On the way back home they made a successful guest appearance on nation-wide ABC TV's *Tennessee Ernie Ford Show.*

Tennessee Ernie Ford's singing career spanned a spectrum of differing song subject matter. Yet, his conclusion was that he was happiest and proudest being able to sing songs of praise and worship in exaltation of the Giver of Life. He made no apology for liberally injecting his Christianity into his music as he said it raised his spirits and his horizons.

The rich, bass baritone of Tennessee Ernie Ford was internationally known to display the appropriate taste, reverence and enthusiasm that the gospel demanded. Consequently over his singing career of fifty years, his style evoked considerable public response to his Christian music.

Despite his early Country and Western tag, there was nothing really rural about his early life. Born on a cold day in February 1919 just after World War 1, he was raised in the industrialized urban area of Bristol, Tennessee. He gave his first vocal solo before an enthralled men's fellowship meeting in his local Methodist Church when Ernie was a mere toddler of three years old.

Tennessee was, of course, the seed-bed of much country music which at an early age seeped into his emotional soul. This plus his church music combined to form a dynamic mix that catapulted him into show business. By 1937 he was on the payroll of a local radio station eager to utilize his clear, penetrating narratives on the news output. By 1939 he was promoted to similar stints in the bigger cities' radio studios as jobs beckoned from Atlanta and Knoxville.

After the Pearl Harbor attack by Japan, the USA entered fully into the conflicts of World War II. Enlisted into the Air Corps, Ernie saw active service in the heavy bombers of the day. When peace was declared, he returned to Bristol, Tennessee with his wife Betty (who he had originally met and married while he was stationed in California). The marriage was to survive until her death in 1989.

Life was tough and employment was thin in the post-war South so they packed up their meagre home and again headed for the gold of California. He was soon snapped up by the west coast radio stations as station announcer and was roped in as a country and western disc-jockey.

Providence was to play its part one day when local country band leader, Cliffie Stone jested on air with Ernie, the announcer, which the latter followed up by vocalizing with a quartet. That's when the legendary Tennessee Ernie Ford was born as he was pressed into Saturday night singing and comic duties on the radio's entertainment output.

In 1947, Capital Records Lee Gillette was captivated by Ernie's rich, mellow voice which he heard on the radio as he drove along. Days later, a record contract was on offer.

Wisely, Tennessee Ernie Ford developed his comic stage act with an alter ego who was a bashful, rejected, country-boy in bib overalls, floppy straw hat and a blacked-out tooth! It gave an enthralling contrast to his more serious song-stylist stage-act.

Recording success started to build in the late forties. *Mule Train, Anticipation Blues, Shotgun Boogie, The Cry Of The Wild Goose, River Of No Return* (from the Marilyn Monroe/Robert Mitchum movie) and, of course, the biggest success of all *Sixteen Tons*. Written by his buddy, Merle Travis, it was to sell in excess of four million copies and establish Tennessee Ernie as an international star. Elected to the Country Music Hall of Fame in 1990, he died a year later.

By the mid sixties, the Blackwood Brothers owned and operated two music publishing companies, the Gospel Quartet Company and the Stamps Quartet Company. Each year, these companies published thousands of copies of gospel songbooks and sheet music in a worldwide marketplace.

Personnel changes continued to plague the group. Joining regulars, Bill Shaw, Cecil and James Blackwood were colorful newcomers, Big John Hall (the 6 foot, five inch bass) and Whitney Houston (on piano). Despite the musical chairs' syndrome the popularity of the quartet continued to build as they headed for their fourth decade.

19   MULTIPLE AWARDS

He that diligently seeks good procures favor:
but he that seeks mischief, it shall come unto him.
Proverbs 11: 27

Record sale volumes continued to rise with the steady acclaim being given to the beloved Blackwood Brothers Quartet over the seventies' decade. For society it would be ten years of agonized re-thinking of traditions and conventions. The very foundations of western culture were being threatened.

The Blackwood Brothers entered the seventies under the guiding genius of a new record producer, Danny Davis. A renowned musician, he had achieved fame with his hit-making Nashville Brass, which gained worldwide exposure.

In 1966, the Blackwoods received the Plaque Award from RCA, representing album sales that had topped one million. They were the first Christian group to ever achieve that status. By 1971, their sales of albums had topped the three million mark!

Throughout their long career but especially in the fifties, the sixties and seventies, the group and individual members received many other honors and distinctions. Indeed, the list is so great it is difficult to list accurately!

ARTHUR GODFREY TALENT SCOUT SHOW
1954   First Place Winners
1956   First Place Winners

DOVE AWARDS
MALE GOSPEL VOCALIST
1969   James Blackwood
1970   James Blackwood
1972   James Blackwood
1973   James Blackwood
1974   James Blackwood
1975   James Blackwood
1977   James Blackwood

MALE GOSPEL GROUP
1973   The Blackwood Brothers Quartet
1974   The Blackwood Brothers Quartet

GOSPEL SONG OF THE YEAR
1970   *The Night Before Easter*
Don Sumner and Dwayne Friend
Recorded on RCA Victor LSP4216 *Fill My Cup, Lord*

BACKLINER NOTES OF A GOSPEL RECORD ALBUM
1973   Eddie Miller *Release Me (From My Sin)*
         Skylite SLP61241
1974   Don Butler *On Stage*
         Skylite SLP6131

ALBUM OF THE YEAR
1970   *Fill My Cup, Lord*
         RCA Victor SLP4216

BEST GOSPEL RECORD ALBUM
1973   *Release Me (From My Sin)*
         Skylite SLP6124

GRAPHIC LAYOUT AND DESIGN OF A GOSPEL RECORD ALBUM
1972   Acy Lehman *L-O-V-E*
         RCA Victor SLP46679
1974   Charles Hooper *On Stage*
         Skylite SLP6131

GOSPEL MUSIC ASSOCIATION
1975   Fan award for Favorite gospel Group
1977   Fan Award for Favorite Gospel Group

ASSOCIATE MEMBERSHIP AWARDS
1974   Blackwood Brothers Quartet
1976   Blackwood Brothers Quartet
1977   Blackwood Brothers Quartet

GRAMMY AWARDS
1966   Best Sacred Recording (Musical)
         With Porter Wagoner *The Grand Old Gospe'* RCA Victor LSP3488
1967   Best Gospel Performance
         With Porter Wagoner *More Grand Old Gospel* RCA Victor LSP3855
1969   Best Gospel Performance
         With Porter Wagoner *In Gospel Country* RCA Victor LSP4034
1972   Best Gospel Performance (Other Than Soul Gospel)
         L O V E RCA Victor LSP4679
1973   Best Gospel Performance (Other Than Soul Gospel)
         Release Me (From My Sin) Skylite SLP6124
1979   Best Gospel Performance, Traditional
         Lift Up The Name Of Jesus Skylite SLP6128
1980   Best Gospel Performance, Traditional
         We Come to Worship Voice Box VB 1080
1981   Best Gospel Performance, Traditional
         The Masters V Skylite SLP 6256
         James Blackwood; Rozie Rozell; Jake Hess; J. D. Sumner; Hovie Lister
1982   Best Gospel Performance, Traditional
         I'm Following You VB 4001
1982   Best Inspirational Performance
         He Set My Life To Music Starsong MCR50
         Barbara Mandrell with the Blackwood Brothers Quartet
         *The Grammys - For The Record by Thomas O'Neil, Penguin Books

NATIONAL QUARTET ASSOCIATION
1977   Favorite Group

GMA HALL OF FAME INDUCTEES
September 1974/James Blackwood was inducted into the Gospel Music Hall of Fame
April 1998/the Blackwood Brothers Quartet was inducted into the Gospel Music Hall of Fame

* All Dove award information courtesy of The Gospel Music Association, Past Winner's

Opportunities to sing abroad started to increase, as Cecil nostalgically recalled.

"It was the height of the Cold War, the relationship of the West with the communist Soviet block was still decidedly frosty. But as is proverbially often said, 'Fools rush in where angels fear to tread'! James, Ken Turner, and Pat Hoffmaster and I decided on the dangerous move to take the gospel to Russia after our Holy Land tour!"

Levon Riley, the organizer responsible for the Israeli trip surprised the group with his offer to arrange a visit behind the feared Iron Curtain.

"Is it gonna be safe?" Ken's question articulated the silent thoughts of the entire group who expectantly then awaited Levon's reply. The opportunity to joke could not be resisted by Cecil as he viewed the seriousness of his colleagues' expressions.

"Perhaps, we can engage the services of James Bond as our Russian tour guide! That oughta keep us safe, guys!"

The frowns turned to smiles. There were some misgivings and protests at first from some members but then Cecil chirped up positively.

"Oh, come on guys! What a great adventure and opportunity it'll be for us to present the gospel in song! It'll be a first! I ain't never heard of any other gospel music artists ever doin' it!"

His colleagues warmed to the proposal. James was the first to agree with Cecil. "Yea, Cecil's right! We should take this as a golden opportunity given to us from heaven itself!"

American gospel music artists had never before been given even a passing whiff of an invitation into this bastion of socialist experimentation located, geographically and culturally, deeply behind, the fearful Iron Curtain.

For the Blackwoods first visit, 1974 was a different time, and Eastern Europe was a different place from what it is as the new millennium breaks. Things were primitive, restricted and sometimes dangerous! Everyday life for everyday folk was undoubtedly tough over there at that time.

It was a crisp, dry, sunny, morning and it was the very first encounter with Cold War politics. Years later, Cecil reminisced accordingly about the great Soviet adventure. That experience will forever be etched indelibly in Cecil's memory.

"We took a party of about forty folks with us. On the Russian border, we advised everyone that we should prudently declare ourselves to be 'folk-singing tourists' rather than 'gospel-singing evangelists'. There was no need to unduly stir antagonism among the guards and officials of this atheistic state!"

Cecil was the first to be quizzed and examined at the border post; but, to his great relief, he was the first to be admitted. After him came James. Then calamity struck.

"Ken Turner let it slip! He admitted that he was a gospel singer! The fearsome guards started to inspect all the American baggage with gleeful zeal. Sure enough, they discovered that our travel party members were carrying a large consignment of Bibles!"

Cecil was duly arrested with cold efficiency and thrown into a dismal cell. Photos were taken of the shaken prisoner with the contraband goods. The aggressive questioning was intimidating and threats were made.

The uncomfortable imprisonment lasted for hours, as Cecil fearfully contemplated what would be his fate at the hands of such a cruel state system. The tempter actively tried to sow seeds of despair and fear, as his thoughts raced.

"How long are these guys gonna keep me here? Was it really the right decision to come to Russia? Are those guards gonna get rough with me? Does God care at all? How can I contact a Western embassy?"

Outside, the tour party prayed earnestly and tearfully, pleading for Cecil's divine protection and release. Their heart-felt, urgent prayers were heard! Quicker than anyone had dared hope, the prison door was swung open.

A shaken, ruffled Cecil was returned to his friends who greeted him with sighs and cries of relieved hallelujahs. With misty eyes, James greeted him with a warm welcoming hug and a broad smile!

"Tell me, Cecil...ha...ha...Who needs James Bond when we've got the 'Commander of the Lord's Host' at our disposal? Praise the Lord for your safe return!"

Forty-eight of the fifty precious Bibles that Cecil was smuggling were rudely confiscated. Later, to his amazement, he discovered that each Bible was disposed of rather than being destroyed.

"We found out later that the guards and officials sold every Bible for about $700 each on the black market. So, I guess those Good Books eventually did get into the hands of some Russian people, after all!"

Reaching their St. Petersburg hotel destination, after a good rest, Cecil asked their Russian guide if she would guide the Blackwood Brothers to the church called The Temple Of The Gospel, where they planned to sing. She refused, worried and frightened about the trouble she would be in with the secret police. Clearly, they would be watching the Americans' movements carefully.

In desperation and frustration, Cecil phoned the church and after several voices, none of whom spoke English, he managed to reach an associate pastor. Sergei Nikolaev spoke pigeon-English through a thick Russian accent but, at least, Cecil could communicate.

Twenty-five years later, with misty eyes and a lump in his throat, Cecil remembered the events with warm nostalgia. "I had previously written about twenty letters and sent boxes of records to the church in advance of our arrival. But, nevertheless, now that we had arrived I was not sure of our welcome. So, on the phone, I was mighty glad to hear the warm greeting and encouraging exclamation!"

"Come on over! Brother Cecil, we're waiting for you all. Welcome to Russia in the name of our dear Savior!"

Cecil's voice trembled with emotion as he told his tired party of the kind words and the welcome that was awaiting them on the other side of the drab city in this Cold War bastion of atheistic repression.

It took ten taxi-cabs to ferry the whole party from the hotel through miles and miles of poor, bleak, grey streets to the unimposing, old, grey, soot-dyed building where the Blackwood Brothers had been booked to sing that day.

"Those bumpy taxis perilously sped through those traffic-empty, city streets at about eighty miles per hour. I do declare them Russian drivers were trying to kill us American boys. On the journey, Ken Turner our comic bass poked his head outside the window and made loud, siren sounds that seemed to add to the drama. But, thank the Lord, we did arrive safely."

Although language communications were difficult, the warm Christian greetings given to the party in the church courtyard were heart-felt. Tears, smiles and hugs said it all!

The hosts warmly and emotionally embraced their visitors. Then the gifts, including the prized Bibles, were distributed followed by an impromptu worship-time as the Christians from East and West praised God together in unison.

Blest be the tie that binds
The saints in Christian love;
The fellowship of kindred minds
Is like to that above.
Before their Father's throne
They pour their ardent prayers;
Their fears, their hopes, their aims are one,
Their comforts and their cares.
They share their mutual woes,
Their mutual burdens bear,
And often for each other flows
The sympathizing tear.
When for a while they part,
This thought will soothe their pain,
That they shall still be joined in heart,
And hope to meet again.
This glorious hope revives
Their courage by the way,
While each in expectation lives,
And longs to see the day.
From sorrow, toil and pain,
And sin they shall be free;
And perfect love and friendship reign
Through all eternity.
John by Fawcett (Trad. arranged Wes Davis / © New Music Enterprises 1999)

They gathered in lines of rough-hewn, narrow pews that quickly filled with work-weary people dressed in layers of hand-patched clothes. Cecil could not help making comparisons.

"How different this is to the plush, theatre-like churches back home. Even the smallest churches back across the Atlantic are carpeted and supplied with smart hymnals."

The worship service that followed was alive but in Russian with some translation. Of course, the Blackwoods could not understand all the words that were being said. The sacred music the Russians sang, however, they did appreciate. Most of the melodies were very familiar, stirring up he nostalgic embers of experiences of their homes and churches in the South.

Eventually, the minister welcomed the Blackwood Brothers and asked them to sing.

Nervously at first, but gaining conviction, James grinned and greeted the smiling congregation. "We are the Blackwood Brothers from Memphis, Tennessee. We are fellow Christians. We are your brothers. We bring greetings from your fellow Christians in America."

Then to the Blackwoods utter amazement, as tears swelled in their American eyes, and their American hearts began to pound, the poorly-dressed, Russian people in the congregation jumped to their feet and waved their hankies. Loud cries of hallelujah echoed around the building in Russian!

"Thank you! Thank you, Jesus! Hallelujah! Praise the Lord!"

The atmosphere was now electric. The Blackwood Brothers music was generally new to the congregation but, where they could, the Russians commenced to sweetly sing along with them. Their traditional, sacred music had tended to lack joy, reflective of the cruel regime they were living under, so the peppy ditties of their visitors were a remarkable departure for them.

"Most songs they got to know well and sang along in Russian!"

The Temple of the Gospel, that day, had a visitation of Holy Spirit baptism. An immensely memorable experience, Cecil recounted with much emotion. "It was very deeply meaningful and a moving episode!"

The lumps in the Americans' throats got bigger and bigger and many felt themselves close to losing control and composure. The spiritual emotion in that drab building that day behind the Iron Curtain, so far removed from the Bible Belt of home, was almost tangible!

While the emotional Blackwoods were singing, they looked around through misty vision, amazed at the sight. That day, the poor congregation shared a few tatty hymnbooks and hand-written songbooks but most would sing the songs of Zion from memory.

The radiant, glowing faces of the people in the uncomfortable wooden pews on the front row stirred the professionals to another uncontrollable surge of deep emotion.

Between two songs, Cecil whispered to James, "Wow, brother, they're glowing witnesses!"

"Yea, Cecil, these are very special people!"

Their radiant countenances just seemed to shine brighter and brighter as the Blackwoods sang.

Later in the church basement, the Russian Christians sacrificially fed their American guests with home-baked cakes and cookies plus pop to drink. What the affluent visitors had not realized back then was that the ordinary citizens of that stark, communist state were enduring severe food shortages. The common Russian people were experiencing great difficulty in obtaining even the basic necessities of life.

The sights, smells and sounds of that memorable day cut deep into the Blackwoods' souls like a two-edged sword! The silent, radiant testimony from the pews challenged them to the core. Their outlook on life would never be the same!

Throughout the moving worship service, the congregation maintained their bright smiles. They glowed as they sang the grand old hymns, and they seemed so hungry to absorb the message. They made a profound, indelible impact on the Americans that day.

The absorbing service over, the Western guests conversed deeply with their Eastern hosts. They told them how people who were committed Christians in Russia had a heavy price to pay! For example, they would be barred from education and forbidden to go to college. The abrasive, State legal system saw their faith in God as a barrier to communist progress.

As in every country in the world, education is the key that unlocks the door of opportunity.

Without adequate training the future looked very bleak for Christians. In all likelihood, they would spend their lives in some sort of low-paying, manual labor or menial job. Any aspirations about being a doctor or lawyer or something of that sort, they could just forget. But it was a cross they gladly bore because they loved the Lord and were publicly taking a stand for Him.

Looking back in deep gratitude, Cecil remembered how he assessed that experience in the context of the direction of his life that day.

The thank yous over, it was time to part. Spontaneously the Russians embraced their emotional guests for the last time then bubbled into Ira Sankey's classic farewell hymn. It was the final good-bye gesture to their American brethren.

God be with you til we meet again!
By His counsels guide, uphold you,
With His sheep securely fold you:
God be with you til we meet again!

'Til we meet, 'Til we meet at Jesus' feet
God be with you til we meet again!

God be with you til we meet again!
'Neath His wings securely hide you,
Daily manna still provide you;
God be with you til we meet again!

God be with you til we meet again!
When life's perils thick confound you,
Put His loving arms around you
God be with you til we meet again!

God be with you til we meet again!
Keep love's banner floating o'er you,
Smite death's threatening wave before you:
God be with you til we meet again!
J.E. Rankin /Trad. arranged Wes Davis / © New Music Enterprises 1999

Ken turned to Cecil, both individuals by now had completely lost their composure and were weeping openly, like most other people there.

"Brother, this sure, eh...this surely feels like, eh...the blessings of heaven are on us today!"

Life-long friendships were forged that day, as Cecil recalled.

"That day secured the Blackwood Brothers' commitment to Russia. Since then we have financially sponsored many Russian pastors on a regular monthly basis. Our on-going vision is for the Blackwood Brothers to continue to go to Russia and help save lost souls as well to bless the saints with our singing!"

20 HOMECOMING INSPIRATION

Without question, the singing Blackwood Brothers have become the legends of gospel music. How I thank God for the blessings that they have brought to millions during a ministry that spans more than half a century.
Pat Robertson

Over the decades, many members of the Blackwood Brothers developed a social conscience and had become politically vocal as well as religiously active. They accepted a prized invitation from Governor Frank Clement to sing the gospel before a joint session of the Tennessee House and Senate. They went on to support Clement and Governor Buford Ellington in their successful political bids with rallies and programs.

The Blackwoods were also recruited to help their cousin, J. P. Coleman in his bid for the Lieutenant Governorship of Mississippi in the fifties. One day in Memphis, he arrived at the radio station where the quartet was broadcasting their program and announced his intention to run for the office of Governor. J. P. obviously recognized the advantage he would have over his opponents, Barnett and Johnson if he could rely on the quartet's considerable promotional skills. He knew that their popularity among the electorate would enhance his bid to get into the runoffs, and then into office.

His canny prediction proved to be correct. Cecil remembered well how he (Cecil), James, J. D., Bill and Jackie "sang at every crossroad and in every town on a flat-bed truck introducing J.P. to the electorate!"

Armed with a very heavy piano that they placed on the top of a flat bed truck, the quartet would drive into a country town, and start singing over the PA to attract a crowd. It worked!

After the singing, J. P. Coleman would then mount the flat bed and speak. His recurring themes were the removal of the famed gambler, Salvatore Petrucci, out of Gulfport and the successful driving of all gambling out of Mississippi. Cecil remembered the political skills and techniques that were mustered.

"He was a great speaker but the Blackwoods drew-in the crowds. He succeeded in getting in the runoffs so we campaigned heavily with him some more. Eventually, he won and became a great and honest governor of the State of Mississippi. Unfortunately in later years, the gambling vice returned to Mississippi!"

Doyle Blackwood, father of Terry and Kaye Blackwood, was elected to the Tennessee State House of Representatives. A beloved gentleman, he died on October 2, 1974. James was originally also asked to run for office but the quartet, according to Cecil, persuaded him against it because of his travel commitments, Doyle ran instead and won.

In June of 1971, Cecil Blackwood and his family were invited to have breakfast with Winfield Dunn at the Governor's Mansion. The invitation was eagerly accepted and Cecil duly summoned all the family in to explain that they should be on their best behavior for the visit!

Their ten year old daughter, Barbara was given special instructions regarding her habit of eating only the inside of her toast and leaving the crust. She was told that, when she went to the Governor's Mansion, she would have to eat the whole thing, crust and all.

When the special day arrived, the plush meal was duly served and young Barbara forgot all about her father's strict instructions and ate only the inside of her toast. In his embarrassment, Cecil then scolded her.

"Barbara, darling, I told you. When you go to the Governor's Mansion, you'll have to eat the entire piece of bread!"

Sensing now the special occasion and feeling the shame of the rebuke from her father, the young girl's eyes misted over as her bottom lip started to quiver. The kindly governor however, was quick to steal the initiative of the deepening drama. Defusing the situation and not wanting to cause any more embarrassment to his young guest and her family, his words were soft and warm.

"Oh that's fine. That sure ain't no problem. No problem at all. She's my special guest and I want her to feel at home, even in this big ole house. Just let her eat it like she wants to."

The renowned evangelist, Dr. Billy Graham was also to have been a guest at the breakfast that day but was unable to attend at the last moment because of another pressing engagement.

Such was the Blackwood Brothers' acclaim, they were named "Tennessee's Ambassadors of Gospel Music" by Governor Winfield Dunn. He went on to proclaim that the week of June 7 through 13, 1971 would be Blackwood Family Week in Tennessee in appropriate recognition of the contributions the family had made to the state of Tennessee!

Through the years, the quartet sang at the invitation of crusade director, Cliff Barrows several times for the globe-trotting evangelist, Billy Graham, at his vast, city-wide missions. The Blackwoods were to lend their considerable support to many other leading evangelists over the years.

How can anyone forget the wonderful, majestic melodies of praise that have characterized the impactive Billy Graham missions of the second half of the twentieth century?

The twentieth century never saw a more powerful songleader than Cliff Barrows. He undoubtedly left his mark on the sands of time with his skills in gospel music, and his dedication to the task of world-wide evangelism. Never one to crave the limelight he would often repeat his choir song, in the words of the blind poet, Fanny Crosby, "To God be the glory, great things He has done."

His lifelong friend, Billy Graham, recalled his first surprising encounter with Cliff in 1945. Cliff was asked to lead the singing for a youth night service at which Billy was to speak. But Billy recalled with a smile, "I must in all honesty say I accepted him dubiously. But my doubts were instantly dispersed by his skill and sunny disposition!. Aided by a fine voice, a trombone and the piano-playing of his beautiful wife, Billie, soon he had the audience singing to their fullest capability!"

So began a historic association as songleader Cliff, preacher Billy Graham, and gospel singer George Beverly Shea hit the road as an evangelistic trio. Their heart-felt quest was to last more than half a century and take them to every continent on earth. Who can begin to measure the harvest ? The seeds of the kingdom were faithfully sown in untold numbers of fertile hearts.

Perhaps only eternity will reveal the full extent of the fruits! Nevertheless, many thousands bore grateful testimony to the life-changing message the trio shared!

Cliff Barrows had a happy- go-lucky exterior that belied his deep sensitivity and discernment. With his ever youthful looks, he was more than just a genial host and songleader. For the giant, globe-trotting, Billy Graham Missions he was actually the person in charge until the evangelist himself stepped forward to deliver his message. Able to command authority among his peers, he was fully equipped for the demanding responsibility he displayed.

Cliff Barrows was born on the sixth day of April 1923, in the little town of Ceres, California (named after Ceres, the pagan goddess of the harvest). His family had a rural background, his father being a humble farmer loved the soil and his work in the fields.

Those boyhood days in the country held affectionate memories for Cliff as he remembered how he toiled alongside his father.

"It was a precious time although I didn't think so at the time. As I reflect back in later life, I respect my dad's work ethic, his love of creation, and his work in the fields of harvest. His love has been a great challenge and inspiration to me!"

Conversion came at the age of eleven as Cliff responded to the claims of Christ, and full-time Christian service beckoned. He met the aspiring young preacher named Billy Graham at the close of World War II in the town of Asheville, North Carolina. They teamed up and a new chapter in church history was to be written from that time.

Songleader, Cliff Barrows single-mindedly devoted his time and efforts into communicating the Good News via a wide variety of media, varying from radio, television, and movies to recordings and concerts.

Always an enthusiast throughout his life-long ministry, he stated, "Every great moving of the Spirit of God has been accompanied by great singing and I believe it always will be!"

As a life-time co-worker, Billy Graham summed his partner up well, "Cliff's dedication and sincerity are immediately evident. He gives Christ the chance to live out his life in Cliff, and the results in terms of Christian witness are wonderful to see."

That other life-time, co-worker with Cliff, his friend, Bev Shea gave his telling assessment too, "Cliff's Christ-centered dedication to his song-leading and choir-directing ministry has given him a much deserved, world-wide reputation!"

The song leading skills of Cliff Barrows are legendary but he is also a first-class songwriter, and an excellent preacher with a warm delivery of the precious gospel of our Lord. More and more, he is being recognized for his insightful interpretation of God's holy word.

Yes, a human being of many skills but on every continent of the globe it is as a songleader that he will be remembered for most! His winning smile and enthusiastic charm have motivated thousands to lift their voices to praise God in song .

Corporately since 1967, the Blackwood Brothers (and Cecil and James Blackwood individually), have won a host of gospel music awards including several Grammys, Dove Awards and Singing News Awards.

Eddie Miller, an outstanding songwriter, remembered the group's recording of his hit songs. He, like many songwriters, was very grateful for the prized exposure and special attention given by the Blackwood Brothers to his songwriting repertoire.

"When James Blackwood and the Blackwood Brothers recorded my composition *Release Me From My Sin,* they forged an entirely new dimension for my song even though the original version had been recorded four hundred times!"

Nominations of the Blackwoods for Grammys have been so plentiful as to be commonplace. Many times, James and Cecil can recall sitting with the rest of the guys at the Award Ceremonies as nominees were called from their seats to the stage. The Blackwood Brothers won eight Grammys as a Quartet, plus one with Barbara Mandrell, and James won a ninth with the Master's V.

Cecil won the Best Baritone award on three occasions against stiff competition in the Singing News awards.

They notched up a total of forty-nine singles on their original White Church label from 1946 to 1951. This was followed by forty-two albums on the Skylite label from 1961-1981, along with many albums for RCA and countless others for lesser known labels. The list continues to expand via the releases of the Blackwood Brothers' group headed by Cecil Blackwood. Their staggering album tally was in the range of about three hundred titles at the beginning of 2000.

It is a reasonable conjecture to assume that because the Blackwood Brothers were signed to RCA Victor at the time, Elvis was influenced to leave Sun Records and sign for that label also. The impact of the quartet on the American, and consequently on the world, pop and country fields is considerable. This influence should not be overlooked when the twentieth century's history of popular music is finally documented.

Along with many of the accepted, established structures of society as a whole, the focus of Christian music had begun to change during the sixties. Accepted norms were under tremendous attack, not least the fashion and art-forms. In essence, it was a substantial social revolution that affected every area of culture, fashion, and even ethics.

Gospel music until this time was aimed primarily at the older church members, but the new, younger generation wanted Christian music to more readily attract and reach all ages. Suddenly, innovative sounds were arising from the likes of Andrae Crouch, Second Chapter Of Acts, Barry McGuire, Dallas Holm, Daniel Amos, Keith Green, Liberation Suite, and many more! It should be noted that the Blackwoods and their so-called traditional associates took leading parts in the facilitating of these changes.

Contemporary composers, arrangers, and producers (such as Michael Omartian, Bruce Herring, Jimmy Owens, and others) started writing modern-style material that was much wider in taste and scope. Performers of the same persuasion also emerged from what became known as the Jesus Movement. On the Californian coast thousands of teens as well as those in their twenties, were turning to Christ as winds of revival and renewal eventually blew worldwide.

The Blackwood Brothers warmly embraced the new changes as their song repertoire and musical arrangements of those days easily illustrate. The quartet continued to push back the established horizons, not only for themselves but also for the new acts and Christian music as a whole.

Up until this time, the Blackwood Brothers were generally considered to be perhaps the most progressive and professional of all Christian groups. With a view to showcasing other new Southern Gospel talent, the Blackwood Brothers and Statesmen together formed the Skylite Record Company.

Most of the Skylite projects were made in the hit-making RCA or CBS studios in Nashville. As the Blackwoods and Statesmen were so busy, Ben and Brock Speer of the Speer Family were put in charge of *'Artists & Repertoire'*. Well qualified, they also usually filled in on bass and electric guitar. Hundreds of recordings followed over later decades from every Southern Gospel quartet, trio, duo, or soloist of any substantial standing or talent.

One Skylite album by the Blackwood Brothers of note was their foresighted, early recognition of the songwriting geniuses of Bill and Gloria Gaither. Entitled *Bill Gaither Songs by the Blackwood Brothers*, it was one of the first album tributes to the later hugely successful video program hosts. There is no doubt that the Gaithers were inspired by the Blackwoods to follow their successful route!

Throughout the last quarter of the twentieth century, their illustrious name has become synonymous with excellence in their particular field. Bill and Gloria Gaither are already heralded by many among the greatest hymn writers of history and listed in the ranks of Fanny Crosby, Isaac Watts, and Charles Wesley.

Classy songs from their pens include *Because He Lives, He Touched Me, Joy Comes In The Morning* and *The King Is Coming*. Many of their heart-warming songs are already found in church hymnbooks around the world - incredible achievements for living songwriters.

The Gaithers' Homecoming video series concept that inspired subsequent audio releases was wondrously simple and winsome! Roots may be in Southern Gospel but the panoramic span of styles extended into almost every gospel form from Thomas Dorsey's *Singing In My Soul* to Fanny Crosby's *Redeemed.*

Under the auspices of song-writing geniuses, Bill and Gloria Gaither, the videos were informal, worship-gatherings of outstanding Christian talent around a studio piano and band. They were there to simply sing and share in the studio. Inevitably, the divine anointing fell and worship took over.

Among those gathered, big song writing names abounded including Dottie Rambo, Vep Ellis, Rusty Goodman, Stuart Hamblen, and Albert Brumley. Beautiful harmony, laughter and tears flowed freely in spontaneity.

The commendable video series drew the viewer almost inevitably into sharing in the remarkable proceedings. Hugely successful audio releases arose from the even more hugely successful secular chart-topping videos.

Big singing names also attended including James Blackwood, Jake Hess, J.D. Sumner, the Speers, Doug Oldham, and Hovie Lister. Some new names in Southern Gospel were also there Ray Boltz, Russ Taff, Jessy Dixon, Joni, and too many more to recount! Among the dignitaries from time to time one could also spot the likes of country stars such as Connie Smith, Larry Gatlin, and Barbara Fairchild, Lulu Roman and others.

Bill Gaither grew up in a rural area of Indiana in a small town of about six thousand people. Coming from a farming family Bill learned to take pleasure in the everyday responsibilities of milking the cows and other essential farm jobs.

"I think this helped", he said, "as far as what I'm doing today. It's helped me develop a sensitivity to life and for the caring of the new-born. When someone speaks about simple, everyday things I know what they're talking about!"

He never planned to do farming as a career because as he jokingly said, "I have always had a bad case of hay fever! That's always been a problem to me even as a child working outside!"

He always loved music but had given up the idea of making a career out of it after high school because he thought he was not good enough to do it full-time.

As a youngster, Bill thrilled to the Blackwoods' 78 single on RCA Victor of *I Won't Have To Cross Jordan Alone* and *Rock My Soul.* He became captivated.

Ace songwriter, Bill was fourteen years old when he first heard the Blackwood Brothers on record, as he explained, he became captivated, as he lovingly recalled!

"As a boy I cannot begin to tell you the impression those records made on my young life. I could not wait to get home from school in the evening to play them, and I had many dreams to one day be able to sing like that. I still have many of those 78's at home.

"I'll never forget when my Dad and Mom took me to Nashville for the first time and I met James Blackwood, personally. What a thrill that was for this young Indiana farm boy.

"Later, in the mid-fifties, when I was in college and our trio had started singing, we sang on the same program with the Blackwood Brothers in a northern Indiana town. Afterward we went out to a restaurant to eat. I remember that James complimented us and said that he thought we had possibilities and some very interesting new ideas. He encouraged us to continue on."

By the age of nineteen, while with the Pathfinders Quartet, Bill was opening for the joint Blackwood and Statesmen concerts. His Pathfinders had ventured into wax with a 78 of Ira Stanphill's *Suppertime* and the spiritual popularized at the time by Frankie Laine, *Rain, Rain, Rain.*

"In those days there were not that many opportunities for a young person interested in full-time music. So what I did was to go to college and major in English. Later, I taught English in public high school for seven or eight years, planning to do that for the rest of my life. That's where I met my wife, Gloria. She was also teaching school at the same place. The thing that stopped my teaching career was when I started writing original songs. Up until then I had not written anything original. I'd always done other people's music I'd heard in the church."

People oft times would ask him, "Where did the poetry come from in your music?" Bill was clear in his reply.

"Well, I think it has to be born in you. I think you can fan the spark, but there must be a natural inclination to understand poetic things, understand the power of poetic suggestion, and to understand signals. I've often said I think everybody has to have a little bit of poetry in him to even make it these days! I think that is where our whole music ministry started - with sensitivity to poetry. You can say very powerful things in a few short words".

Surprisingly, Bill said that he never found himself being in the top of the class in things like poetry and his school friends were amazed at the way he developed this talent. Gloria, however, graduated from college with honors in French, English and Sociology.

Later, Bill and Gloria, with Bill's brother Danny (an outstanding song-stylist before cancer attacked his throat) formed the world-renowned Bill Gaither Trio. His love for quartet music was ultimately fulfilled in the Gaither Vocal Band.

At the start of the third millennium, the Gaithers' home town was still Alexandria, Indiana, and it was plagued with pilgrimages from Gaither enthusiasts. They had an ever increasing stream of people coming by to see the various places that the Gaithers' spoke about in albums and concerts, down through the years.

Bill laughed and said, "I don't think our people look on us as stars. I think people who follow us look on us more as fellow strugglers who are going through some of the same things as they are. I know I don't even feel famous. We've found a few answers that we share but we haven't all the answers!"

The Gaithers have written several hundred gospel songs, not a lot when compared to Charles Wesley and Fanny Crosby who wrote thousands! Time, however, is on their side, grace permitting! The great songwriters of previous generations, of course, came to their greatest attention after they were gone. With the power of modern media available, the Gaithers have already become a legend in their lifetimes.

How does it make them feel to be classed among the ranks of history's great hymn writers? "You know", Bill modestly stated, "in something as sensitive as Christian ministry I don't think one can even think about that very long because the Lord blesses and the Lord adds to the increase. The only reason we're here in the first place is because God chose to bless the ministry. History will take care of itself and then the people can be the final judge as to what will live and be meaningful over a period of time. We're just thankful that what has happened has happened. But it can all go away tomorrow, and I don't think it would change our love for each other and for our family. To me the family is more important than the acceptance of people."

To their credit, the Gaithers were uncompromising in their approach to their music ministry down through the years. They maintained a consistency and an integrity that helped them to remain spiritually sharp and culturally relevant.

Such was the high esteem in which the Blackwood Brothers Quartet was held, a museum was established dedicated to the Blackwood Brothers in the state capital in Jackson, Mississippi.

In the third millennium, plans were also underway to erect a permanent memorial in honor of the quartet at the Pyramid, the largest auditorium in Memphis. The Ellis Auditorium was slated to be demolished and a Grammy Hall of Fame was to be placed in the Pyramid. A special section was to be dedicated to the Blackwood Brothers.

The Blackwoods' inspiring story reads amazingly at times as if it were fiction. It is a human tale full of passionate and heart-warming sentiment, spiritual idealism, and blood, sweat and tears! The story has its balanced share of achievements and mistakes.

Do ye not know that they which minister about holy things live of the things of the temple?

and they which wait at the altar are partakers with the altar?

Even so hath the Lord ordained that they which preach the gospel should live of the gospel. Corinthians 9:13-14

21 CRITICISM AND CONTROVERSY

Favor is deceitful, and beauty is vain: but a ...man that fears the LORD...he shall be praised. Give (him) of the fruit of (his) hands; and let (his) own works praise (him) in the gates.
Proverbs 31: 30-31

Down through the decades of the twentieth century, it is remarkable to observe how many Blackwood family members of succeeding generations have been actively involved in the gospel music and the entertainment industry. It is amazing to count the number of clan members who have eked out a living in these apparently divergent activities.

Nothing is forever, and the eventual attacks on the Blackwood Brothers' unrivalled supremacy of half-a-century was to be anticipated. Factors that mounted attacks against the Blackwood Brothers as leaders in the field were many and varied but not least of which was the fickleness of public taste and demand. The winds of change blow constantly through all departments of life especially fashion, culture, and...musical taste. In truth, the Blackwoods weathered the attacks and fashion-culture-storms with great success.

The unstoppable advent of the greater influence of television, in particular syndicated television, precipitated a refocus of priorities for gospel groups. Costs of television production were considerably higher than in the media of concerts and radio.

The Blackwood Brothers had the financial capability to professionally and successfully enter the growing television medium. Around them, it could be observed that the times proliferated the overwhelming advent of newer, amateurish groups who entered the limited market place. The considerable range of new choices arising from the proliferation of Christian music groups in the sixties and seventies increased the competition for bookings. The Blackwood Brothers, however, never skipped a beat or suffered any reversal throughout those years.

Years later, Cecil recalled how the Blackwood Brothers exploited the media of TV exposure.

"We had great successes with *At Home With The Blackwood Brothers* in the fifties, and *The Glory Road plus Singing Time In Dixie* in the sixties and seventies."

Initially made in black and white and jointly hosted by Hovie Lister and James Blackwood, *Singing Time In Dixie* featured the Blackwoods along with the

Statesmen and the Speer Family. The one hour syndicated show at its height was on one hundred stations, coast to coast. When color television took over, the show went to thirty minutes duration and was titled The Glory Road.

In 1975, Cecil drew up plans for further TV shows and approached Christian networks accordingly. There was not complete unanimity, however, as Cecil remembered. "James and Jimmy Blackwood were not sure that it was wise to do more television. They wanted to spend more time at home."

Support for Cecil's ideas did come from John Cox and Ken Turner. New shows were commissioned via Lesea Broadcasting with Cecil acting as host. Syndicated, they were broadcast to over one hundred terrestrial stations and via cable networks. The Blackwoods' show was aired ten times per week on the PTL network over a period of about five years plus about two years on the 700 Club network. Then for eight years, recorded in South Bend, Indianapolis, the shows featured the Blackwood Brothers (Cecil, Jimmy, Ken Turner, and Pat Hoffmaster) with James as a special guest. Later, John Cox substituted for Pat. Later still, Pat returned again to the Blackwoods' fold.

The shows via the networks were beamed to millions, coast to coast. Cecil remembered how well the shows were received.

"It seemed that everywhere we went, in shopping malls and streets, we'd meet people who'd say, 'I saw your television show. It's great! Our family never misses it.'"

In 1985, television production costs spiraled to great heights. But it was the intolerable weight of time investment that had to be addressed. Time and work combined became so much of a consumer that the TV idea was rested for a while. In the late nineties, Cecil put the idea back on the Blackwood Brothers' future agenda. Plans are in train to introduce a new series of Blackwood Brothers' television programs for the third millennium.

From the early fifties, the Blackwood Brothers performed some of their sacred material to a rock 'n' roll beat, somewhat revolutionary for the day! Even the King of Rock 'n Roll would agree that the Blackwood Brothers preceded his rock 'n roll by several years. Indeed, he would say that they even inspired it in him. But it was too early a revolution in Christian music for many denominations to readily accept.

It was not until the late sixties that conservative attitudes changed substantially with the advent of contemporary Christian music. This movement was spearheaded by a younger generation who saw themselves as being the church of tomorrow. Although the Blackwood Brothers had always sung with a popular beat, in a very real way they represented the old guard. Young faces as well as young music were demanded. Thanks to the dedicated efforts of the Blackwood Brothers over half a century, these young faces inherited a thriving legacy of a solid audience base, an ever growing touring circuit, and a Gospel Music Association still growing in status and clout.

Piously perceived, but nonetheless, quietly creeping up on all gospel music acts, was a highly subtle factor emerging that sought to dilute the power that the Blackwood Brothers wielded. It was the move away from Christian performers who overtly displayed what was seen as the unbecoming techniques and theatrics of show-business. The Blackwoods were quick to respond.

Years later as he looked back, Cecil commented philosophically on the Quartet's changes of direction that occurred in the Seventies. "We started avoiding the all night sings with the multiple quartets because we could draw big crowds by ourselves. We just didn't need the support of the other quartets. This also helped with our financial situation!

"We started going into more and more local churches in the seventies. We called such bookings a One Night Crusade with the Blackwood Brothers, and it was a crusade! We sang the hymns of the church, then Dwayne Friend, an evangelist, would play guitar and sing. Then he would give a gospel message. He was one of the best speakers ever! Sometimes, James or I would speak.

"We have never really changed our format since then. Over the years, we've become more and more evangelistic in our work. Winning souls for Christ was, and is now, the main thrust of our work!"

Before these changes to local evangelism in the gospel music arena, the extrovert style and attire of the exuberant group were giving cause to greater and greater misgivings. Sometimes this led to mistrust, however unfounded. Perhaps in retrospect, the usually astute Blackwood Brothers were slow to respond to the churches' demand for greater displays of piety and greater emphasis on ministry rather than entertainment. There is little doubt that there were times when the Blackwood Brothers were accused of displaying a lack of wisdom and discern-ment in this area. Cecil disputed this, arguing that the Blackwoods (Cecil, Jimmy, Ken, Pat and James) were quick to switch to "church work and a new style at home and abroad." The Blackwood Brothers Evangelistic Association has now worked in a staggering forty-seven countries.

In 1971 came a most directly, damaging factor that temporarily and margin-ally tarnished the Blackwood Brothers' reputation and standing in Christian circles. It also left a bad taste in the mouth of some of the music industry and in the public domain as a whole. It was the accusation of rigging the Dove Awards.

That year, the Blackwood family swept the board of Dove Awards at Nashville's Gospel Music Association banquet. The Dove Awards were the Association's Oscar-type way of recognizing the various achievements in the what was by then called the Gospel Music Industry.

James won the Outstanding Male Vocalist Award and other family members also won awards including Most Promising New Gospel Talent (Kaye Blackwood); Outstanding Mixed Vocal Group (the Blackwood Singers); Out-standing Gospel Instrumentalist (Billy Blackwood) and last but not least Outstanding Male Vocal Group (the Blackwood Brothers Quartet).

Two weeks after receiving the awards from the Gospel Music Association directors, the same directors revoked them accordingly, on the allegation of over-zealous politicking. The move sent minor shock waves throughout the music industry and a few naughty tongues wagging overtime in churches throughout the nation.

The shocked Blackwoods and their associates were accused of the over-active solicitation of votes via their mail, broadcasts and personal communication.

The Blackwood Brothers solicitation practice was the same as all others. However, in truth, the Blackwoods were much better at it! Courageously, the Blackwood patriarch, James Blackwood, conceded the possibility of over zealousness and reluctantly recognized the invalidation, returning the awards accordingly. It was doubtless a brave act of damage limitation. A lengthy war over the matter would have left many individual and corporate casualties in its wake.

At the end of the century, James recalled the incident philosophically. "We returned the awards voluntarily. No rules or regulations were broken! But in the interests of harmony, we returned them! Les Beasley, the Gospel Music Association's president said we should not return them but I did to prevent any splits in the gospel music industry!"

A soft answer turneth away wrath:
but grievous words stir up anger.
The tongue of the wise useth knowledge aright:
but the mouth of fools poureth out foolishness.
The eyes of the LORD are in every place,
beholding the evil and the good.
Proverbs 15:1-3

Long standing jealousies regarding the Blackwood Brothers' ascendance over the gospel music scene were most likely highly contributing factors that fuelled the gossip and allegations made. All this type of controversy was understated at the time because of James' relatively quick action.

The vast fan base that the boys enjoyed exceeded all other acts considerably. This would clearly have been what some critics would see as unfair advantage in the Gospel Music Association's public, mail-vote system.

The minor controversy had the potential to severely damage or even to ultimately destroy both the Gospel Music Association and the Blackwood Brothers. This was avoided in no mean part because of the wise, conciliatory responses of James Blackwood that defused the crisis, and by the handing back of the awards.

Even after thirty years, Cecil Blackwood remained adamantly defensive about the Blackwoods' position, as he argued, "No Dove Award rules were broken. The Gospel Music Association begged the groups to sign-up as many subscriptions to the *Good News* newspaper as possible. Then when people did sign up they were prone to vote for their favorite group, even as they do nowadays!

"In 1969 and 1970, the Oak Ridge Boys won many awards. Willie Wynn (their tenor) told me that they had pushed the *Good News* subscriptions! In 1970, the Oaks sold 666 subscriptions thus giving them 666 possible votes because their fans would most likely vote for them via mail!

"I thought it would be a good idea for the Blackwood Brothers to push the subscriptions harder. We had the forms on the record tables but we started to announce them as being available every night."

Cecil's announcement from the platform, night after night, informed the audiences that the GMA had a publication available for them via subscription.

Such subscriptions then entitled subscribers to vote in the awards poll. Like all, or many groups to some degree, the Blackwoods invited their admirers to vote for them.

In 1971 the Blackwoods sold about 1200 subscriptions for the GMA, a staggering achievement. Consequently, this swayed the poll via the mail considerably in their direction! Cecil remains to this day most convinced about the innocence of the Blackwoods' position and somewhat grieved that the awards were rescinded.

"The GMA had asked all their artists to sell subscriptions, and like all the groups, that's what we did! All the groups, with any ambition, also asked their admirers to vote for them. Even today in 1999, groups who win sell the most subscriptions!"

It was generally accepted that the letter of the law had not been transgressed but debate continues as to whether it was broken in spirit. Questions about whether such award polls have a tendency to promote unhealthy and unbecoming competitive rivalry, jealousy, and pride among the servants of God will rage on and on.

Thirty years later, Cecil expressed his perspective on the 1971 affair. "We should not have given the awards back! The GMA did not take them back! J.D. Sumner wanted to give them back and James gave in to him. Later, J.D. said he was wrong and wanted to ask for the awards back. Those who win today in 1999 are the ones who sell the most subscriptions. Those who do not sell do not win!"

The Gospel Music Association survives to this day bigger and grander than ever despite the adverse publicity of 1971. The GMA Annual Awards continue to be awarded and, in subsequent years, the Blackwood Brothers were to win further awards of both Doves and Grammys. Problems started to hit the group on several fronts in the years to come. Feeling the stain of touring and ill health, James decided to retire from the Blackwood Brothers only to join the Masters V later (in 1981). He was replaced in the Blackwood Brothers by Jimmy Blackwood (James' son).

Cecil remembered how early in 1970 it became apparent that James' health was failing. "One night, James came to my room in some distress and with blood-shot eyes. He explained that he'd had a mini stroke or something. Clearly, he was going to have to slow down. He said that he would like to bring his son, Jimmy into the quartet to help do some of his singing and ease some of his load. James even offered to pay Jimmy out of his own salary. I said, 'No, James! We should bring Jimmy in but pay him the same amount that he was making in the Stamps Quartet!'

"So we had two lead singers for many years. Then, James started slowing-up and doing some evangelistic work on his own. Eventually, he did TV shows in California and finally went on to sing with the Masters V."

This may have had some adverse effect on the Blackwoods' popularity. Good as he was, Jimmy could never fill the shoes of Mr. Gospel Music, the man who had been in the Blackwood Brothers since 1934.

Well loved and a quality vocalist in his own right, Jimmy was singing baritone with the Stamps Quartet before joining the Blackwood Brothers. Through no fault of his own, the change in personnel did not initially, go down well with the audience. For some years, the Quartet's popularity temporarily waned. The going was tough at times but the group overcame it in time.

Jimmy loyally stayed with the Blackwoods for sixteen years, until 1985. Then he was diagnosed as having cancer of the pancreas, a very serious and potentially fatal type of cancer. When news came to James of his son's plight, he was at a church in Spokane, Washington. Medical authorities feared that surgery would not be survived. Heart-broken, it was reported, that James cried out, hands and eyes raised heavenward, "Oh, gracious, merciful, Heavenly Father, please, please save my boy!"

God heard his prayers and Jimmy was divinely healed. He left the Blackwood Brothers in 1985 to pursue a successful, fruitful, solo ministry of his own.

Following basses, J.D. Sumner, Big John Hall and London Paris, came the popular bass, Ken Turner who served for sixteen years (from 1971 to 1986). After he married a girl from the Carolinas his traveling was curtailed so he retired from the group.

The celebrated name of the Blackwood Brothers Quartet continued into the new millennium under the shrewd leadership of Cecil Stamps Blackwood. An early Sunday school buddy of Elvis Presley, he received the mantle of baritone when his brother R.W. perished in the tragic aircrash of 1954. He has been the three-times, proud winner of the Favorite Baritone fan award presented by the *Singing News* magazine annually.

The busy, well-loved group made many changes in response to the ups and downs of life in the late eighties and early nineties but eventually consolidated. Commendably constant throughout all the winds of change, since the plane crash of 1954, was the durable Cecil.

Mark Blackwood (Cecil's son) also helped stabilize the group membership as the group's lead singer. Cecil continued as the baritone and manager of the group. Then Cecil's grandson, Chris Blackwood joined the group at the age of seventeen.

Later in 1986, Mark moved to Knoxville, Tennessee and not wanting to continue with so much travelling started the Blackwood Voices group. Replacing him was Mike LoPrinzi from West Virginia who sang the lead part.

In 1994, Steve Warren left the Stamps to join Cecil's Blackwood Brothers Quartet as lead singer and arranger. At the time, the group included Cecil's wife, Francine Blackwood and Penny Burke. Francine studied voice and piano for many years, and she had also sung for her father who was an evangelist. Penny had sung in a quartet and was a former church pianist and choir arranger. For a while the Blackwoods were a mixed group that included the two ladies.

Steve Warren from Houston, Texas was destined to eventually inherit the tenor position. Several albums of his piano-playing had been released. He joined the Blackwood Brothers after serving with the Masters V for over four years followed by six years with J.D. Sumner and the Stamps Quartet.

A multi-instrumentalist, songwriter, arranger, and record producer, Steve was also an accomplished tenor known as the voice.

Ironically, his earliest musical recollection was of hearing the Blackwood Brothers Quartet singing on radio. He himself began singing at the tender age of three years old when incredibly, he sang in front of an audience of ten thousand people! He began playing the piano at five years of age and later guitar when he was twelve.

Steve's musical heritage dates back to his paternal grandparents. His grandmother was a child star on the Vaudeville stage, while his grandfather was a bass singer in barbershop quartets.

His father, the late Larry Warren, was the promoter of the gospel quartet concerts in Houston Texas, his hometown. Combining the facts that his dad was an accomplished singer and his mother a skilled pianist (who incidentally was Steve's first piano teacher), his has truly been a musical family-world.

Later, Steve went on to be one of the founder members of The Royals. From The Royals came such renowned singers as Larry Gatlin and the Blackwood Brothers' former tenor, the late Pat Hoffmaster.

In 1982, Steve became tenor for Gospel Music's first super group, the Master's V. After the Masters V disbanded and J. D. Sumner reformed the Stamps Quartet, Steve became the tenor for that celebrated group. He then became pianist, vocal arranger and featured soloist for the renowned Wayne Newton Show. Finally, he came full circle when he rejoined the Blackwood Brothers Quartet.

In 1999, Steve had been happily married for two full decades to the girl he described as the love of his life, Shirley. They boasted two married sons and he considered himself most richly blest.

His music abilities were recognized by the music industry with his nomination for nine Grammy Awards in three categories and also by being inducted into the Gospel Music Hall of Fame in three positions as well.

Steve unhesitatingly gives the credit and honor for his many talents to God, as he recounted, "I am most richly blest. First, to have been given the abilities that I have by my Heavenly Father. Then secondly, to have had the rich heritage of music that I've been privileged to have, starting with the group I now perform with, the Blackwood Brothers Quartet."

Chris Blackwood is Cecil's grandson, a fourth generation Blackwood, no less. He sings with the group and organizes the product sales.

Low bass, Eric Winston, a licensed minister, followed the pastoring example of his Arkansas based grandfather. Cecil reported that Eric is reputed to have recorded the lowest bass note in gospel music (double low C).

Eric said that he always treasured the desire to preach and sing the gospel. Even at a very early age, he would dress up in his smart, little suit and hold pretend services for his friends! Becoming a Christian at the early age of nine, he developed a love of gospel quartet music at about the same time. From then on, all he ever wanted to do in life was to sing! His first choice in his dreams was always to sing, if possible, with the Blackwood Brothers.

He first auditioned for Cecil Blackwood when he was fifteen years of age but was unsuccessful. But nine years later, he auditioned again and realized his greatest dream that was to sing bass with the Blackwood Brothers Quartet.

At the age of sixteen, Eric was one of Arkansas' youngest, radio disc jockeys. He indulged himself by majoring on gospel quartet sounds, particularly from the Blackwood Brothers. After graduating from high school, Eric worked as an undertaker in the funeral profession, leaving in 1992 to preach.

He recorded his debut, solo album when eighteen years old, produced by ex-Blackwoods' bass, London Parris. Sadly, London passed away on Labor Day 1992 . Eric recalled with some satisfaction how well the album turned-out.

On one song, I sang a double low B flat and then dropped down to an F off the keyboard! As far as I know, no one else has ever reached that note!"

Eric's inspiration was always J. D. Sumner, who died in November 1998. So Eric's 1999 solo project was a warm album tribute to J.D.

Rick Price first joined the Blackwood Brothers at the age of nineteen, then left after a few years to follow his own independent ministry, rejoining at the age of forty-three!

In 1998 and 1999, the Blackwood Brothers sang at the Elvis Presley Restaurant in their hometown of Memphis, Tennessee. Cecil followed this appearance by sponsoring a Blackwood Brothers' Reunion Concert at the Theatre of Memphis. At this concert, they celebrated James Blackwood's eightieth birthday, Cecil's sixty-fifth birthday and the Blackwood Brothers' sixty-fifth anniversary. Featured on the program were the Blackwood Brothers, the Blackwood Voices, the Blackwood Singers, James Blackwood, Cecil Blackwood, Andy Childs (Cecil's country singing son-in-law), the Blackwood Mixed Group and others. It was a sold-out crowd and was such a success that Cecil said that plans would be made to present the Blackwood Brothers' Reunion Concert in various cities across the USA. Plans were also set in motion to pilot a Blackwood Brothers' Reunion Concert television show.

It worthy of note that, since 1954 to the third millenium's dawn, Cecil has not missed a single Blackwood Brothers' concert, television show or album recording. He has remained the one constant common denominator in the group.

Enthusiastic as ever, Cecil was upbeat in his comments. "The Blackwood Brothers of the year 2000 still present approximately 275 gospel concerts each year in auditoriums and churches across the USA!

"Our crowds in the nineties are on average bigger than they were in the fifties, sixties, and seventies. Back then, we had our hot spots of 5000 and 6000 people but church crowds were smaller. Nowadays, we don't sing with other groups, and attendances range from 400 to 800 per night.

"We're as busy as ever, doing our part in fulfilling the Great Commission! Many pastors report that the Blackwood Brothers still draw the largest crowds in the histories of their churches. Praise the Lord on high!"

From 1997 to 2000, the composition of the on-going quartet was, therefore, Cecil Blackwood, Steve Warren, Chris Blackwood, Eric Winston, and Rick Price. They released three very commendable gospel albums entitled *Learning To*

Lean, Beulah Land, and *Songs That Elvis Loved.* The latter album holds particular connotations for Cecil.

"These songs, on *Songs That Elvis Loved,* were actually the numbers that Elvis got from us in the early fifties and recorded. He went on and won three Grammy awards singing Blackwood Brothers and Statesmen music."

Donnie Sumner (J.D.'s nephew) was reported to observe that he considered them to be three of the Blackwood Brothers' finest! Sales continued to be pleasing. Mr. Dunn, President of Crystal Inc, the CD and tape manufacturer for many gospel artists, reported the Blackwoods to be their top seller saying that "the Blackwood Brothers' business was as solid as a rock!"

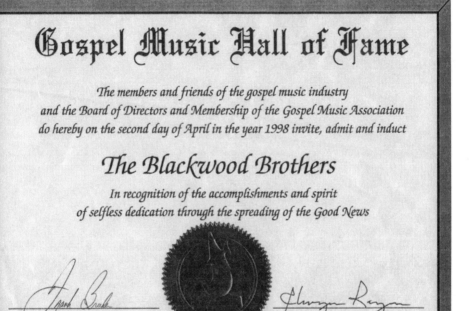

22 MR. GOSPEL MUSIC

My son, forget not my law;
but let thine heart keep my commandments:
For length of days, and long life,
and peace, shall they add to thee.
Let not mercy and truth forsake thee!
bind them about thy neck;
write them upon the table of thine heart!
So shalt thou find favor and good understanding
in the sight of God and man.
Proverbs 3:1-4

At the end of the twentieth century, there was only one surviving member of the original Blackwood Brothers Quartet. Few would dispute that by then he thoroughly deserved the unique, patriarchal role he fulfilled in Christian music as Mr. Gospel Music.

James Blackwood was semi-retired by 1971 but still retained a keen interest and dedication to the cause of gospel music, particularly with reference to matters that involved the Blackwood name. Jimmy, his son, replaced James as the quartet's lead singer for sixteen years, although James appeared with the group as a featured soloist. Then in 1981 he went full-time with the Master V.

Throughout the exciting second half of the twentieth century, the name of the Blackwood Brothers had been synonymous with Southern gospel music. During his long-lasting, illustrious career that commenced in 1934, James and his renowned group received twenty-eight consecutive Grammy Award nominations, and won nine Grammy Awards. They had also been awarded seven Dove Awards, many Singing News Fan Awards and The Marvin Norcross Award.

Tributes about his music and lifestyle from fellow performers were plentiful as the comments of the outstanding tenor, Larry Ford illustrated in 1999.

"James has always been a role model for me since I was five years of age and learned my first songs from the Blackwood Brothers. I thank God for allowing me to be a small part of James' music and life!"

As unchallenged patriarchal head of the Blackwood dynasty, James Blackwood had an unprecedented reputation. Rather than turn his head, he remained highly focused with reference to spiritual matters and their associated priorities.

A country boy, James was certainly not born with the proverbial silver spoon in his mouth but he had wisely and duly acknowledged his loving Creator in the days of his youth. His surrender in early years to divine leading gave him long life and a great, satisfying sense of fulfillment.

Remember now thy Creator
in the days of thy youth,
while the evil days come not,
nor the years draw nigh,
when thou shalt say,
'I have no pleasure in them.'
Ecclesiastes 12:1

In rural poverty, Mother Blackwood gave birth to him on a humble share-cropper farm near the Choctaw County seat of Ackerman, Mississippi on the fourth day of August 1919. It was the year after the cessation of World War I hostilities, and his struggling parents were in their mid-forties. Money was scarce, and the war-weary world was fast heading for a severe economic depression. The humble family to be fed and housed was large which made life tough! Nevertheless, God blessed James' faithful parents with long life. Father Blackwood died in 1951 and Mother Blackwood died in 1963.

James was the fourth child and the third of three boys. By the time baby James was born, his sister Lena was sixteen, Roy, the oldest, was nearly nineteen, and baby Doyle was already eight years old!

Clearly the family age span was considerable. Indeed, brother Roy's son named R.W., was to become more of a brother than a nephew to James. R.W. was a whole two years younger than James. They were to be great buddies at play and later close co-workers together with Christ as long as life was to last.

James was converted to Christ at the tender age of seven in the Mount Olive Church in rural Mississippi. Later, he was baptized by immersion firstly in his home state, and much later still in 1977, as an act of rededication, in the Holy Land's Jordan River.

At the close of the twentieth century, looking back on James, as a performer, he is widely recognized as a quality song-stylist and an excellent, enthusiastic lead singer of his day. In live concert performance, his expressive face typically reflected the whole gamut of emotions required from the front persons of this particular genre of gospel music. Seriousness, fun, excitement and enthusiasm were all clearly exhibited in his face and deeply felt in his sincere personality.

Since 1934 to the dawn of the twenty-first century, through all the changing scenes of quartet life, his smiling face and commanding presence have been ever enduring constants. The wide-flung, Blackwood dynasty, over which he presided, had for several generations provided a rich gold mine of talented relatives and descendants. They served the Southern Gospel Music cause (and in some cases the secular music industry) with great skill and dedication. However, best of all, many served the cause of Christ's Kingdom honestly, earnestly and sacrificially. Great was the harvest of their labors.

Big in personality and high in integrity as he was, conversely James was a small, slightly built gentleman. When he spoke or sang, he had a distinctive, melodic ring and accent in his crystal-clear voice. Vocally, his special, unique quality of enunciation and tone was immediately recognizable in virtually all of the Blackwood Brothers' multiple recordings.

Even in advancing years, the sophisticated James conducted himself with great class and considerable dignity. Tenor, Larry Ford (of the James Blackwood Quartet) described this as tantamount to royalty! Fashionably and smartly dressed, dignified and well-spoken, his genuine class could easily be mistaken for aloofness or ego. But not so! Truly, he had earned his worthy reputation as a Southern Christian gentleman of integrity and faith.

Without hesitation or solicitation, many of his associates, some close and some not so close, happily testified to this writer that James sacrificially took quality-time and gave dedicated-attention to ordinary people in all walks of life.

In his post-prison autobiography, the ex-TV-host evangelist, Jim Bakker speaks highly of James as he was one of the very few to visit him in prison. Bakker's friends and associates deserted him in multiple numbers when he dramatically fell from the pinnacle of his multi-million-dollar Heritage USA Retreat Centre, losing his wife, fortune, dignity, faith and freedom. Imprisoned initially in 1989 for an incredibly ridiculous forty-five years, Bakker hit rock bottom. Amid his abject despair, loneliness and humiliation, most so-called Christian friends treated him shamefully. But not James Blackwood, as Bakker exclaimed!

"What a wonderful day it was when James Blackwood came to the Jesup prison and brought his quartet to perform a gospel concert on the prison's loading dock. The prison guard even allowed me to visit with them on their bus, though he had to accompany me!"

Highly worthy of note was James' long surviving marriage (since May 4, 1939) to Miriam Grantham, of Weathersby, Mississippi. Such longevity in marriage was, and is sadly, rare in the second half of the twentieth century even in the Christian music department of show business. Their long lasting marriage-bond gave laudable testimony to their high fidelity, consistency of quality character, and sheer determination to see things through!

Always patiently supportive, the soft-spoken Miriam was content to stay home, keeping the home-fire burning, doing the administration of the office affairs, and last but not least, raising two sons. These two sons gave her four grandchildren and four great-grandchildren to thoroughly spoil from time to time, as all good matriarchs do!

Despite the ups and downs of life that all are subject to, James and his dear wife were successful survivors; role-models to many. It was evident that in matters of family values, Miriam and James' marriage partnership had successfully raised two sons of whom they could be proud.

Jimmy and Billy, like their devoted parents, were men of integrity and faith. They displayed also no mean talent when it came to musical expression, and an on-going passion for the gospel of Christ! Jimmy became a notable singing preacher throughout the USA, and Billy was to serve fruitfully on the pastoral staff of the Hendersonville Chapel in Nashville.

James was always an astute business man. This was well illustrated when James kept a cool head in 1951 in lofty discussions with the legendary Steve Sholes. The RCA Victor king-pin desperately wanted to sign up the Blackwood Brothers and James wanted a contract as well. Not overwhelmed, James did more than secure a prestigious recording contract. He and Sholes also signed to a distributor deal for the entire range of RCA gospel products while amazingly retaining the right for the Blackwood Brothers to continue their custom record label.

The wide exposure in secular quarters given to Christian music as a whole, because of James Blackwood's astute deal, should not be under-emphasized. It laid the foundation for the thriving Christian music industry and touring circuits that came in the subsequent fifty years. For that, the Blackwoods, and James in particular, should be duly credited!

After half a century of constant personal appearances, the rigors of being on the road, and all that it entailed, started to become burdensome. James reluctantly conceded that he should slow-up in 1971, formally retiring from the Blackwood Brothers Quartet in 1981...but not from singing and not for long!

Itchingly restless, he joyfully returned to singing the unchanging gospel with the prestigious group he started called the Masters V. It was composed of well-known, long-serving, gospel-quartet contemporaries such as Hovie Lister, J.D. Sumner, Rosie Rozell, and Jake Hess, all in the eventide of their great careers.

In Memphis, his comfortable, living room's trophy case overflows with industry, church and fan awards of every shape and size. Among them is the Memphis State University Award of Excellence in Arts and Communication that he was awarded in 1985.

He enterprisingly turned his hand to acting of a sort in 1992. After careful selection, he was invited to portray the late R.W. Blackwood several times on stage in a series of Mississippi Chautaugua programs. These were sponsored by the Mississippi Humanities Council and entitled *Mississippi's Musical Heritage.* It was a role that James enjoyed and after all, no one knew R.W. better than James himself!

At the dawn of the twenty-first century, he still lived in Memphis with his dear Miriam and continued an active concert schedule both as a soloist and as the featured artist of the James Blackwood Quartet. The line-up in 1999 was James Blackwood, Ken Turner, Larry Ford, Ray Shelton and Brad White (pianist). Deservedly riding high on the heritage of the Blackwoods, the James Blackwood Quartet carried the banner onward!

In mid-1999, his sixty-sixth year in gospel music, he was still performing frequently in live concerts and church services nation-wide and occasionally abroad.

James and Miriam Blackwood were blessed with a close clan of loving family and dear friends. She exclaimed that she was genuinely grateful that James had used his unique, God-given talent to be a heavenly blessing to countless people all over the world. Still enthusiastic, Miriam faithfully considered that James' voice was the most beautiful she had ever heard.

Asked how she coped with him being away from home so often during their marriage, she delighted to borrow the answer of Mrs. Billy (Ruth) Graham about her husband, Billy. Miriam declared that she would rather be with James part of the time than with anyone else all the time!

Asked in the eventide of his life what was the highlight of his lengthy career,

James reply was moving and surprising in the light of his history.

"There have been several high spots like winning the national Arthur Godfrey TV talent show and singing to thousands for Dr. Billy Graham. If I had to pick the best it would be one night in Greenville, South Carolina before six thousand folk.

"I was singing *I Will Meet You In The Morning* and decided to leave the platform and shake hands with people in the audience as far as my microphone chord would allow. People started rising and coming down to meet me from high up in the auditorium.

I will meet you in the morning
Just outside the Eastern Gate,
Then be ready, faithful pilgrim,
Lest for you it be too late!

Full the joy of that great morning
With the saints who for us wait,
There a blessed, happy morning,
Just inside the Eastern Gate!

I will meet you in the morning,
I will meet you in the morning
Just inside the Eastern Gate over there!
I will meet you in the morning
I will meet you in the morning
I will meet you in the morning over there!
Rev I. G. Martin / Trad. arranged by Wes Davis / © New Music Enterprises 1999

"Then I saw a little, gray-haired lady on crutches advancing down the aisle, tears flooding her face. As she came up close, she embraced me with a loving hug. Then she spoke emotionally! 'James, I will...I will meet you in the morning!'...It was Ken Turner's dear mother!...

"I still choke up when I picture that scene. She reminded me of my little, old mother, four feet nine inches tall, who barely came up to my shoulder.

"She always remained faithful in prayer, a prayer warrior to the end. She called it 'praying through' meaning 'until she felt her prayer had been heard in heaven'.

My dear mother went to be with the Lord in 1963 at the age of eighty-three. That elderly, little lady in the aisle reminded me of her, which makes the memory sweet and special."

The specific choice made by James Blackwood of the highlight of his illustrious, music career silently speaks volumes. It remains highly reflective of where his heart was anchored! In reality, James' career was a ministry all the time, as he explained.

"It has been said that music is the language of the angels. If this is true, surely it must be doubly true of sacred songs and gospel music! Christian music tells of heaven, the life hereafter and the reunion with loved ones. It gives testimony of the peace and happiness found in serving God in this life.

"This is the music that the Blackwood Brothers have been dedicated to. In music, as in everything else, fads come and go. This happens even in gospel music! But our style has not changed appreciably during the years. I believe that the message in a gospel song is as eternal as that of the preached Word and the Bible itself. If it is presented sincerely and performed by dedicated singers, it will be an inspiration to all who listen."

On a personal note, this writer must document his thanks to James. It is to his credit that I found him to be a man who walked his talk when it came to going the extra mile! Unsolicited, he gave of his time, hospitality, energy and substance in great abundance in the research for this book.

23 THE FAMILY VOCATION CONTINUES

And the LORD said unto Moses,
'Behold, thy days approach that thou must die:
call Joshua, and present yourselves in the tabernacle of the congregation,
that I may give him a charge.
And Moses and Joshua went,
and presented themselves in the tabernacle of the congregation.
And the LORD appeared in the tabernacle in a pillar of a cloud:
and the pillar of the cloud stood over the door of the tabernacle.
And the LORD said unto Moses,
*   'Behold, thou shalt sleep with thy fathers...*
Now therefore write ye this song for you,
and teach it the children of Israel:
put it in their mouths, that this song may be a witness for me....
And it shall come to pass, when many evils and troubles are befallen them,
that this song shall testify against them as a witness;
for it shall not be forgotten out of the mouths of their seed....!'
Moses therefore wrote this song the same day, and taught it the children of Israel.
And he gave Joshua the son of Nun a charge, and said,
'Be strong and of a good courage:
for thou shalt bring the children of Israel into the land which I sware unto them:
and I will be with thee!'
And Moses spake in the ears of all the congregation of Israel
the words of this song, until they were ended.
Deuteronomy 32: various

At the dawn of the new millennium, Cecil Blackwood was the ever-present, effervescent leader of the Blackwood Brothers. Heading for his golden jubilee with the group, he was as enthusiastic as ever about what he saw as a God-given vocation.

Cecil, hard-working and visionary, was the son of Roy, one of the quartet founders. A nephew of James, he was the younger brother of the late, legendary, baritone R.W. In 1954, at the age of nineteen, immediately after R. W .'s death in the plane-crash, Cecil stepped into his brother's spot in the quartet. He had cut his harmony teeth with the Memphis-based, Songfellows Quartet.

Grateful for his Blackwood Brothers heritage, the current, very talkative leader of the Blackwood Brothers was in nostalgic mood as he contemplated the family ministry.

"I praise God that I was born into a family that loved the Lord and dedicated their lives to the ministry. Because of a family revival in 1917, no less than thirty of my own kinfolk became committed to serving their Lord. Since then, untold numbers of people have come to a saving knowledge of Jesus Christ as a result of that commitment."

Cecil married the attractive and very beautiful Francine who was half-Native American and Dutch. Born on the sixth day of December 1944 on a Native American reservation, her father was an Indian Chief and preacher, singer and evangelist. Her mother was of Dutch descent and met her husband at Bible college where they were both studying. Francine traveled and sang with her family all her young life. She later sang with Cecil in the Blackwood Brothers for six years, pitching her voice between the tenors.

Francine, who accepted Christ at the age of seven, was once employed by the US Health and Human Services to work in its Indian Health Agency. The mother of John and Lisa, according to Cecil, Francine will always be the apple of his eye.

"Francine is a good, loving wife and mother!...She can also drive the Blackwood Brothers' bus, cook a gourmet dinner, and head up the Blackwood Brothers' business affairs....She is the wind beneath my wings!"

In 1954, members of the original Blackwood Brothers Incorporated were James Blackwood, Cecil Blackwood, J. D. Sumner, Bill Shaw and Jackie Marshall. In the new millenium, Cecil Blackwood remained the only incorporated member left of the original quartet still singing and carrying on the tradition of the Blackwood Brothers Quartet. Cecil's hope was that the Blackwood Brothers' evangelistic ministry would continue until, as he said, 'the return of the Lord!'

"We're in our fourth generation now! The Blackwood name has become so popular in America that I believe the name can be carried on. I know of no other gospel group that has so many family members serving the Lord in gospel music!"

Continuing the family tradition, as well as Cecil's Blackwood Brothers, are the Blackwood Voices (headed by Cecil's son) and the Blackwood Singers (headed by Cecil's nephew).

Cecil Blackwood was born on October 28, 1934 in an old, timber house situated on four acres of land that his grandfather had bought for one hundred dollars in Mississippi. Before Cecil was born, his father, Roy E. Blackwood was a well traveled evangelist and North Carolina state overseer of the Churches of God pentecostal movement, that had its headquarters in Cleveland, Tennessee.

Roy was converted to Christ in 1917 in a family revival of about thirty members. The paternal family side were Blackwoods and maternal side were Halls. The spiritual experience revolutionized both sides of the close Christian family as many enlisted in evangelistic work.

For a while, the pioneering Roy pastored a church in Forth Worth, Texas and then one in Morgan Town, Mississippi. Before that, he pastored in West Virginia, Kentucky and Alabama. Parallel to the pastoring work, the singing ministry was still being diligently pursued.

The Blackwood Brothers started in 1934 and in 1938, went full time.

They were interrupted by World War II, Roy became a riveter in San Diego, and R.W. and James were welders in an aircraft factory also in San Diego. Doyle Blackwood returned to Chattanooga, Tennessee as his health was bad, but he continued to broadcast on radio.

Cecil's first marriage was at the age of eighteen and Mark was born when Cecil was nineteen. The first marriage broke up in 1973 and that left Cecil to raise three teenagers single-handed in his home.

Cecil has not been, of course, without his personal difficulties or heavy crosses to bear.

My grace is sufficient for thee:
for my strength is made perfect in weakness.
Most gladly therefore will I rather glory in my infirmities,
that the power of Christ may rest upon me.
Therefore I take pleasure in infirmities,
in reproaches, in necessities, in persecutions, in distresses for Christ's sake:
for when I am weak, then am I strong.
2 Cor.12:9-10

A very special person in the Cecil Blackwood family is his beloved daughter, Regina Monette Blackwood.

Regina was born mentally handicapped and thus unable to read or write. Eventually however, she was able to care for herself, albeit slowly. As Cecil stated, in her own way, she was happy.

At the age of fifteen years, the worried family was advised that she should undergo a preventative hysterectomy and other operations followed. Sadly, the stress of all the surgery caused her to have a total nervous breakdown. For several years after that she became a bedridden case and knew nothing or no one for several years. She was eventually transferred between three or four hospitals and saw numerous doctors, all to no avail.

During one of her father's tours, Regina was put in the care of her brother, Mark. He concluded that she was not receiving the necessary care for her to progress any further. He bravely made the decision, in his father's absence, to take her out of the hospital and against the doctors advice brought her home with him. The hospital then refused to have any more to do with her and warned him that in their opinion Regina would never be able to care for herself nor get any better.

Refusing to accept their diagnosis, and putting all their faith in the God of the impossible, the family continued to pray for her and nursed her back to better stability and saw progress accordingly!

With supervision, she was totally enabled to care for herself, doing light housework in and around the house. She also worked for the Blackwood Brothers on the road, setting up the concert-sales table and keeping the bus tidy, among other things. Regina also worked in the Blackwood Brothers' headquarters in Memphis.

As Cecil proudly asserted, "Regina loves Jesus and is a source of real joy, a blessing and a great testimony proving what the power of God can do."

Based live in Cordova, Tennessee, Cecil's youngest daughter, Barbara Blackwood Childs married country singer and businessman, Andy Childs and is the proud mother of two boys, Daniel and Cameron. Before her marriage to Andy, Barbara was the Blackwood Brothers' booking agent.

The new millennium's Blackwood Brothers' group consisted of Cecil Blackwood, Steve Warren, Rick Price, Chris Blackwood and Eric Winston. The age-range of their family audiences still extended from the very young to the old, although the appeal tended to be in the older category. The younger members of the group tended to successfully draw younger people to the venues. Many of the audiences attended following the successes of the Bill and Gloria Gaither videos during the nineties.

"The type of program we give in 2000," declared Cecil, "is evangelistic. Many years ago we tended to just do one song after another and get as loud and sing as high as we could! Often we tried to outdo other groups!

"We no longer feel in competition with other guys. Instead, we try to present Jesus Christ through music. We are preachers and evangelists giving the message in our songs!"

Cecil was clear in his views with reference to the vexed question of whether the Blackwoods are ministers or entertainers.

"We are singers, number one! I have to admit we entertain Christian people mostly but over and above that we are ministers! I and the bass singer are ordained and we minister in our program. We don't take a text and preach for an hour but we share about the Lord between songs. We are Christian entertainers who sing the gospel! The programs usually finish after an altar call and we have seen thousands accept the Lord over the years!"

Asked whether the Blackwood Brothers were ever tempted to go secular, Cecil's response was adamant. "I was born into a gospel music family, that's all I know! Gospel music was and remains my first love! We have never sought the opportunity to go secular. We have never tried the doors because God has provided us with this living and this calling!

"I don't criticize those who go secular but our desire is to sing the gospel and reach as many as possible with the gospel. We do like other music, of course. I'm not narrow minded!...But for me, I believe, God has ordained me and the Blackwoods to sing gospel!"

Cecil owned and continued the group into the new millennium. Their average, annual work-rate had been 280 to 300 concerts per year since the early fifties. The quartet had presented the gospel in forty-seven countries.

Cecil's Blackwood Brothers still love to sing the old-song favorites but they have been given a little face lift. For instance, *I Bowed On My Knees and Cried Holy* was an old Blackwood favorite from the fifties. Like other groups, including the Gaither Vocal Band, the boys have changed it somewhat in tempo keeping up with the times. The current Blackwoods also do updated versions of *How Great Thou Art, Until Then,* and even the old English hymn, *I Love To Tell*

The Story.

"In the late Seventies," Cecil recalled, "we tried to go more contemporary and won Grammy Awards doing so. But our fans did not like the idea of full concerts of that kind! They always liked to hear a sampling of some of the older songs too!"

Cecil stated that the first qualification he looks for in a new member of the Blackwood Brothers is that he should be a Christian. Secondly, that he has the ability to sing and reach people in ministry. Thirdly, he needs to be able to travel.

"We've had great singers who can't travel because of their family commitments. Our road schedule is three weeks of travel and then one week off. With kids and home to deal with, that's sometimes difficult! Lastly, we also need the professional appearance of being clean-cut and appealing to the people!"

The type of repertoire that the Blackwood Brothers looked for in their choice of songs were themes that would bless the people, be fun to sing, pleasing on the ear, and would be commercial (in record sales terms).

"Ultimately, we want songs that will help our audience find a closer walk with God."

Cecil admitted he did get weary of the road, especially as he did some of the bus driving. "I'm not complaining 'cause it's the same for missionaries....The road does get weary!...But the benefits outweigh the negative!"

Asked when he planned to retire, he answered humorously. "I have no plans to retire. So many people retire and then just die. I think I'd probably die if I did not have my work. I want to keep working 'til the Lord comes back! Yes, as long as health permits, I will continue singing!"

Cecil also admitted that gospel singers often did not have the financial foundation that allowed them to retire easily. Unless they had been very foresighted and prudent in early years they would not have an adequate pension.

"I have about thirty people in our set-up who need my support including missionaries in Russia. In 1989, we helped start a church there that has nine pastors needing support. We also help many other missionaries in different parts of the world! Our main focus is the Temple Of The Gospel in St. Petersburg, Russia where Dr. Sergei Nikolaev is the head pastor. The church started with twenty nine people in 1989 and today boasts a congregation numbering three thousand members! We have a fully accredited college from which about five hundred missionaries graduated to go throughout Russia with the good news of the gospel of Jesus Christ."

Most of the pastors at the Temple of the Gospel Church in St. Petersburg were solely supported by Cecil Blackwood and the Blackwood Brothers Quartet.

Cecil's daughter, Barbara Blackwood Childs is married to country singer, Andy Childs who also sings Christian gospel music. He has performed at Blackwood Brothers' Homecomings.

"The inheritor of the Blackwood Brothers' group is my grandson, Chris Blackwood. He is in line. My son, Mark chose to go a different route with his own group. I am trying to train Chris as a leader to keep the group going after I'm gone!"

Chris Blackwood was born on the sixth of February, 1976, in Memphis, Tennessee. The son of Cecil Mark Blackwood, and Cecil Stamps' grandson, Chris was separated from the rest of the Blackwood family at the age of five and raised in Nashville, Tennessee. During the summer and vacations, Chris would travel with the family or stayed with his father in Memphis, but deep-down always felt his place was with the Blackwood family.

As Chris grew into his teens, he began to desert his Christian roots and go his own way. Like the Prodigal Son, bowing to peer pressure, he became entangled and involved with the wrong crowds. At the age of eighteen years, he left home and moved in with his cousins and other friends.

He was taught how to buy and sell drugs by his friends who would send him into the rough areas of Nashville to ply his trade. Eventually, Chris reached rock bottom and was practically living on the streets.

Chris's grandfather, the well-traveled Cecil, heard of the dire situation his grandson was in and planned to seek him out when the Blackwood Brothers next toured the Nashville area. What he found appalled and shocked him to the core. Chris had grown to 6'2" yet weighed only 140 pounds. Wearing an ear-ring, he was unwashed, his hair was shaved three inches above his ear, his clothing was disheveled and dirty and he had not eaten for three days.

Cecil's grandfather's heart was filled with compassion for his wayward grandson whom he dearly loved so he decided to take Chris on the Blackwood Brothers' touring bus with him. Chris was at first reluctant to go but, because of his deep-rooted love for his grandfather, he was persuaded to get on the bus.

Then a life changing transformation began to take place in Chris' young life. He immediately started eating and gained twenty pounds within two weeks. His hair on his shaven head grew back and the ear-ring was removed. But Chris still had a problem, as Cecil recalled.

"He was still hooked on rock music! He did not want to hear about God as he had never been raised in church. He would wait outside in the parking lot whenever he was taken to hear the quartet sing. All Chris' life consisted of was his love of rock music!

"But the love of God, and the testimony and love shown to him by the Christians around him had its effect on Chris' life. One day he completely surrendered himself to the claims that Christ made on him. He received Him as his Lord and Savior, much to the delight and joy of this grandfather!

"Transformed, Chris nowadays stands tall like a man, wears a smart suit, and is singing gospel music. Chris' main aim in life now is no longer rock music and the pitfalls of his earlier life! Instead, he works to win souls for Christ, to sing gospel music with his family.

"He is proud to carry on the tradition of the Blackwood Brothers Quartet, started all those long years ago by his great grandfather Roy E. Blackwood!"

On a personal note, this writer must document his thanks to Cecil. He remains to this day, a great enthusiast eager to sacrificially provide details of his considerable, first-hand experience plus his memories in great measure in the research for this book.

24 THE LEGACY THAT REMAINS!

By their fruits ye shall know them.
Matthew 7:20

The outspoken singing preacher, Hovie Lister, of the Statesmen Quartet used to laughingly joke that God never intended for Christianity to sing the blues or wear a long face.

The realities of everyday life, however, sometimes dictate somewhat differently, as seasons inevitably must change from sunshine to rain. Yes, truly, according to wise old King Solomon, "there is a time to laugh and a time to weep."

Doubtless, the tragic crash of the Blackwood Brothers' twin-engine plane in 1954 devastated the group's enthusiasm and joy but only for a season. They slowly had to come to workable terms with losing two well-beloved, sincere, family men and quartet colleagues.

Such a blow was devastating but not crushing!

The deceased overnight became legends of gospel music and the remaining, replenished group bounced back into the limelight of a steadily-growing and prosperous Christian music industry and circuit. Truly the genre came into its own, in good measure, as a result of the Blackwood Brothers' enterprises.

Yes, in essence, the Blackwood Brothers' role should not be an underestimated contribution to the emergence and building of the successful, gospel music circuit and industry of the latter quarter of the twentieth century! Their part was not merely crucial but fundamental.

The quartet recovered remarkably well in the mid-fifties and went on to sing well into the dawn of the twenty-first century. They continued to bring innovation to their trade and amassed a trophy display-case brim full of awards.

The Blackwood Brothers Quartet's earth-breaking energy, unprecedented professionalism, and sheer quality became the pattern for thousands of aspiring "wannabes" in the Christian music sphere.

Attitudes, fashions and tastes have inevitably changed with the passage of time. Yet the Blackwood Brothers' innovative professionalism in the music ministry survived the ravages of circumstance and time. They have also received priceless promotion via the phenomenally successful Bill and Gloria Gaither videos.

The Gaithers' strategic television exposure in the nineties was to dramatically resurrect many dormant or waning careers, reviving interest in gospel performers of historic importance. They did not come anymore important than the

Blackwoods.

Musical styles have come and gone with every changing wind of fashion but the solid, underlying Christian message that the Blackwood Brothers broadcasted continued and endured.

"Our songs were mainly testimony songs," James recalled. "My God truly is real! I hope we never lose the testimony songs. There is a movement today towards only praise and worship songs. But testimony songs speak to the unsaved. We should remain missionaries for the gospel."

Since 1934 until the dawn of the next century, the Blackwood Brothers displayed an entertaining, edifying and evangelistic singing partnership at conventions, concerts and missions that took them all over the world. They performed to hundreds of thousands, dressed in their immaculately tailored, plush dress-suits and shiny footwear.

Just like Barnabus of the early first century church, the Blackwoods can take also take rightful credit as encouragers and facilitators of hundreds of other Christian acts for whom they blazed a trail!

James Blackwood sincerely believed, as he looked back, that if ever a group was raised and endowed for a special work by the Divine Master, that group was the Blackwood Brothers!

From the early thirties to the third millennium, their days of heavy travel were filled with dedicated, hard-work as they sought to fulfil the Great Commission's task.

Before their time, psalms and hymns and some gospel songs played the most important part of Christian services. Christian music seldom jumped the secular fence. Thus no substantial impact had been made by Christian music on show business until the Blackwood Brothers came along.

The Blackwood Brothers popularized, among the general public, a Christian music industry that provided a new style of pleasing gospel songs. Such repertoire was designed to stir cold hearts and challenge honest seekers with the gospel while, at the same time, thoroughly entertain.

Along the way, the Blackwoods upset more than a few who were fearful of mixing ministry with entertainment. Most contentious of all was the vexed issue of commercialization of a free gospel.

Without fear or favor, the Blackwood Brothers progressed their daring strategy and continued to popularize their powerful Christian ditties.

The Blackwood Brothers' inspiring performances, subjectwise, spanned a diverse panorama of sentiment and emotion that appealed to and touched successive generations. The Blackwood Brothers musical moods shifted at great pace from early rock and roll to lazy Hawaiian waltzes to toe-tapping spirituals to singalong country to old time hymns plus, along the way, many more styles!

Innovative and flexible, at times, they were renowned to be as effective gospel communicators as their preaching associates.

Throughout the years since 1934, untold multitudes heard their rich, full, inspiring voices on uplifting songs like the peppy *Give The World A Smile Each Day*, the reflective *Peace In the Valley*, the majestic *How Great Thou Art*, and the moving *I Will Meet You In The Morning*. Such songs have since become well-beloved, evergreen standards inside and outside the church.

Vast family audiences were entertained, uplifted, or even convicted and challenged by their harmony and message. Their talents were able to stir even some of the most apathetic or hard-hearted who would remain unmoved by powerful preaching from the pulpit.

No other Christian performers have advanced the gospel music cause so daringly or progressively as the Blackwood Brothers. Today's thriving Christian music industry, gospel-concert circuit, and the Gospel Music Association are living legacies of the dedicated, enthusiastic, ground-breaking vision, persevering hard-work, and success of the Blackwood Brothers.

In the latter half of the twentieth century, many thousands gladly bore testimony to the convicting, stimulating power of the Blackwood Brothers' utterance. Since their time there have been many imitators and successors who have successfully ploughed their gospel-singing fields.

The Blackwood Brothers were truly ground-breakers, of that there is no doubt! This attribute of the Blackwood Brothers was uniquely documented and saluted by the Statler Brothers, one of the greatest country music groups of all time.

At their nostalgic, harmonic-best, the Statlers' Mercury recording was their personal testament; a foot-tapping, story-telling ballad aptly entitled *The Blackwood Brothers*. It was a remarkable, fitting tribute, the type of which is rare in the harsh, dog-eat dog world of show biz.

The Blackwood Brothers' story is a simple, sublime account of how the delicate, sensitive balance between the commercial business of entertainment and the sacrifice of ministry in sacred song can generally, successfully be struck.

Sometimes they failed, occasionally spectacularly. In doing so, they upset, or conversely delighted, some scoffing religionists along the way, eager to magnify human imperfection, question motives, and generally seek to find fault.

When one flies high and lives daringly as the Blackwood Brothers did, one can expect some spectacular falls from time to time. Just a casual reading or appreciation of scripture will assure one that all God's human agents are indeed human! Even exalted names, like Noah, Moses, David, and Peter, illustrate the point conclusively!

That paragraph is not written to make excuse but rather to understand! God in His providence can turn all the saints' troubles to their credit.

And we know that all things
work together for good
to them that love God,
to them who are the called
according to his purpose.
For whom he did foreknow,
he also did predestinate
to be conformed to the image of his Son,
that He might be the firstborn among many brethren.
Romans 8:28-29

No one, except the Divine Master Himself, is without fault. No matter how pious, committed, or sincere one may be, we all fail the test of ultimate perfection.

Overall, taking all into account, this writer, to quote the much-respected Christian music sage, Bill Gaither (who in turn used the Apostle Paul's terminology), considered that the Blackwood Brothers finished the race well!

Their dedicated music added a new, thrilling chapter to the triumphs of the gospel. Their music ministry is a precious, sacred-song legacy to those who faithfully follow in their gospel music train.

Let us hear the conclusion of the whole matter:
Fear God, and keep his commandments:
for this is the whole duty of man.
For God shall bring every work into judgement,
with every secret thing,
whether it be good, or whether it be evil
Ecclesiasties 12 :13-15

PAUL DAVIS (copyright : December 1999)

25 THE BLACKWOODS BROTHERS' VOICE

The Blackwoods were a voice, a persuasive voice,
That traveled the world-wide through.
Old and young pointed to paths of the true!
Their gospel songs flew on beams of light,
Speaking to folk with a gentle might,

The Blackwood Brothers' sound
Traversed over land and sea,
To human hearts, they brought the Key,
Telling His story and singing His song!
Praising the right, and blaming the wrong.

The Blackwoods were a voice, a consoling voice,
That traveled on the wings of the air.
Their gospel songs snapping chains of despair!
In homes, rich and poor, they'd gently seek,
His calm and truthful words to speak!

Southern-gospel's message did abound,
Lovingly broadcast all around,
Enriched by the Blackwood Brothers' sacred sound.
Warming hearts with enduring pain,
Encouraging all to look up again!

The Blackwoods were a voice, a convincing voice,
That traveled with Spirit Wind.
Pointing the way to heaven's new dawn,
Love's song melted hearts, sadly torn,
With unhappiness, spite and scorn.

Establishing peace and Christian virtue
So helping evil thoughts subdue
The Blackwood Brothers' sound
Rode the thunder-crash
Into blinded conscious flashed.

The Blackwoods were a voice, an Evangel voice,
That traveled the world around.
Where men to false gods were bowed,
They'd publish in notes both loud and long,
The Gospel's joyful sound!

Proclaiming peace via the Only Way,
The Blackwood Brothers' sound
Flew on the wings of the day,
So bidding the saddened world rejoice!
Thank God for their voice, the precious Evangel voice.

(Paul Davis - Wes Davis / © New Music Enterprises 1999

Gospel Music Hall of Fame

The members and friends of the gospel music industry
and the Board of Directors and Membership of the Gospel Music Association
do hereby on the second day of April in the year 1998 invite, admit and induct

The Blackwood Brothers

In recognition of the accomplishments and spirit
of selfless dedication through the spreading of the Good News

President
Gospel Music Association

Chairman
GMA Hall of Fame Committee

26 LONG-PLAY ALBUM DISCOGRAPHY

(VINYLS, TAPES AND COMPACT DISCS)
(NOTE: This list may not be completely exhaustive due the sheer volume of titles involved)

1958 *FAVORITE GOSPEL SONGS AND SPIRITUALS*
(RCA VICTOR LPM3082 /10 inch vinyl)
Take My Hand Precious Lord/Wanta Rest/(There'll Be) Peace in the Valley/It Is No Secret/He Bought My Soul At Calvary/My Journey to the Sky/Mansion Over The Hilltop/Swing Down Sweet Chariot
Dan Huskey; James Blackwood; R. W. Blackwood; Bill Lyles; Jack Marshall

1956 *HYMN SING*
(RCA VICTOR LPM1255 Mono)
I Saw A Man/He Knows Just What I Need/Heavenly Love/Wonderful Saviour/I Wanta Go There/I Don't Mind/I Just Can't Make It by Myself/Stop and Pray/Inside the Gate/The King and I Walk Hand in Hand/I Bowed on My Knees and Cried Holy/Wonderful
Bill Shaw; James Blackwood; Cecil Blackwood; J. D. Summer; Jack Marshall

1956 *GOSPEL SONGS AND SPIRITUALS*
(RCA VICTOR LPM1351 Mono) (Twelve inch re-issue of RCA LPM3082)

1957 **I'M BOUND FOR THAT CITY**
1958 (RCA VICTOR LPM1488 Mono)
He Lifted Me From Sin/Peace of Mind/Farther Along/Jesus Lifted Me/I'm Bound for That City/Give Me the Strength to Stand/Jesus Is Mine/No Tears In Heaven/I Was There When It Happened/There's One/You Are the Finger of God/I Will Lift Up Mine Eyes Unto the Hills
Bill Shaw; James Blackwood; Cecil Blackwood; J. D. Sumner; Jack Marshall

1958 *HANK SNOW SINGS SACRED SONGS*
(RCA VICTOR LPM 1638 Mono)
The Glory Land March/Invisible Hands (with Blackwood Brothers)/He'll Understand And Say "Well Done"/My Religion's Not Old Fashioned (But It's Real Genuine)/My Mother/I'm Glad I'm on the Inside (Looking Out) (with Blackwood Brothers)/The Alphabet/I'm In Love With Jesus/These Things Shall Pass/Pray/Little Children (Hope of the World)/I'm Moving On to Glory
Bill Shaw; James Blackwood; R.W. Blackwood; Bill Lyles; Jack Marshall

1958 *HIS HANDS*
(RCA VICTOR LPM1705 Mono)
God Made a Way/His Hands/I'm, Happy and Free/Gentle Hands/I'll follow Where He Leads (Night and Day)/Inside your Heart/Invisible Hands/He's My King/I'm Free/Tho' I'm Unworthy/On the Other Side of Jordan/Take Me Home
Bill Shaw; James Blackwood; Cecil Blackwood; J. D. Sumner; Jack Marshall

1959 *THE STRANGER OF GALILEE*
(RCA VICTOR LPM1892 Mono)
The Stranger of Galilee/Amazing Grace/Tell someone About Jesus/Shall I Crucify Him?/Who Is That/The Old Rugged Cross/Sweet Peace/What A Friend/Medley: The Last Mile of the Way, When I make My Last Move, When I Take My Vacation in Heaven/Rock of Ages/When I'm Alone/Whispering Hope
Bill Shaw; James Blackwood; Cecil Blackwood; J. D. Sumner; Jack Marshall

1959 *PARADISE ISLAND*
(RCA VICTOR LSP2033 Living Stereo/LPM2033 Mono)
Beyond God's Horizon/Paradise Island/My Lord Goes With Me/Land Called Heaven/Dreams of Tomorrow/He Will See You Through/Each Step I Take/Behind Your Tears/My All I Give/Do You Know My Jesus?/Do You Go to Church/?Pay as You Go
Bill Shaw; James Blackwood; Cecil Blackwood; J. D. Sumner; Jack Marshall

1959 *THE BLACKWOOD BROTHERS*
(RCA CAMDEN CAL544 Mono)
Take a Look in the Book/Christ Is a Wonderful Saviour/At The End of the Trail/He Knows Just How Much You Can Bear/My Saving King/The Soul Spangled Banner/The Lord Is a Busy Man/ The Workshop of the Lord/I Don't Care What the World May Do/will Heaven be Heaven Without You/How Many Times/If I pray
Bill Shaw; James Blackwood; Cecil Blackwood; J. D. Sumner; Jack Marshall

1959 *GIVE THE WORLD A SMILE*
(Skylite SSLP5966 Life-like Stereo/SLRP5966 Mono)
A Beautiful Life/Just a Closer Walk with Thee/Looking for a City/Peace Like a River/Tell My Friends/where Could I Go/Over The Moon/That Glad Reunion Day/Life's Railway to Heaven/A Mail order from Heaven/Give the World a Smile/Want to be More Like Jesus
Bill Shaw; James Blackwood; Cecil Blackwood; J. D. Sumner; Wally Varner

1960 *THE BLACKWOOD BROTHERS IN CONCERT*
(RCA VICTOR LSP2137 Living Stereo/LPM2137 Mono)
I'm Thankful/Not My Will/Hide Me Rock of Ages/I Get Happy/I Wouldn't Trade/How Great Thou Art/Never/Then I Met the Master/Dear Lord, Remember Me/The Devil Can't Harm a Praying Man/He's All I Need/what a Morning
Bill Shaw; James Blackwood; Cecil Blackwood; J. D. Sumner; Wally Varner

1960 *BEAUTIFUL ISLE OF SOMEWHERE*
(RAC VICTOR LSP-2248 Living Stereo/LPM-2248 Mono)
Eternal Paradise/On That Happy Golden Shore/I'll Be True/I Want To Meet You Up in Heaven/I Found God/Heaven For Me/Aloha Time/A Land Where Milk and Honey Flows/Jesus Fills My Every Need/Paradise Island/What a Glorious Morning That Will Be/Beautiful Isle of Somewhere
Bill Shaw; James Blackwood; Cecil Blackwood; Wally Varner

1960 *SUNDAY MEETIN' TIME*
(SKYLITE SRLP-5967 Mono)
Saviour Gently Take Me Home/Sunday Meetin' Time/It Took A Miracle/Just a Little Talk With Jesus/Lord, Keep Your Hand On Me/Everyday Will Be Sunday By and By/Where No One Stands Alone/I Am A Pilgrim/How Long Has It Been/In My Father's House/I Shall Be at Home with Jesus/He's Everywhere
Bill Shaw; James Blackwood; Cecil Blackwood; J. D. Sumner; Wally Varner

1960 *STATESMEN-BLACKWOOD FAVORITES*

(SKYLITE SSLP5980 Life-like Stereo/SRLP5980 Mono)
(Side One)Lead Me to That Rock/I'm Bound for the Kingdom/This World Is Not my Home/He'll Understand and Say, "Well Done"/Rolling, Riding, Rocking/* What A Friend We Have in Jesus/ My Heavenly Father Watches Over Me
(Side Two)My Heavenly father Watches Over Me/Good-bye, World, Good-bye/Somebody Bigger Than You and I/the Love of God/Just a Closer Walk with Thee/* When the Saints Go Marching In
Bill Shaw; James Blackwood; Cecil Blackwood; J. D. Sumner; Wally Varner
Side one Blackwood Brothers; Side two Statesmen; *Combined quartets

1961 *ON TOUR*

(RCA VICTOR LSP2300 Living Stereo/LPM2300 Mono)
Crossing Chilly Jordan/because of Him/Bell of Joy Keep ringing/Because of the Love of the Lord for Me/Happy People/When I Stand with God/Some Wonderful Day/Only Believe Him/The Prodigal Son/Dear Jesus, Abide with Me/Pablo/The Old Country Church
Bill Shaw; James Blackwood; Cecil Blackwood; J. D. Sumner; Wally Varner

1961 *THE PEARLY WHITE CITY*

(RCA VICTOR LSP2397 Living Stereo/LPM2397 Mono)
The Way of the Cross/In Times Like These/Something Took Hold of Me/What a Homecoming Day/These Drops of Blood/Sorrow Not/Until Then/To Tell About His Love/childhood Memories/ To Me, He's Everything/If You Know The Lord/The Pearly White City
Bill Shaw; James Blackwood; Cecil Blackwood; J. D. Sumner; Wally Varner

1962 *PRECIOUS MEMORIES*

(RCA VICTOR LSP2506 Living Stereo/LPM2506 Mono)
I Feel Like Travelling On/Is It Well with Your Soul?/For I've Got the Lord/There Is a Change/I'll Keep walking in the King's Highway/I Dreamed I Searched Heaven for You/sing Your Blues Away/ Way Down Deep In My Soul/I Know the Lord/It's Just Like Heaven/I Do, Dear Jesus, I Believe/ Precious Memories
Bill Shaw; James Blackwood; Cecil Blackwood; J. D. Sumner; Wally Varner

1962 *SILVER ANNIVERSARY ALBUM*

(RCA VICTOR LSP 2585 Living Stereo/LPM2585 Mono)
Joyfully, I'll Travel on/When the Clouds Roll By/My Non stop flight to Glory/I Could Never Tell You (What God Has Done for Me)/He'll Be There/In That Land/Keep Me/Take a Moment and Live/Let Him In/One Day/Mammy's Boy
Bill Shaw; James Blackwood; Cecil Blackwood; J. D. Sumner; Wally Varner

1962 *A MUSICAL MERRY CHRISTMAS*

(James Blackwood and the Blackwood Brothers with Hovie Lister and The Statesmen)
(RCA VICTOR LSP2606 Living Stereo/LPM2606 Mono)
O Come All Ye Faithful (Combined)/Silver Bells (Blackwoods)/Go Tell It on the Mountain (Statesmen)/Praises to Our King (Blackwoods)/White Christmas (Statesmen)/Christmas Means Christ to Me (Blackwoods)/Joy to the World (Combined)/Christmas Time Is Here (Statesmen)/O Little Town of Bethlehem (Blackwoods)/Away In A Manger (Statesmen)/O Holy Night (Blackwoods)/ Silent Night! Holy Night! (Statesmen)

1962 *THE KEYS TO THE KINGDOM*

(RCA CAMDEN CAL618 Mono)
Walkin' and Talkin' with My Lord/The Keys to the Kingdom/I'm Feelin' Fine/I Won't Have to Cross Jordan alone/Wonderful Love/Without A Prayer/His Love/Rock A My Soul/His Hand in Mine/There Is a God/Peace Like a river/Every Day Will Be Sunday By and By
Bill Shaw; James Blackwood; Cecil Blackwood; J. D. Sumner; Wally Varner

1962 *AT HOME WITH THE BLACKWOODS*
(SKYLITE SSLP5995 Life-Like Stereo/SRLP5995 Mono)
I'm Free Again/What A Saviour/He/When God's Chariot comes/the Love of God/Lord, Build Me a Cabin in Glory/Sing, Be Happy/beyond the Sunset/Give Me Time/There's a God Somewhere/ 'Tis Wonderful to Me/When They Ring Those Golden bells for You and Me
Bill Shaw; James Blackwood; Cecil Blackwood; J. D. Sumner; Wally Varner

1963 *ON STAGE! (Recorded at Municipal Auditorium, Long Beach, California)*
(RCA VICTOR LSP2646 Living Stereo/LPM2646 Mono)
I Want to Know More About My Lord/It Don/t Mean a Thing/Wait Awhile/Old Time Religion Song/Lord, Teach Me How To Pray/He Means All the world to Me/I Will See Him There/Camp Meetin' time/I Never Knew Till Now/From Now On/He'll See You Through/Somebody Loves Me
Bill Shaw; James Blackwood; Cecil Blackwood; J. D. Sumner; Wally Varner

1963 *THE NATIONAL GOSPEL QUARTET CONVENTION*
(RCA VICTOR LSP2728 Living Stereo/LPM2728 Mono)
I'm Free Again/I'll Be All Right Someday (Blackwood Quartet)/I Found the Way/The Love of God (Stamps Quartet)/Jesus Is the Reason/When I Come to the End of the Road (Oak Ridge Quartet)/ I'm Saved and I know That I Am/Trying to Get a Glimpse (Of My Lord) (Statesmen)/This is a Mean World/I'm Looking for Jesus (Kingsmen)/When I Think of Calvary/Let's Make a Joyful Noise (Speer Family)/Amazing Grace (All Quartets and Audience)
Bill Shaw; James Blackwood; Cecil Blackwood; J.D. Sumner; Wally Varner

1963 *THE BLACKWOOD BROTHERS QUARTET FEATURING THEIR FAMOUS BASS J.D. SUMNER*
(RCA VICTOR LSP2752 Stereo/LPM2752 Mono)
I've Got to Walk That Lonesome Road/Jesus Is the Reason/I Shall Arise/Precious Is He to Me/It Must Be the Man in the Sky/Back Home/There's a Light/Jesus Cared for Me/Lord, Send Me/I Must Have Jesus/Victory Road/Today, I've Been with Jesus
Bill Shaw; James Blackwood; Cecil Blackwood; J.D. Sumner; Wally Varner

1963 *GIVE US THIS DAY*
(RCA CAMDEN CAL735 Mono)
Give Us This Day/I've Got It (You Can Have It)/Someone to Care/Angels Watching Over Me/Led by the Master's Hand/Live Right, Die Right/Walking in the Light/Jesus Holds the Keys/Footprints of Jesus/Brush the Dust Off the Bible/Jesus the Way Maker/For My Good Fortune
Bill Shaw; James Blackwood; Cecil Blackwood; J. D. Sumner; Jack Marshall; R.W. Blackwood; Bill Lyles; Dan Huskey;

1964 'BLACKWOOD FAMILY ALBUM'
(SKYLITE SSLP6026 Life-Like Stereo/SRLP6026 Mono)
I Can Tell You The Time/Do You Know Him?/I Need the Prayers/Well Done My Child/I've Had a Talk with Jesus/Echoes of the Past/* This Little Light of Mine/* The Devil's Gonna Get You/** I'll Be Ready/** Nobody/** At the Altar/** If I Follow
Bill Shaw; James Blackwood; Cecil Blackwood; J. D. Sumner; Wally Varner
*The Blackwood Little Brothers: Billy & Mark Blackwood, Garry, Doug & Greg Pilant.
**The Junior Blackwoods: James & R.W. Blackwood Jr., Phil Enloe, Jim Brown, Everett Reece

1964 'THE BLACKWOOD BROTHERS QUARTET FEATURING JAMES BLACKWOOD'
(RCA VICTOR LSP2838 Stereo/LPM2838 Mono)
Roamin' River/Give me This Mountain/I'll Never Walk alone/Turn to the Lord/The Lord's Prayer/ Medley: How Beautiful Heaven Must Be, The Unclouded Day, when I Get to the End of the Way, I'll See You Over There/There Is a Higher Power/Nobody/Christ Is the Answer/somebody Prayed for Me/Use Me/I Walked Today Where Jesus Walked
Bill Shaw; James Blackwood; Cecil Blackwood; J.D. Sumner; Wally Varner

1964 'THE BEST OF THE BLACKWOOD BROTHERS QUARTET'
(RCA VICTOR LSP2931 Stereo/RCA VICTOR LPM2931 Mono)
I've Got to Walk That Lonesome Road/One Day/In Times Like These/Paradise Island/The Lord's
Prayer/The Old Country Church/Eternal Paradise/He Means All the World to Me/Precious
Memories/How Great Thou Art/* The Stranger of Galilee/God Made a Way
Bill Shaw; James Blackwood; Cecil Blackwood; J.D. Sumner; Wally Varner; *Jack
Marshall

1964 'THE BLACKWOOD BROTHERS QUARTET'
PRESENT THEIR EXCITING TENOR BILL SHAW
(RCA VICTOR LSP2938 Stereo/RCA VICTOR LPM2938 Mono)
The Angels Must Have Cried/Everybody Ought to Love/I Serve a Living God/I'm Gonna Walk,
Talk, and Sing/Only One Touch/The Holy city/Welcome to Glory Land/All I Do Is Ask the
Lord/Down From His Glory/What a Wonderful Saviour/My Wonderful God/Sunrise
Bill Shaw; James Blackwood; Cecil Blackwood; J.D. Sumner; Whitey Gleason

1964 'GLORYLAND JUBILEE'
(RCA CAMDEN CAL794 Mono)
A Wonderful Time Up there/How About Your Heart/Gloryland Jubilee/I Can't Stand Up Alone/
I've Found the Way/The Touch of His Hand/Something Old, Something New/One Step (Toward
the Lord)/Good News/All Upon the Altar/Joy, Joy, Joy (To My Soul)/Supper Time
Bill Shaw; James Blackwood; Cecil Blackwood; J.D. Sumner; Wally Varner; *R.W.
Blackwood; Bill Lyles; Jack Marshall;

1964 'TV REQUESTS'
(STATESWOOD SW404 Mono)
I'm Free Again/Give the World a Smile (Blackwood Brothers)/New Born Feeling/Jesus Fills My
Every Need (Statesmen Quartet)/Keep Me/Is My Lord Satisfied with Me You/From Now On
(Rebels Quartet)/When I Come to the End of the Road/I'm Gonna See Heaven (Stamps Quartet)
Bill Shaw; James Blackwood/Cecil Blackwood/J.D. Sumner; Wally Varner

1965 'SOMETHING OLD - SOMETHING NEW'
(RCA VICTOR LSP3334 Stereo/LPM3334 Mono)
Echoes from the Burning Bush/The Home-coming Week/Heaven Will surely Be Worth It all/I
Can Tell You the Time/Time Has Made a Change/Lord, Build Me a Cabin in Glory/When I Get
to Heaven/He's Everything to Me/His Grace Reaches Me/He Took My Troubles Off My Mind/At
the Altar/Take Your Troubles to the Lord
Bill Shaw; James Blackwood; Cecil Blackwood; J.D. Sumner; Whitey Gleason

1965 'THE BLACKWOOD BROTHERS QUARTET
FEATURING CECIL BLACKWOOD'
(RCA VICTOR LSP3439 Stereo/LPM3439 Mono)
Ol' Brother Noah/Above the Clouds/Close to the Master/The Sweetest Name I Know/Promise
You'll Meet Me/From This Moment On/I'm Happy now/Wonder of °Wonders/God Is
Everywhere/Let Me Touch Him/Walk, Talk and Live/I will Never Walk Alone
Bill Shaw; James Blackwood; Cecil Blackwood; S.J. Sumner; Whitey Gleason

1965 'DO YOU THANK THE LORD EACH DAY?'
(RCA CAMDEN CAS854e Electronic Stereo/CAL 854 Mono)
O Lord, Hear My Prayer/I Will Lean on His Arm/When we Look on His Face/Paradise
Awaits/Thank God for Calvary/O rock of Ages/God Is right/Church Twice on Sunday/He Will
Deliver Us/Do You Thank the Lord Each Day?

1966 'THE GRAND OLD GOSPEL'
PORTER WAGONER AND THE BLACKWOOD BROTHERS QUARTET

(RCA VICTOR LSP3488 Stereo/LPM3488 Mono)
When I Reach That city/Hide Me, Rock of Ages/The Family Who Prays (Never Shall Part)/My Last Two Tens/If We Never Meet Again/Good Mornin' Neighbor/Trouble In the Amen Corner/There's A Higher Power/I See A Bridge/I'm Using My Bible for a Road Map/A House of Gold/Wait a Little Longer, please Jesus
Bill Shaw; James Blackwood; Cecil Blackwood; Big John Hall; Whitey Gleason

1966 'HOW BIG IS GOD?'
(RCA VICTOR LSP3521 Stereo/SLP3521 Mono)
How Big Is God/My Heart Is Reserved for the Lord/Tho' I'm Unworthy/That Happy Feeling/His Name Is wonderful/Because He Died/Somebody touched Me/Undying Love/Our Troubles will Be over/He Has Surely Borne Our Sorrow/We Are on God's Side/Ten Thousand Angels
Bill Shaw; James Blackwood; Cecil Blackwood; Big John Hall; Whitey Gleason

1966 'THE SOUND OF GOSPEL MUSIC'
(RCA VICTOR LSP3625 Stereo/LPM3625 Mono)
I Asked the Lord/Forever and Ever/No One Cared So Much/Everybody's Gonna Love Everybody/I Know My Lord Will Walk with Me/May the Good Lord Bless and Keep You/Climb Every Mountain/Wherever I Go/The Christ of Every Crisis/There Is This Need/Faith Can Work Miracles/America, the Beautiful
(RCA VICTOR LSP3625 Stereo/LPM 3625 Mono)
Bill Shaw; James Blackwood; Cecil Blackwood; Big John Hall; Dave Weston

1966 'ON THE JERICHO ROAD'
(RCA CAMDEN CAS933 Stero/CAL933 Mono)
On the Jericho Road/Some Day I'm Going Home with Jesus/You Can Know/If You Want Happiness/Lead Me Higher/A Beautiful Life/Tell Me why/I'll Walk Along With Jesus/I Gave My Heart to Jesus/My Heart Is Set on Heaven
Bill Shaw; James Blackwood; Cecil Blackwood; Big John Hall; Whitey Gleason

1967 'THE BLACKWOOD BROTHERS QUARTET
FEATURING THE VOICE OF BIG JOHN HALL'
Deep is the River/The Church Triumphant/No One Else/Fall on Us/Don't Spare Me/For God So Loved/God Is Not Dead/By the Cool Waters/Higher Hands/The Latch Is on the Inside/All Hail the Power/Medley: A Child of the King, Child of the King
Bill Shaw; James Blackwood; Cecil Blackwood; Big John Hall; Dave Weston

1967 'SINGS FOR JOY'
(RCA VICTOR LSP3851 Stero/LPM3851 Mono)
Come On and Ride This Train/Open Your Heart/He's Not A Stranger/Perfect Peace/Whosoever' Meaneth me/My Jesus. I Love Thee/In That Great Judgement Day/The Unveiled Christ/surely Goodness and Mercy/You Must Run the Race (With Patience)/Hide Me Behind Calvary's Cross/The Saviour Is Waiting
Bill Shaw; James Blackwood; Cecil Blackwood; Big john Hall; Dave Weston

1967 MORE GRAND OLE GOSPEL
PORTER WAGONER AND THE BLACKWOOD BROTHERS QUARTET
(RCA VICTOR LSP3855 Stereo/LPM 3855 Mono)
Where No One Stands Alone/Rank Strangers to Me/You're Not Home Yet/Lord, Build Me a Cabin in Glory/There'd Be No Need for a Heaven/Where the Soul Never Dies/Beautiful wings/God Walks These Hills with Me/Day of Wrath/God's Wonderful Way/I'll Fly Away/Thirty Pieces of Silver

1967 SURELY GOODNESS AND MERCY
GEORGE BEVERLY SHEA WITH
THE BLACKWOOD BROTHERS QUARTET
(RCA VICTOR SLP3864 Stereo/LPM 3864 Mono)
Surely Goodness and Mercy/Where the Roses Never Fade/Jesus Walks among Us/Heavenly Sunlight/O Day of Rest and Gladness/Tell It Again/bringing in the Sheaves/Thanks to God/Just a Wayward lamb/With Christ as My Pilot/Take My Life and Let It Be/Amazing Grace

1967 THE BEST OF THE BLACKWOOD BROTHERS QUARTET (VOL.2)
(RCA VICTOR LSP3868 Stereo/LPM 3868 Mono)
Ol' Brother Noah/Ten Thousand Angels/Aloha Time/His Grace Reaches Me/Deep is The River/I Get happy/I Feel Like Travelling On/Until Then/From This Moment On/The Holy city/Pablo/ Climb Every Mountain
Bill Shaw; James Blackwood; Cecil Blackwood; J.D. Sumner; Wally Varner; Whitey Gleason; Dave Weston

1967 WITH A SONG ON MY LIPS (AND A PRAYER IN MY HEART)
(RCA CAMDEN CAS 2115 stereo/CAL2115 Mono)
With a Song on My Lips (And a Prayer in My heart)/Without Him/God Is Alive/Heaven Came Down and Glory Filled My Soul/What a Day That Will Be/brighten the Corner Where You Are/ He Touched Me/There's No Other Way/Take the Hand of the Lord/All the Way
Bill Shaw; James Blackwood; Cecil Blackwood; Big John Hall; Dave Weston

1968 THE FABULOUS BLACKWOOD BROTHERS QUARTET
(RCA VICTOR LSP3923 Stereo/LPM 3923 Mono)
I Believe In The Old-Time Way/One More Mountain/I found Him/I'll Never be Lonely/Jesus Means All the World to Me/He the Pearly Gates Will Open/The Shepherd of the Stars/Thy Hand Shall Lead Me/He's Everything to Me/The Master's Voice/I Wouldn't Take Nothin' for My Journey/Marvellous Grace
Bill Shaw; James Blackwood; Cecil Blackwood; John Hall; Dave Weston

1968 YOURS FAITHFULLY
(RCA VICTOR LSP4029 Stereo)
Way Up in Glory Lane/The Heartbeat (From the Old Rugged Cross)/Zion's Hill/Sawdust and Folding Chairs/I Believe/This Love is Mine/What a Wonderful Change/to Be Used of God/Step by Step/One of these Days/Will There be Any Stars?/I Know It's So
Bill Shaw; James Blackwood; Cecil Blackwood; London Parris; Dave Weston

1968 IN GOSPEL COUNTRY
PORTER WAGONER AND THE BLACKWOOD BROTHERS QUARTET
(RCA VICTOR LSP4034 Stereo)
I'm going That Way/Lord, I'm Coming Home/Pastor's Absent on Vacation/Canaan's Land/Dreaming of a Little Cabin/If Jesus Came to your House/I'll meet You in church Sunday Morning/Mama's bible/The Finer Taste of Man/The wings of a Dove/Suppertime/From the Cradle to the Grave
Bill Shaw; James Blackwood; Cecil Blackwood; London Parris; Dave Weston

1968 IN THE SWEET BY AND BY
(RCA CAMDEN CAS 2194 Stereo)
In The Sweet By and By/Ivory Palaces/We've Got a Great Big Wonderful God/In the Shelter of His Arms/Camping in Canaan's Land/I'll Walk with God/Who Am I/Open Up Your Heart (Accept the Saviour Today)/Happy Day/Lead me Back to Calvary
Bill Shaw; James Blackwood; Cecil Blackwood; Big John Hall; Dave Weston

1968 ALL DAY SINGING

(SKYLITE SLP6068 Stereo)

Go Right Out/*I Love to be Alone with Jesus/I'll be Listening/I'm Winging My Way Back Home/ There's A Little Pine Lo Cabin/Won't We be Happy/When He Put a Little Sunshine In/Heaven Now Is in View/I've Never Been Sorry/Did You Ever Go Sailin'/Blessed Jesus Loves You Too/All The Day Long

Bill Shaw; James Blackwood; Cecil Blackwood; John Hall; Dave Weston; *London Parris

1969 THE HEAVENLY HARMONY OF
THE BLACKWOOD BROTHERS QUARTET

(RCA VICTOR LSP4117 Stereo)

The Broken Vessel/Happiness/On the Battlefield/Let Me Call Upon the Lord/Sweet, Sweet Spirit/ This Is Our Lane/Daddy Sang Bass/After Awhile/How Sweet It Is (To Know the Lord)/Going Away Someday/Homecoming/If I Knew There'd Be No Tomorrow

Bill Shaw; James Blackwood; Cecil Blackwood; London Parris; Peter Kaups; Dwayne Friend

1969 JAMES BLACKWOOD SINGS HIS FAVORITE GOSPEL SOLOS

(RCA VICTOR LSP4165 Stereo) (Re-issued in 1973 as You'll Never Walk Alone)

Now I Have Everything/I Met the King/As Flows the River/It's Been a Good Trip/Empty Hands/I'd be there/You'll Never Walk Alone/Follow, I will Follow Thee/Unworthy/he Looked beyond My Faults (And Saw My Need)/On My Journey Home/The Things That Matter

1969 FILL MY CUP, LORD

(RCA VICTOR LSP4216 Stereo)

Fill My Cup Lord/Something Worth Living For/I Want to Get Closer/I Came Here to Say/Now I Have Everything/That Meeting in the Sky/The Night Before Easter/There Is Power in the Blood/ Race with Time/Less of Me/God Made a Way/Victory in Jesus

Bill Shaw; James Blackwood; Cecil Blackwood; London Parris; Peter Kaups; Dwayne Friend

1969 JUST A CLOSER WALK WITH THEE

(RCA CAMDEN CAS2292 Stereo)

Just a Closer Walk with Thee/It Will Be Worth It All/It Matters to him/We Can Still See His Footprints (In the Sands of Time)/When the Saints Go Marchin' In/Get Right, Live Right, Stay Right/Do You Know Jesus?/Hear Me When I Call/the Richest Man I Know/The Rainbow of Love

Bill Shaw; James Blackwood; Cecil Blackwood; London Parris; Dave Weston

1969 O COME ALL YE FAITHFUL

(RCA CAMDEN CAS2361 Stereo)

O Come All Ye Faithful (Combined Quartets)/Silver Bells (Blackwood Brothers)/Go Tell It on the Mountain (The Statesmen)/Praises to Our King (Blackwood Brothers)/White Christmas (The Statesmen)/Christmas Means Christ to Me (Blackwood Brothers)/Joy to the World (Combined Quartets)/Christmas Time Is Here (The Statesmen)/O Little Town of Bethlehem (Blackwood Brothers)/Away in a Manger (The Statesmen)/O Holy Night (Blackwood brothers)/Silent Night! Holy Night! (The Statesmen)

Bill Shaw; James Blackwood; Cecil Blackwood; J.D. Sumner; Wally Varner

1970 GOSPEL CLASSICS

(RCA VICTOR LSP4279 Stereo)

The World the Way I Want It/He's The Lily of the Valley/Keep On the Firing Line / If We Never Meet Again/Above All/Created in His Image/Closer to Thee/He's a Good Guy Now/If I Can Help Somebody/I'm Just a Stranger Here/I've Got a Determination/Little Boy Lost

Bill Shaw; James Blackwood; Cecil Blackwood; London Parris; Peter Kaups; Dwayne Friend; Larry Davis

1970 MY GOD AND I
(RCA VICTOR LSP4403 Stereo)
My God and I/Little boy from the Carpenter Shop/I Walk in the New Jerusalem Way/When He Reached Down His Hand For Me/If It Keeps Getting Better and Better/Try a Little Kindness/Oh How I Love Him/I Believe He'd Go (to Calvary for Me)/Talk About the Good Times/If That Isn't Love
Bill Shaw; James Blackwood; Jimmy Blackwood; Cecil Blackwood; London Parris; Peter Kaups; Dwayne Friend; Larry Davis; Billy Blackwood

1970 OH HAPPY DAY
(RCA CAMDEN CAS2376 Stereo)
Oh Happy Day/Work for Peace/it's Been a Good Trip/Jesus Is Coming Soon/Have You Told Anyone About Jesus/?In Twain He Rent the Vail/I've Been Born Again/I'll Meet You in the Morning/Since Jesus Passed By/A Better Tomorrow
Bill Shaw; James Blackwood; Cecil Blackwood; London Parris; Peter Kaups; Dwayne Friend

1970 SKYLITE PRESENTS THE BEST OF THE BLACKWOOD BROTHERS
(SKYLITE SLP6092 Stereo)
How Long Has It Been?/Give The World A Smile/What a Savior/Blessed Jesus Loves You Too/Peace in the Valley/it is No Secret/He'll understand and Say, 'Well Done'/Looking for a City/Where No One Stands Alone/Every Day Will be Sunday/More About Jesus/Glad Reunion Day
Bill Shaw; James Blackwood; Cecil Blackwood; J.D. Sumner/Wally Varner; John Hall; Dave Weston

1971 THE BLACKWOOD BROTHERS QUARTET FEATURING LONDON PARRIS
(RCA VICTOR LSP4484)
Daddy Was an Old-Time Preacher man/If God Is Dead (Who's That Living in my soul)/Rise and Shine/Jesus Loves me/Some Day soon/the King is Coming/I Know/ICannot find the Way Alone/You Sho Do Need Him Now/Joybells
Bill Shaw; Cecil Blackwood; London Parris; Peter Kaups; Larry Davis; Billy Blackwood

1971 HE'S STILL THE KING OF KINGS AND LORD OF LORDS
(RCA VICTOR LSP4589)
He's Still the King of Kings (And Lord of Lords)/the Next Thing I See/Jesus. Hold My Hand/I find No Fault In Him/Won't We Be Happy Up There/I'll have a New Life/The Eastern Gate/I've Got Confidence/Standing at the Crossroads/I Can Feel the Touch of His Hand
Bill Shaw; James Blackwood; Jimmy Blackwood; Cecil Blackwood; London Parris; Peter Kaups; Larry Davis; Billy Blackwood

1971 SHELTERED IN THE ARMS OF GOD
(RCA CAMDEN CAS2446)
Sheltered in the Arms of God/Precious Memories/The Old Rugged Cross Made the Difference/Way Down Deep in My Soul/My Name is Jesus/Thank god I'm Free/I Have a Friend/God Is Just a Prayer Away/sing Your Blues Away
Bill Shaw; James Blackwood; Jimmy Blackwood; Cecil Blackwood; London Parris; Peter Kaups; J. D. Sumner; Wally Varner

1971 AMAZING GRACE
(RCA CAMDEN CAS2504)
Amazing Grace/Put Your Hand In the Hand/Thy Hand Shall Lead Me/What a Friend/Whispering Hope/Bridge Over Troubled Waters/I Cannot Hide from God/The Voice of the Lord/I believe in the Old-Time Way/Sweet Peace
Bill Shaw; James Blackwood; Cecil Blackwood; London Parris; Peter Kaups; Larry Davis; Billy Blackwood; J.D. Sumner; Jack Marshall; Wally Varner

1972 L-O-V-E
(RCA VICTOR LSP4679)
L-O-V-E (Everything Living Needs Love)/I Should Have Been Crucified/I Just Love My Jesus/
Through It All/The Man of Galilee/Song for the Man/Because He Lives/Talk About Jesus/Praise
God Anyhow/I'd Rather Be an Old-Time Christian
Bill Shaw; James Blackwood; Jimmy Blackwood; Tony Brown; Larry Davis; Billy Blackwood

1972 THIS COULD BE THE DAWNING
(RCA VICTOR LSP4764)
Heaven/(Take Away My Worldly Gain, But)Give Me Jesus/Jesus Will Outshine Them All/The
Lighthouse/Redemption Draweth Nigh/This could Be the Dawning of That Day/Satisfied
Feeling/Who Can We Turn To? (If We Can't Turn to God)/he Hideth My Soul/I Want to Walk
Just as Close as I Can
Bill Shaw; James Blackwood; Jimmy Blackwood; Cecil Blackwood; Ken Turner; Tommy
Fairchild; Larry Davis; Billy Blackwood

1972 MIGHTY CLOUDS OF JOY
Mighty Clouds of Joy/I'll Fly Away/That Resurrection Morn/Walk with the Lord/What the
World Needs Now Is Love/What a Glorious Morning That Will Be/Sunrise/Above the Clouds/
Open Your Heart/I've Got To Walk That Lonesome Road
Bill Shaw; James Blackwood; Jimmy Blackwood; Cecil Blackwood; London Parris; Tony Brown;
Larry Davis; Billy Blackwood; J. D. Sumner; Wally Varner; Whitey Gleason; John Hall; Dave
Weston

1972 ROLL ON JORDAN
(SKYLITE SLP6118)
Roll on Jordan/the Joy of Heaven/He's a Saviour to be Proud Of/I Need the Prayers/Land Where
Living Waters Flow/If You've Never learned to Pray/Living with Jesus/I'm Glad My Saviour Was
Willing/Shelter from the Storms/I've Had a Talk with Jesus
Bill Shaw; James Blackwood; Jimmy Blackwood; Cecil Blackwood; Ken Turner; Tommy
Fairchild; Larry Davis; Billy Blackwood

1972 RELEASE ME (FROM MY SIN)
(SKYLITESLP6124)
Release Me (From My Sin)/Said I Wasn't Gonna Tell Nobody/I Knew Jesus (Before he Was a
Superstar)/For Me/At the Crossing/God Showed His Love to Me/Leaning on the Arms of Jesus/
Blessed Jesus/I Like What's Happened to Me/Something Took Hold of Me
Bill Shaw; James Blackwood; Jimmy Blackwood; Cecil Blackwood; Ken Turner; Tommy
Fairchild; Larry Davis; Billy Blackwood

1972 MEMORIAL ALBUM
(MEMORIAL RECORDS VOL.1 BB-1001)(Mono Radio Recordings)
It Took A Miracle/The Robe/I Want to be More Like Jesus/There Must be A God
Somewhere/What Could I Do/My Desire/Working on the Building/You Sho Do Need
Him Now/Roll On Jordan/Lead Me to That Rock
Bill Shaw; James Blackwood; R.W. Blackwood; Bill Lyles; Jack Marshall; Alden Toney; Hilton
Griswold

1973 HOW GREAT THOU ART
(RCA CAMDEN CAS2601)
How Great Thou Art/Way Up in Glory Lane/how Big Is God/Undying Love/I'm Bound for That
City/Until Then/Somebody Touched Me/What a Wonderful Change/Echoes from the Burning
Bush/The Way of the Cross
Bill Shaw; James Blackwood; Cecil Blackwood; J.D. Sumner; Wally Varner; Jack Marshall; John
Hall; Whitey Gleason; London Parris; Dave Weston;

1973 ON STAGE
(SKYLITE SLP6131)
I'll Soon be Gone/Will You Be Among the Missing?/It's Worth It All/Peace in the Valley/When the Saints Go Marching In/Heaven/How Great Thou Art/I'll Meet You In the Morning/Give the World a Smile/Old Country Church
Bill Shaw; James Blackwood; Jimmy Blackwood; Cecil Blackwood; Ken Turner; Tommy Fairchild; Larry Davis; Billy Blackwood

1973 IT'S WORTH IT ALL
(BLACKWOOD BROTHERS DRP)
I'll Soon Be Gone/After Calvary/Just a Rose Will Do/When the Roll Is Called Up Yonder/Will You Be among the Missing?/It's Worth It All/At Calvary/Till the Storm Passes By/Lovest Thou Me/The Church's Finest Hour
Bill Shaw; James Blackwood; Jimmy Blackwood; Cecil Blackwood; Ken Turner; Tommy Fairchild; Larry Davis; Billy Blackwood

1973 HALLELUJAH TO THE KING
(BLACKWOOD BROTHERS DRP7223)
Hallelujah to the King/He's More Than just A Swear Word/What A Happy Day/While Ages Roll/That Day Is Almost Here/When We All Get to Heaven/His Grace Is Sufficient for Me/I'm as Poor as a Beggar/I've Been to Calvary/I'm gonna Make It
Bill Shaw; James Blackwood; Jimmy Blackwood; Cecil Blackwood; Ken Turner; Tommy Fairchild; Larry Davis; Billy Blackwood

1973 THE BLACKWOOD BROTHERS FEATURING CECIL BLACKWOOD
(BLACKWOOD BROTHERS DRP7348)
The Way That He Loves/Wasted Years/I'd Rather Have Jesus/Those Tender Hands/Shady Green Pastures/Born to Serve the Lord/now I Know Why/He Washed My Eyes With Tears/The Love of God/The Family of God
Bill Shaw; James Blackwood; Jimmy Blackwood; Cecil Blackwood; Ken Turner; Tommy Fairchild; Larry Davis; Billy Blackwood

1973 TURN YOUR RADIO ON
(ARTCO LPG106)
He Set Me Free/i Just Stead Away and Pray/I Couldn't begin To Tell You how Beautiful Heaven Is/Turn Your Radio On/The Prettiest Flowers Will Be Blooming/I'll Meet You by the River/It's Really Surprising (What the Lord Can Do)/Her Mansion Is Higher Than Mine/We'll Meet a Lot of Friends and Neighbours/When We Sing Around the Throne Eternal/Never Say Good-bye/When I Look Up and He Looked Down
Bill Shaw; James Blackwood; Jimmy Blackwood; Cecil Blackwood; Ken Turner; Tommy Fairchild; Larry Davis; Billy Blackwood

1973 MEMORIAL ALBUM
(MEMORIAL RECORDS VOL.II BB1002)(Mono Radio Recordings)
He'll understand and Say, 'Well Done'/Somebody Knows/Go Right Out and Keep Singing/I believe/Swing Down Chariot/Bend A-Way Down Low/What A Friend/I Know the Lord/I Can Tell You the Time/I Love to Be Alone with Jesus
Bill /Shaw; James Blackwood; R.W. Blackwood; Bill Lyles; Jack Marshall; Cat Freeman; Hilton Griswold

1973 MY SWEET SAVIOR'S LOVE
(ARTCO LPG949)
Walking in the Sunshine of My Sweet Savior's Love/I Cannot Fail the Lord/Reunion in Heaven/I'm Nearer Home (Than I Was yesterday)/The Walls Came Tumbling Down (Joshua)/He Fills a Longing/At The End of My World/In the Upper Room/so Many Reasons/he Cares for You/I'm Too Near Home/In This Little House By the Side of the Road
Bill Shaw; James Blackwood; Jimmy Blackwood; Cecil Blackwood; Ken Turner; Tommy Fairchild; Larry Davis Billy Blackwood

1973 BEST OF THE BEST OF
(ARTCO DRP7224)
I Won't Have to Worry Anymore/Get Acquainted with the Lord/Ten Thousand Years/Beyond the Gates/I Know Who Holds Tomorrow/Where the Roses Never Fade/Palms of Victory/He Will Pilot Me/I'm Living in Canaan Now/I've Been Changed/Hand in Hand with Jesus/Jesus Use Me
Bill Shaw; James Blackwood; Jimmy Blackwood; Cecil Blackwood; Ken Turner; Tommy Fairchild; Larry Davis; Billy Blackwood

1973 A FATHER'S PRAYER
(SKYLITE SLP6134)
A Father's Prayer/Travelling On and On/It Was I/My Heart is Filled with Jesus's Love/Keep Holding On/Touring That City/One Day Too Late/He Is My Everything/I Am The Reason/I Never Shall Forget the Day
Pat Hoffmaster; James Blackwood; Jimmy Blackwood; Cecil Blackwood; Ken Turner; Tommy Fairchild; Larry Davis; Billy Blackwood

1973 THE BLACKWOOD BROTHERS FEATURING CECIL BLACKWOOD
(SKYLITE SLP6137)
The Way That he Loves/Wasted years/I'd Rather have Jesus/Those Tender Hands/Shady Green Pastures/Born To Serve the Lord/Now I Know Why/He Washed My Eyes with Tears/The Love of God/The Family of God
Bill Shaw; James Blackwood; Jimmy Blackwood; Cecil Blackwood; Ken Turner; Tommy Fairchild; Larry Davis; Billy Blackwood

1973 HALLELUJAH TO THE KING
(SKYLITE SLP6138)
Hallelujah to the King/He's More Than Just a Swear Word/What a Happy Day/While Ages Roll/That Day Is Almost Here/When We All Get to Heaven/his Grace Is Sufficient For Me/I'm as Poor as a Beggar/I've Been to Calvary/I'm Gonna Make It
Bill Shaw; James Blackwood; Jimmy Blackwood; Cecil Blackwood; Ken Turner; Tommy Fairchild; Larry Davis; Billy Blackwood

1973 IT'S WORTH IT ALL
(SKYLITE SLP6139)
I'll Soon be gone/After Calvary/Just a Rose Will Do/When the Roll Is Called Up Yonder/Will You Be Among the Missing/It's Worth It All/At Calvary/Till The Storm Passes By/Lovest Thou Me/The Church's Finest Hour
Bill Shaw; James Blackwood; Jimmy Blackwood; Cecil Blackwood; Ken Turner; Tommy Fairchild; Larry Davis; Billy Blackwood

1974 KEN TURNER SINGS HIGH AND LOW
(CAM 1420)
Long Haired Hippie Preacher/Green Grass of Home/I'm On My Way/It Is No Secret/Praises To Our King/If You Need A Friend/Why Me/Thanks To Calvary/Which Road Do you Take?/Repay For Calvary/Canaan Land

1974 LET'S MAKE A JOYFUL NOISE
(RCA CAMDEN CXS0573)(re-issue of RCA VICTOR LSP272)
I'm Free Again/I'll be Alright Someday/I Found The Way/The Love of God (Stamps Quartet)/Jesus is The Reason/When I come to the End of the Road (Oak Ridge Quartet)/I'm Saved and I Know That I Am/Trying to Get a Glimpse (Of My Lord) (Statesmen)/This Is a Mean World/I'm Looking for Jesus (Kingsmen)/When I Think of Calvary/Let's Make a Joyful Noise (Speer Family)/Amazing Grace (Quartets and Audience)
Bill Shaw; James Blackwood; Cecil Blackwood; J.D. Sumner/Wally Varner

1974 THERE HE GOES
(SKYLITE SLP6142)
There He Goes/brother I'll Not Be Far Behind/The Road to Emmaeus/Gettin' Ready to Leave/
One Day Closer/One Day at a Time/(Jesus will be What Makes It) Heaven for Me/Go Down/
He's Still Living/Jesus Held On to My Hand

1974 FAMILY SINGING TIME
(POWER PAK PG1713) (Re-issue of SKYLITE SSLP6026)
I Can Tell You the Time/Do you Know Him?/I Need the Prayers/Well Done My Child/I've Had
a Talk with Jesus/Echoes of the Past/This Little Light of Mine/The Devil's Gonna Get You/I'll Be
Ready/Nobody/At the Altar/If I Follow
Bill Shaw; James Blackwood; Cecil Blackwood; J.D. Sumner; Wally Varner

1975 GOSPEL WITH A TOUCH OF COUNTRY
(Skylite SLP6156)
Brother Galloway/Just A Closer Walk With Thee/I'll Fly Away/I Was Lonely Without Jesus/I Am
A Pilgrim/I Saw The Light/Where No One Stands alone/The Gospel Ship/His Name is Jesus/
Someone Who Loves Me

1975 WHAT A BEAUTIFUL DAY FOR THE LORD TO COME
(SKYLITE SLP6147)
What A Beautiful Day (For the Lord to Come Again)/More to Go to Heaven For/The Most He
Had to Offer Me/Lord I'm Not Ashamed (of Loving You So Much)/I'd Rather See a Smile/
Stepping on the Clouds/Life is so Fragile/My Burdens Rolled Away/Tears Will Never Stain (The
Streets of That city)/The First Look
Pat Hoffmaster; James Blackwood; Jimmy Blackwood; Cecil Blackwood; Ken Turner; Tommy
Fairchild

1975 BEAUTIFUL ISLE OF SOMEWHERE
(CAMDEN CXSO831) (re-issue of RCA VICTOR LSP2248)
Eternal Paradise/On That Happy Golden Shore/I'll be True/I Want To Meet You Up in Heaven/I
Found God/Heaven For Me/Aloha Time/A Land Where Milk and Honey Flows/Jesus Fills My
Every Need/Paradise Valley/What a Glorious Morning That Will Be/Beautiful Isle of Somewhere
Bill Shaw; James Blackwood; Cecil Blackwood/J. D. Sumner; Wally Varner

1975 KEEP ON SINGING FEATURING JAMES BLACKWOOD
(SKYLITE SLP6152)
Keep On Singing/Hallelujah Square/Come On Down/Happy Side of Living/Statue of Liberty/
Nearing The Shore/To Remember Calvary/Over The Next Hill/I Never Knew/The Last Song
Pat Hoffmaster; James Blackwood; Jimmy Blackwood; Cecil Blackwood; Ken Turner; Tommy
Fairchild

1975 HALLELUJAH MEETIN'
(SKYLITE SLP 6155)
Hallelujah Meetin'/Leave a Well in the Valley/He Has The Answer/Restore My Soul/He's All I
Ever Need/I'm Never Going Back Again/The Joy of Knowing Jesus/I'll See you in the Rapture/
Lord, I'm Unworthy/I Found Jesus Today
Pat Hoffmaster; James Blackwood; Jimmy Blackwood; Cecil Blackwood; Ken Turner;Tommy
Fairchild

1975 HYMNS OF GOLD
(SKYLITE SLP6158)
Without the Blood/he Hideth My Soul/Lead Me Gently Home, Father/His Eye Is on the
Sparrow/It Is Well with My Soul/An Evening Prayer/Lead Me to Calvary/Blessed Assurance/My
Heavenly Father Watches Over me/How Great Thou Art
Pat Hoffmaster; James Blackwood; Jimmy Blackwood; Cecil Blackwood; Ken Turner; Tommy
Fairchild

1975 CHILDRENS' ALBUM
(Skylite SLP6188)
The Preacher and The Bear/Laughin' Song/Let The Church Roll On/Sounds All Around/Danny Boy - Instrumental/Dogs In Harmony/This Old House/Sounds All Around/Rollin' and Kicking in The Noon Day Sun/Make The Guitar Talk

1976 LEARNING TO LEAN
(SKYLITE SLP6161)
Learning to Lean/That's Worth Everything/Brush Arbor Meeting/By Faith/Take Me As I Am/Just a Little Talk with Jesus/I'll Glory in the Cross/The Stranger/When he Reached Down His Hand for Me/Hold on Till Jesus Comes
Pat Hoffmaster; James Blackwood; Jimmy Blackwood; Cecil Blackwood; Ken Turner; Tommy Fairchild

1976 LORD WE PRAISE YOU
(SKYLITE SLP6166)
There's a Whole Lot of People/Jesus, I Love You/Praise the Lord Everyday/Brotherly Love/Praise the Lord/Lord, We Praise You/You Must Decide/rise and be Healed/Jesus Is Lord to me/The Greatest of all Miracles
Pat Hoffmaster; James Blackwood; Jimmy Blackwood; Cecil Blackwood; Ken Turner; Tommy Fairchild

1977 SPOTLIGHTING JAMES BLACKWOOD LIVE! FROM NASHVILL'E
(SKYLITE SLP6173)
I Want To be More Like Jesus/His Grace Reaches Me/He's Still the King of Kings/Release Me (From my Sins)/I'll Meet You in the Morning/The Night Before Easter/He Is my Everything/I Can Feel the touch of His Hand/The King Is Coming/theEastern Gate
Pat Hoffmaster; James Blackwood; Jimmy Blackwood; Cecil Blackwood; Ken Turner; Tommy Fairchild

1977 BILL GAITHER SONGS
(SKYLITE SLP6175)
Jesus Is Lord of All/because He Lives/Jesus, We Just Want To Thank You/The Family of God/He Touched Me/Something Beautiful/It is Finished/We Have This Moment Today/songs That Answer Questions/Leet's Just Praise the Lord
Pat Hoffmaster; James Blackwood; Jimmy Blackwood; Cecil Blackwood; Ken Turner; Tommy Fairchild

1977 JESUS LET ME WRITE YOU A SONG
(SKYLITE SLP6182)
Jesus, Let me Write You a Song/All in the Name of Jesus/Who Am I/Jesus, Be Lord of All/The Anchor/He Was There All the time/Lost/Remember Me, Oh Lord/More Than My Share/The First Step
Pat Hoffmaster; James Blackwood; Jimmy Blackwood; Cecil Blackwood; Ken Turner; Tommy Fairchild

1977 SIXTEEN ALL-TIME FAVOURITES
(STARDAY SD3009)
Old Time Religion/I Want to be More Like Jesus/now I Have Everything/This Little Light of Mine/I Can Tell You the time/Just a Closer Walk with Thee/O, What a Saviour/When the Saints Go Marching In/Fill My Cup/Good-bye, World, Good-bye/I've Had a Talk with Jesus/Over in the Gloryland/Well Done My Child/Mansion Over the Hilltop/I'm Feeling Fine/the Devil's Gonna Get You

1978 HIS AMAZING LOVE
(SKYLITE SLP6187)
His Amazing Love/It Wouldn't Be Enough/Soon and Very Soon/the Loaves and The Fishes/Jesus Is Precious/What the World Needs Is Jesus/One day at a Time/Jesus Is Coming Soon/He Is as Close/ Come Unto Jesus
Pat Hoffmaster; James Blackwood; Jimmy Blackwood; Cecil Blackwood; Ken Turner; Tommy Fairchild

1978 LIFT UP THE NAME OF JESUS
(SKYLITE SLP6197)
Lift Up The Name of Jesus/He Is the Lily of the Valley/I Found It all in Jesus/It Is No Secret/Home Beyond the Blue/Holy Spirit, Thou Art Welcome/Standing on the Solid Rock/Amazing Grace/I Saw Jesus When He Died/Love Grew Where the Blood Fell
Pat Hoffmaster; James Blackwood; Jimmy Blackwood; Cecil Blackwood; Ken Turner; Tommy Fairchild

1979 KEN TURNER'S FAVOURITE HYMNS
(Voice Box VB0897)
If I Could Hear My Mother Pray Again/The Old Rugged Cross/Where You There?/Heaven Will Surely Be Worth It All/Do Not Pass me By/Whispering Hope/Softly and Tenderly/Farther Along/ He'll Understand and Say Well Done/Lord, I'm Coming Home/When They Ring Those Golden bells/In The Garden

1979 PAT HOFFMASTER - TAKE ANOTHER LOOK
(Voice Box VB0379)
Jesus Is My Best Friend/I Got Victory In Jesus/Blessed Assurance/I Am Lord/Take Another Look/I Never Gave Up/Restore My Soul/You Loved Me/He Was There All The Time

1979 LIVE! IN MUSIC CITY USA
FEATURING THE LEGENDARY JAMES BLACKWOOD'
(SKYLITE SLP6204)
My Song/This Is the Time I Must Sing/Come Listen to My Story/Inside the Gate/Tell My Friends/ Down From His Glory/It Is Finished/The Holy City/I Walked Today Where Jesus Walked/There he Goes
Pat Hoffmaster; James Blackwood; Jimmy Blackwood; Cecil Blackwood; Ken Turner; Tommy Fairchild

1979 HYMNS BY THE BLACKWOOD BROTHERS
(SKYLITE SLP6207)
I Must Tell Jesus/Close to Thee/O, How I Love Jesus/My Jesus I Love Thee/Near the Cross/God Will Take Care Of You/More About Jesus/'Tis So Sweet/I Gave My Life for Thee/Nearer By God To Thee
Pat Hoffmaster; James Blackwood; Jimmy Blackwood; Cecil Blackwood; Ken Turner; Tommy Fairchild

1979 LIVE! AT THE NATIONAL QUARTET CONVENTION
(SKYLITE SLP6212)
Soon and Very Soon/The Light House/He Was There all the Time/Because He Lives/Jesus Is Coming Soon/Rise Again/Restore My Soul/His Grace Reaches Me/How Great Thou Art/learning to Lean
John Cox; James Blackwood; Jimmy Blackwood; Cecil Blackwood; Ken Turner; Tommy Fairchild

1979 MERRY CHRISTMAS FROM THE BLACKWOOD BROTHERS
(VOICE BOX VB0779)
White Christmas/The First Noel/O Holy Night/Chestnuts Roasting/Silent Night! Holy Night!/It Came Upon a Midnight Clear/Joy to the World/Hark! The Herald Angels Sing/O Come All Ye Faithful/Away in a Manger
John Cox/James Blackwood/Jimmy Blackwood/Cecil Blackwood/Ken Turner/Tommy Fairchild

1980 ON THE JERICHO ROAD
(SKYLITE SLP6229)
On The Jericho Road/Come Quickly, Lord Jesus/Because of Calvary/There's a Brand New Anointing/I found My World/He Rose Again/You Could Have Stopped, Lord/Something Happened To Me/The Marriage Supper/God Is My Friend
John Cox; James Blackwood; Jimmy Blackwood; Cecil Blackwood; Ken Turner; Tommy Fairchild

1980 HYMNS OF THE CHURCH
(SKYLITE SLP6232)
Alleluia/I Surrender All/Near To the heart of God/Just a Closer Walk/Revive Us Again/Just a Closer Walk/Revive Us Again/Sweet Hour of Prayer/Cleanse Me/abide with Me/Higher Ground/I Am Thine, O Lord
John Cox; James Blackwood; Jimmy Blackwood; Cecil Blackwood; Ken Turner; Tommy Fairchild; Larry Davis; Rick Price;

1980 UNTIL THEN
(SKYLITE SLP6237)
Until Then/Jesus Now/Patriotic Medley: Why Not Give Jesus Your Life, I'm Happy/ I'll Fly Away/Jesus Is right/He's coming Soon/Lord, I Need your Love/When Morning Comes
John Cox; James Blackwood; Jimmy Blackwood; Cecil Blackwood; Ken Turner; Tommy Fairchild

1980 WE COME TO WORSHIP
(VOICE BOX VB1080)
We Come to Worship/God Is Alive/Closer to Jesus/Shine Through Me/It's My Desire/Lord, I Need You Now/all the Way Home/I Never Gave Up/It's a Joy/Take Away the Stone
John Cox; James Blackwood; Jimmy Blackwood; Cecil Blackwood; Ken Turner; Tommy Fairchild

1981 HITS OF THE CENTURY
(SKYLITE SLP 6250)
Lead me to That Rock/His Hands/I'm Bound for That City/I bowed on My Knees and Cried Holy/He's all that I Need/I Wanna Rest/He Bought My Soul at Calvary/Peace Like a River/Then I Met the Master/The Old Country Church
Pat Hoffmaster; James Blackwood; Cecil Blackwood; Ken Turner; Tommy Fairchild

1981 THE JOY OF KNOWING JESUS
1982 (SKYLITE SLP6259)
Redemption Draweth Nigh/Rise Again/It's Real/the Joy of Knowing Jesus/Restores My Soul/We Shall Wear a Crown/He Touched Me/Ship Ahoy/Jesus, I Love You/Because You believed in Me
Pat Hoffmaster; James Blackwood; Jimmy Blackwood; Cecil Blackwood; Ken Turner; Tommy Fairchild

1982 KEN TURNER/DONNA DOUGLAS - HERE COME CRITTERS
(Skylite SLP6286)
Joshua Fit De Battle/Noah's Ark/Go Jonah/Swing Low Sweet Chariot/David And Goliath/ Animals Visit The Christ Child

1982 THROUGH THE YEARS...LIVE!
(SKYLITE SLP6261)
Give the World a Smile/Holy Spirit, Thou Art Welcome/He Rose Again/It is Finished/There He Goes/Because he Lives/Lord, I'm Not Ashamed of Loving You/Until Then/When Morning Comes/More About Jesus
Pat Hoffmaster; James Blackwood; Jimmy Blackwood; Cecil Blackwood; Ken Turner; Tommy Fairchild

1982 JOY COMES IN THE MORNING
(SKYLITE SLP6267)
Joy comes in the Morning/I Will Serve Thee/He's Still Working on Me/Someone to Care/Peace in the Valley/Praise the Lord/The Blood Will Never Lose Its Power/I Want to be More Like Jesus/ The Touch of His Hand/It Is Well with My Soul
Pat Hoffmaster; James Blackwood; Jimmy Blackwood; Cecil Blackwood; Ken Turner; Tommy Fairchild

1982 RISE 'N BE HEALED
(SKYLITE SLP6278)
Rise 'N Be Healed/How He Loves You and Me/There's a Whole Lot of People/More Than You'll Ever Know/Brotherly Love/There's Life in Jesus Name/Jesus, Let Me Write You a Song/More than My Share/Our Lord's Return/What Sins Are You Talking About?
Pat Hoffmaster; James Blackwood; Jimmy Blackwood; Cecil Blackwood; Ken Turner; Tommy Fairchild

1982 HOW GREAT THOU ART
(SKYLITE SLP6283)
How Great Thou Art/The Greatest Miracle/You could Have Stopped Lord/It Took a Miracle/Lead Me Gently Home/Jesus I Love You/On the Jericho Road/I Found My World/Praise the Lord Everyday/Praise the Lord
Pat Hoffmaster/James Blackwood/Jimmy Blackwood/Cecil Blackwood/Ken Turner/Tommy Fairchild

1982 FOLLOWING YOU
(VOICE BOX VG4001)
I'm Following You/My Tribute/Gentle Rain/Let Jesus happen To You/Easter Song/Reach for the Faith/Little Boy From the Carpenters Shop/Sweet, Sweet, Smile/Lord I Believe/Bless You Lord
Pat Hoffmaster; James Blackwood; Jimmy Blackwood; Cecil Blackwood; Ken Turner; Tommy Fairchild

1983 LEARNING TO LEAN
(SKYLITE SLP6293)
Learning to Lean/By Faith/Brush Arbor Meeting/The First Step/Blessed Assurance/He Was There All The Time/Who Am I/Until Then/Come Quickly, Lord Jesus/He Hideth My Soul
Pat Hoffmaster; James Blackwood; Jimmy Blackwood; Cecil Blackwood; Ken Turner; Tommy Fairchild

1983 BECAUSE HE LIVES
(SKYLITE SLP6300)
Because He Lives/Let's Just Praise the Lord/God will Take Care of You/When Morning Comes/O, How I Love Jesus/Something Beautiful/I Must Tell Jesus/More About Jesus/Because of Calvary/Something Happened to Me
Pat Hoffmaster; James Blackwood; Jimmy Blackwood; Cecil Blackwood; Ken Turner; Tommy Fairchild

1983 THE FAMILY OF GOD
(SKYLITE SLP6310)
The Family of God/God Will Take Care of You/Jesus Is Lord of All/'Tis So Sweet/We Have This Moment/Jesus, We Just Want to Thank You/Nearer My God to Thee/He Rose Again/My Jesus I Love You/Come Quickly, Lord Jesus
Pat Hoffmaster; James Blackwood; Cecil Blackwood; Ken Turner/Tommy Fairchild

1983 PERFECT HEART
(MUSIC BOX MBR3803)
Searching/Perfect Heart/I'm So Glad (With Jeanne Johnson)/The Galilean/Surely the
Presence/We Shall Beyond Him/I Believe in a Hill Called Mount Calvary/The Man Upstairs/Oh
How Sweet/The Same Old Fashioned Way (With Jeanne Johnson/Beaulah Land/Yesterday
Pat Hoffmaster; James Blackwood; Cecil Blackwood; Ken Turner; Tommy Fairchild;

1983 SECOND TO NONE
(VOICE BOX VB4012)
If You Only Knew/God's Patient Grace/New and Improved/Come Unto Me/Right Again/It
Never Even Crossed My Heart (with Andrea Blackwood)/He Could Never/Blessed be the Name/
Daddy's Girl/Second to None
Robert Crawford; James Blackwood; Cecil Blackwood; Ken Turner; Jeff Stice

1984 RELEASE ME (FROM MY SIN)
(SKYLITE SLP6322)
He Was There All the Time/Release me (From my Sin)/Cleanse Me/Leaning on the Arms of
Jesus/One Day Closer/Go Down/Sweet Hour of Prayer/Brother, I'll Not Be Far Behind/God
Showed His Love to Me/The Anchor
Pat Hoffmaster; James Blackwood; Jimmy Blackwood; Cecil Blackwood; Ken Turner; Tommy
Fairchild

1984 HE TOUCHED ME
(SKYLITE SLP6332)
He Touched Me/I'll Soon Be Gone/Just a Rose Will Do/Will You Be Among the Missing/Gettin'
Ready to Leave/Heaven for Me/It's Worth It All/'Til the Storm Passes By/Jesus Hold on to My
Hand/At Calvary
Pat Hoffmaster; Jimmy Blackwood; Cecil Blackwood; Ken Turner; Tommy Fairchild

1984 THE FINAL CURTAIN
(Live Concert in Gulfport, Mississippi, 1954, by Original Blackwood Bros. Quartet)
(BLACKWOOD COLLECTORS SERIES VOL.1)
Hide Me Rock of Ages/The Robe/How About Your Heart/I'm Feeling Fine/I Want to be
More Like Jesus/Asleep in the Deep/How About You/Gloryland Jubilee/Keys to the
Kingdom/Over the Moon

1984 GOSPEL 1
(OUT OF TOWN OTD 8627)
I Wanna Rest/he's All That I Need/Lead Me to That Rock/The Old Country Church/He Is the
Lily of the Valley/Rise and be Healed/Jesus Is Lord of All/It Is No Secret/I Saw Jesus When He
Died/Love Grew Where the Blood Fell
Pat Hoffmaster; Jimmy Blackwood; Cecil Blackwood; Ken Turner; Jeff Stice

1984 LITTLE CRITTERS IN CONCERT
(Skylite SLP6314)
Jesus Loves The Little Children/Train And The Bus/Critters Joke Telling Lesson/alligator Boots/
Cross Eyed Rat/Lighthouse Beam/Helicopter and Airplane Fight/Everything Is Beautiful/Raining
Cats and Dogs/Allelujah

1984 TURNER FAMILY - MORE THAN EVER
(Skylite SLP6330)
Now More Than Ever/Your Love/No Other Word For Grace/Look For Me/I'm The Lamb/
Seeking/Standing On Holy Ground/No other Name/Amazing Grace/Forever In Your Arms

1985 BLACKWOODS/STATESMEN
(RCA CAMDEN CAK2361)
O, Come All Ye Faithful/Silver Bells/Go Tell It On The Mountain/Praises To The Coming King/
White Christmas/Christmas Means Christ To Me/Joy to The World/Christmas Time is Here/O,
Little Town Of Bethlehem/Away In A Manger/O, Holy Night/Silent Night

1985 ONE DAY CLOSER
(OUT OF TOWN OTD8652)
Jesus, I Love You/Praise the Lord Everyday/The Greatest of All Miracles/Holy Spirit, Thou Art
Welcome in This Place/Standing on The Solid Rock/Our Lord's Return/O, How He Loves You
and Me/there's Life in Jesus' Name/He Looked Beyond My Faults
Pat Hoffmaster; Jimmy Blackwood; Cecil Blackwood; Ken Turner; Jeff Stice

1985 JAMES BLACKWOOD - 50 GOLDEN YEARS
(Skylite SSC6337)
Don't Be Knocking/Six Feet of Earth/I Can Hear The Harbor Bells/Heaven's Harmony/Roy's
Prayer/I've Never Been Sorry/When We Sing Around The Throne Eternal/His Hand In Mine/
Majesty/Sheltered In The Arms Of God/One Day/Oh, What A Moment/Heaven's Sounding
Sweeter

1985 ONE DAY AT A TIME
(SKYLITE SLP6338)
One Day At a Time/When He Reached Down His Hand For Me/'Til The Storm Passes By/Jesus
Is Lord to Me/I'll glory in the Cross/Just a Little Talk With Jesus/Jesus Will Be What Makes It
Heaven for Me/It's Worth It All/Lovest Thou Me?/You Must Decide
Pat Hoffmaster; Jimmy Blackwood; Cecil Blackwood; Ken Turner; Tommy Fairchild

1985 OLD TIME SINGING
(SKYLITE SLP6344)
The Joy of Knowing Jesus/Then I Met the Master/Leave a Well in the Valley/Lord, I'm
Unworthy/I Wanna Rest/Old Country Church/Lead Me to That Rock/I Bowed on My
Knees and Cried 'Holy'/I Want to Be More Like Jesus/Restore My Soul
Pat Hoffmaster; Jimmy Blackwood; Cecil Blackwood; Ken Turner; Tommy Fairchild

1985 SAFE IN THE ARMS OF JESUS
(SKYLITE SLP6350)
Safe in the Arms of Jesus/First Day in Heaven/O For A Thousand Tongues/I Never
Gave Up/I'm Feeling Fine/His Name Is Jesus/Turn your Radio On/Beaulah Land/Good Bye,
World, Good Bye/Fill My Cup, Lord
R.W. Blackwood; Jimmy Blackwood; Cecil Blackwood; Ken Turner; Jeff Stice

1985 THAT BRIGHTER DAY
(VOICE BOX VB4014) (re-released on Riversong ZLP8509 1985)
That Brighter Day/Lift Me Again/God Bless the USA/My Quiet Time/Vessel of Love/Only a
Matter of Mercy/Blessed Be the Name/Lord, I Need Your Love/The Lord is My Light
Robert Winston Blackwood; Jimmy Blackwood; Cecil Blackwood; Ken Turner

1985 ALL THEIR BEST
(VOICE BOX VB4030)
New and Improved/Valleys Are for Learning/We Come to Worship/Reach for Your Faith/I'm
Following You/Heir to it All/It Never Even Crossed My Heart/It's a Joy/I Never Gave Up/He
Could Never
Robert Winston Blackwood; Jimmy Blackwood; Cecil Blackwood; Ken Turner

1985 I BOWED ON MY KNEES AND CRIED HOLY
(VOICE BOX VB5801)
Inside the Gate/Softly and Tenderly/O, When I Met You/Search me Lord/My Desire/What A
Morning/I Bowed Down on My Knees and Cried 'Holy'/Christ Is So Wonderful/'Til I Found the
Lord/I Heard About a City/My Saving King/Where Thou Goest
Bill Shaw; James Blackwood; Cecil Blackwood; J. D. Sumner; Wally Varner

1985 SPEAK HIS NAME
JAMES BLACKWOOD QUARTET
What Kind of Christian Are You/How About Your Heart/Speak His Name/Every Need Supplied/
Mighty God/Old Fashioned Meeting In This Place/Little Is Much/I've Got That Old Time
Religion/The War Is Over/No Less Than Me

1985 CHRISTMAS WITH THE CRITTERS
(Skylite/Temple TEM8516)
Jingle Bells/Critters Christmas Song/Twelve Days of Christmas/Frosty The Snowman/Rudolph
The Red Nosed Reindeer/Critters Christmas Story/Silver Bells

1986 AND NOW - JEFF STICE
(Skylite SLP6370)
Chariots of Fire/When God Dips His Love In My Heart/In The Garden/Goodbye World,
Goodbye/Bye and Bye/You Light Up My Life/When We All Get To Heaven/The One For Me/
Allelujah, Jesus Reigns

1986 JEFF STICE ON PIANO
(Skylite SLP6375)
In The Garden/Just A Closer Walk With Thee/Medley/While Ages Roll On/Church In The
Wildwood/When They Ring Those golden bells/Somebody Touched Me/Glorious Church of
God/There Is A Fountain/F# Can Be Fun

1986 BEST OF KEN TURNER
(Temple TEM8528)
One Day Too Late/One Day Closer/Tears Will Never Stain The Streets/Lead Me Gently Home/
Lord, I'm Unworthy/Brotherly Love/Who am I?/His Amazing Love/I'm Never Going Back
Again/When He Reached Down His Hand

1986 THE ANSWER -12 inch Radio Disc
(Calvary SPCN007)
The Answer/Radio Interview/Cecil Blackwood by Rick Jarrent/Station ID's and Promos

1986 THE ANSWER
(Calvary SPCN750851999)
The Answer/Show Me Your Way/That's Wrong/Talk To The King/My God Is Real/His Name Is
Wonderful/Man of Sorrow/Medley- Jesus Lifted Me/Kum Ba Ya/On The Wings Of the spirit

1986 BEST OF THE BLACKWOOD BROTHERS
(Arrival NU 2094)
We Come To Worship/An Heir To It All/I Never Gave Up/It Never Even Crossed My., Heart/
Blessed be The Name/New & Improved/Right Again/It's A Joy/Daddy's Girl/Come Unto Me

1986 WITH A SONG ON MY LIPS (AND A PRAYER IN MY HEART)
BLACKWOOD BROTHERS QUARTET
(RCA CAMDEN CAD2115)
With a Song on My Lips (And A Prayer in My Heart)/Without Him/God Is Alive/Heaven Came
Down & Glory Filled My Soul/What a Day That Will Be/Brighten the Corner Where You Are/
He Touched Me/There's No Other Way/Take the Hank of the Lord/All the Way

1986 THE ANSWER
(CALVARY SPCN7501851999)
The Answer/Show Me Your Way/That's Wrong/Talk to the King/My God Is Real/His Name Is wonderful/Man of Sorrows/Medley: Jesus Lifted Me, Kum-Baya, On the Wings of the Spirit
Robert Winston Blackwood; Jerry Trammell; Cecil Blackwood; Ken Turner

1986 THING CALLED LOVE
THE BLACKWOOD BROTHERS PRESENT JIMMY LAMAR
(SKYLITE SLP6369)
Thing Called Love/If I Can help Somebody/Light at the End of the Darkness/Through It All/ Will They Love Him Down in Shreveport?/Room of Prayer/I Lift Up Holy Hands/Who Am I/ Welcome to My world/You Should have Come Sooner
Robert Winston Blackwood; Jimmy Blackwood; Cecil Blackwood; Ken Turner; Jeff Stice

1986 CECIL BLACKWOOD OF THE BLACKWOOD BROTHERS
(SKYLITE SLP6371)
Until Then/By Faith/Go Down/Leave a Well/Because He Lives/More About Jesus/Rise and Be Healed/Something Took Hold of Me/Fill My Cup, Lord/I'll See You in the Rapture
Robert Winston Blackwood; Jimmy Blackwood; Cecil Blackwood; Ken Turner; Jeff Stice

1986 OLD COUNTRY CHURCH
(Skylite SSC 6356)
Old Country Church/Holy Spirit Thou Art Welcome/He's The Lily of the Valley/My Jesus, I Love Thee/He Bought My Soul/Blessed Assurance/Lead Me To That Rock/Peace Like A River/ He's all I Need/God Will Take Care of You

1987 IN CONCERT
(Skylite SSC6360)
Give The World A Smile/He Rose Again/Holy Spirit/It Is finished/There He Goes/Because he Lives/Lord, I'm Not Ashamed/Until Then/When Morning Comes/More About Jesus

1987 THE MASTERS V PRESENT JAMES BLACKWOOD IN ALOHA TIME
WITH BUD TUTMARC
(Skylite SSC6379)
Aloha Time/Morning Communion/Over the Sunset Mountains/Eternal Paradise/Hawaiian Wedding Song/Paradise Island/Cast Your Bread On The Water/Over The Moon/I Owe It All To Jesus/He's Coming Soon

1988 FEATURE CECIL STRINGER
(Skyline BO241)
I Love To Tell The Story/Rainbow Of Love/How Great Tho Art/What A Friend/A Beautiful Life/Impossible Dream/Somebody Bigger Than you And I/I Love You Lord/He Looked Beyond My Faults

1989 USA TOUR VOL.1
(CSB 1089)
Holy Spirit/Lily of The Valley/Heaven/Then I Met The Master/Learning To Lean/Just A Little Talk With Jesus/Walk With Me/How Great Thou Art

1989 USA TOUR VOL.2
(CSB 1271989)
Hide Me, Rock of Ages/Until Then/The Robe/I Wanna' Know/Someone to Care/The Old Rugged Cross/In The Garden/Give The World A Smile/Just A Closer Walk With Thee/The Love of God

1989 TURNING THE SOIL
(CSB Records)
Turning The Soil/Old Ship Of Zion/Rolled Away/Leaning On The Rock/Fill My Cup
Have You Seen A Miracle/Higher Power/Leavin' On Out/Old Country Church

1989 HE IS MY EVERYTHING
JAMES BLACKWOOD WITH THE BLACKWOOD BROTHERS
(Skylite SSC6394)
A Father's Prayer/His Hands/There He Goes/Sweet Beulah Land/It Was I/He Is My Everything/I
Saw Jesus When He Died/Without the Blood/He/I Found It All In Jesus

1989 ORIGINAL RECORDINGS OF THE 50's BLACKWOOD BROTHERS
(BLACK INC. RECORDS BIC11888)
Sunday Meetin' Time/I am a Pilgrim/Give the world a Smile/Just a Closer Walk With Thee/
Looking for a City/Peace Like a River/I Want to be More Like Jesus/Tell My Friends/A Mail
order from heaven/Over the Moon/Life's Railway to Heaven/Saviour, Gently Take Me Home/Just
a Little Talk with Jesus/Lord, Keep Your Hand on Me/Every Day will be Sunday/Where No One
Stands Alone/How Long Has it Been?/I Shall Be at Home with Jesus/He's Everywhere/A
Beautiful Life
James Blackwood; Cecil Blackwood; Bill Shaw; J.D. Sumner

1990 THE UNFORGETTABLE PAT HOFFMASTER
(Skylite SSC6396)
I Must Tell Jesus/Learning To Lean/He Touched Me/He Hideth My Soul/Jesus, I Love You/He Is
Lord Of All/He Was There All The Time/Holy Spirit, Thou Art Welcome/Blessed Assurance/The
Joy Of Knowing Jesus

1990 HERE COMES THE VOLKSWAGON
(CSB Records 3925)
Little House By The Side Of The Road/O Know Who Holds Tomorrow/Wandering Aimlessly/
Life's Railway To Heaven/Here Comes The Volkswagen/The Lighthouse/Peace In The Valley/I
Won't Have To Live Here/I've Been Accepted By The Lord/Last Mile Of The Way

1990 BLACKWOOD BROTHERS CLASSICS VOL. 1
(CSB Records)(Produced by Steve Warren)
What A Morning/His Love/Never/Wonderful Love/He's All That I Need/Wonderful Saviour/I
Don't Mind/Inside The Gate/Night And Day/God Made A Way

1990 BLACKWOOD BROTHERTS CLASSICS VOL. 2
(CSB Records) (Produced by Steve Warren)
On The Other Side of Jordan/Walking and Talking With My Lord/Each Step I Take/Behind Your
Tears/Paradise Valley/On That Happy Golden Shore/I Want To Meet you Up In Heaven/My All I
Give/One Day/Christmas Christ To Me

1990 BLACKWOOD BROTHERS CLASSICS VOL. 3
(CSB Records) (Produced by Steve Warren)
In That Land/Keep Me/I Shall Arise/For I've Got The Lord/Something Took Hold of Me/The
Sweetest Name I Know/Childhood Memories/Give Me Time/Give Me This Mountain/When
The Clouds Roll By

1991 JAMES BLACKWOOD & GABRIEL
(Skylite Sing Records SSC6416)
Patriotic Medley/I'm Winging My Way Back Home/When He Was On The Cross/Because He
First Loved Me/We Shall Beyond Him/God Bless The USA/I've Got That 'Old-Time Religion/
He's The Giver Of Life/Electricity/No More Night

1991 JAMES BLACKWOOD WITH THE MASTERS V
(Skylite SSC6384)
It Is Finished/More Than Wonderful/I Can Feel The Touch Of His Hand/His Eye Is On The Sparrow/The Battle Was Won in Gethsemane/It Is Well With My Soul/The Haven of Rest/ Worthy The Lamb/His Amazing Love/The Holy City

1991 THE LEGENDARY JAMES BLACKWOOD
(Heartwing HW0100)
Learning to Lean/I'm Free/Because he Lives/It Wasn't Nails/Those Are The Valleys/Some Glorious Morning/I Will Serve Thee/Land Of Living/God Still Loves The World/I Have Heard Of A City

1991 BLACKWOOD BROTHERS CLASSICS VOL.4
FEATURING JAMES BLACKWOOD
His Love/I've Got It (You Can Keep It)/Walking in the Light/When I Stand with God/ He'll Be There/One Day/It Must Be The Man (In The Sky)/I Must Have Jesus/Roamin River/I'll Never Walk Alone

1991 BLACKWOOD BROTHERS CLASSICS VOL. 5
FEATURING JAMES BLACKWOOD
The Lord's Prayer/Everybody Ought To Love/There's A Higher Power/I Walked Today Where Jesus Walked/Time Has Made a Change/Let Me Touch Him/Tho' I'm Unworthy/I Asked The Lord/In That Great Judgement Morn/Don't Spare Me

1991 BLACKWOOD BROTHERS CLASSICS VOL. 6
FEATURING JAMES BLACKWOOD
What A Glorious Morning/I Want To Walk/It Will Be Worth It All/Marvellous Grace/The Broken Vessel/Something worth Living For/Above All/I Believe He'd Go To Calvary/Love/ Through It All

1992 BEST OF THE BLACKWOOD BROTHERS RCA
(RCA07863)
One Day/Old Country Church/How Great Thou Art/God Made A Way/That Lonesome Road/Paradise Island/Eternal Paradise/Precious Memories

1993 I'LL FLY AWAY -CECIL BLACKWOOD FAMILY/FRIENDS
(CSB21593)
Learning To Lean/I'll Fly Away/Without Him/Just A Closer Walk With Thee/Mansion Over The Hilltop/He/Until Then/Where Could I Go?/Life's Railway To Heaven/Just A Little Talk

1994 'FIRST CLASS FLIGHT
JAMES BLACKWOOD QUARTET
(SUMNER & ASSOC.)
Rock My Troubles Away/For What Earthly Reason/God Is Still In Control/Lay Them Down/First Class Flight/It Was for Love of Me/Mama's Song Book/I Am Strong/Brag About the Son/Love Found a Pardon
James Blackwood; Ray Shelton; Larry Ford; Ken Turner; Brad White

1994 STEVE WARREN - RECITAL
In The Garden/Something Good Is About To Happen/Mountain/America The Beautiful/Pass Me not/All Praise To God Victorious/I Shall Be At Home With Jesus/Old Rugged Cross

1994 STEVE WARREN - THE VOICE
The Hallelujah chorus/Stand Up/There Is A Savior/The Battle Was Won At Gethsemane/The Wonderful Spirit Of It All/Midnight Cry/There Rose A Lamb/Wish You Were Here/Temporary Home/God Shall Wipe Away All Tears/Up In Chicago/When You Pray, Pray For America

1994 STEVE WARREN - RELEASED
Release Me/O My lord What A Time/It Must Have Rained In Heaven/You Never Showed Me/
Rock of Ages/A House of Gold/Would They Love Him in Shreveport/Heaven, Home of the Soul/
A Day In the Life/All Things Good for Aron

1994 GOSPEL CLASSICS FROM THE 59's, 60's & 70's
THE BLACKWOOD BROTHERS FEATURING CECIL BLACKWOOD
(Crystal Incorporated 438793.12)
Its' Almost Tomorrow/Without A Prayer/There is A God/Only believe Him/When the Clouds Roll
By/The Love of God/Sing, Be Happy/It Took A Miracle/Only One Touch/He's Everything to Me/
Ol' Brother Noah/From This Moment On/Close to The Master/I Will Never Walk Alone/Tell Me
Why/Because He Died/Climb Every Mountain/By the Cool Water/Take the Hand of the Lord/
Perfect Peace/In the Shelter of His Arms/It Matters to Him/I'll Soon Be Gone/Oh How I Love
Him/Because He Lives/Jesus Will Outshine Them All/The Little Boy From the Carpenter Shop

1994 FANTASTIC LIVE VOL.7 - SOUTH BEND
(CSB Records)
We Come To Worship/He Hideth My Soul/He's Coming Soon/When I Lift Up My Head/This
Old House/I Never Gave Up/He Was There All The Time/Lead Me To That Rock/I Want To Rest/
It's A Joy

1994 FANTASTIC LIVE VOL.8 - SOUTH BEND
(CSB Records)
Until Then/It's My Desire/Jesus, I Love Thee/Jesus Is Coming Soon/I Never Gave Up/More Of
You/God Is Alive/Medley/I Have No Song/Medley/I Want To Be More

1994 FANTASTIC LIVE VOL.9 - SOUTH BEND
(CSB Records)
I Want To Be More Like Jesus/Eastern Gate/Old Country Church/Take Away The
Stone/It Is Finished/How Great Thou Art

1994 LIVE IN 1975 VOL.1
(CSB Records)
He Hideth My Soul/the Lighthouse/because He Lives/What A Beautiful Day/He Touched Me/
Restore My Soul/The Eastern Gate/I Can Feel The Touch Of His Hands/Get On The Happy Side
of Living

1994 LIVE IN 1975 VOL.2
(CSB Records)
Come On Down/Hallelujah Square/James Gives History of Blackwood Bros./Nearing The Shore/
One Day At A Time/I Am The Reason/I'm Not Ashamed/Without The Blood/One Day Too Late

1995 THE WAY OF THE WORLD
BLACKWOOD BROTHERS PRESENT MARK BLACKWOOD
(New Voice Box)
The Way of the world/Life me Again/No Matter What You're Going Through/He Alone is the
Cornerstone/Keep On Running/Keep Me/Just A Touch/Speak His Name/I'm going to Heaven/Just
For Me/That's What's Wrong/My Friend, My Guide

1995 MASTERPIECE - PRESENT STEVE WARREN
Hallelujah Chorus/Amazing Grace/I Walked Today Where Jesus Walked/The Holy City/How
Great Thou Art/It's Almost Over/I Believe/Old Rugged Cross

1997 PRECIOUS MEMORIES
JAMES BLACKWOOD
(Mark Goodman Productions 100697-4)
How About Your Heart/Till The Storm Passes By/Great Is Thy Faithfulness/Then I Met The Master/Until Then/Beaulah Lane/His Hand In Mine/Leaving On My Mind/My Jesus I Love Thee/ Precious Memories

1997 KEEP LOOKIN' UP
THE TEXAS SWING SESSIONS
JAMES BLACKWOOD & THE LIGHT CRUST DOUGHBOYS
(Doughboys DB1010)
This Ole House/The Unclouded Day/Wayfaring Stranger/The Big Boss/Trouble in the Amen Corner/This World Is Not my Home/The Chair That Never Got Mended/I am A Pilgrim/That's The Way it Used to Be/Riding the Range For Jesus/When All God's Children Go Marchin In/ Sheltered in the Arms of God/Six Days/Life's Railway to Heaven/Beautiful Texas/Lord, Take all of Me/Washed in the Blood Medley/Keep Lookin' Up

1997 'REMEMBERING THE BLACKWOOD BROTHERS
SMOOTH & CLASSY'
(Memory Lane Gospel MLGCD1013)
Ev'ry Day Will Be Sunday By and By/Take My Hand Precious Lord/I Just Rose to Tell You/I Feel it in My Soul/Peace in the Valley/Jesus is a Waymaker/It is No Secret/Lead Me to That Rock/He'll Understand and Say 'Well Done'/Come On in the Room/Satisfied/He Bought My Soul at Calvary/ Didn't It Rain/Keys to the Kingdom/I'll Walk Dem Golden Stairs/It took a Miracle/Working on the Building/On the Jericho Road/My God is Real/What Could I Do?

1997 'GAITHER GOSPEL SERIES - THE BLACKWOODS'
(SPRING HOUSE SHD4905)
Angels Watches Over Me/It Is No Secret/He Bought My Soul At Calvary/Swing Down Chariot/ The Hand of God/He Knows Just How Much You Can Bear/Someone to Care/Gloryland Jubilee/ I'm Feelin' Fine/His Hand in Mine/Jesus the Way Maker/Brush The Dust Off the Bible/The Man Upstairs/How About Your Heart/Live Right, Die Right/Give Us This Day/God Made a Way/His Hands/The Stranger of Galilee/Paradise Island/The Pearly White City/the Old Country Church

1997 'MAGNIFICENT SOUNDS'
JAMES BLACKWOOD QUARTET
God Is Good/Eastern Gate/Walk With Me/I Want To Be More Like Jesus/Until You've Known The Love of God/I Just Can't Make it By Myself/The Ground Is Level At Calvary/The Keys to the Kingdom/Just a Little Talk with Jesus/Oh, What a Saviour

1997 STILL ALIVE
(CSB Records)
First Day In Heaven/I'm Feelin' Fine/I Can't Stand up alone/Angels Watches Over Me/When I Stand In The Presence/Matter of Mercy/Blessed be The Name/I'm going Home/Everyday/ Whosoever Will

1997 ON THE JERICHO ROAD -FEATURE ERIC WINSTON
(CSB62097)
When The Saints Go Marching In/When I Wake Up To Sleep No More/On The Jericho Road/ Reprise/Show A Little Love And Kindness/Turn your Radio On/I Feel Like Travelling On/Farther Along/ Oh, How I Love Jesus/Suppertime

1998 'THEY GAVE THE WORLD A SMILE - STAMPS QUARTET TRIBUTE ALBUM' JAMES BLACKWOOD QUARTET AND THE LIGHT CRUST DOUGHBOYS

(DOUGBOYS DB1014)

What A Saviour/Give the World a Smile/I Want to be More Like Jesus/Precious Memories/No Tears in Heaven/Where Could I Go (But to the Lord)/Turn Your Radio On/Farther Alone/On The Jericho Road/Low Singin' Bass Where We'll Never Grow Old/We'll Soon Be Done With Troubles and Trials/The Eastern Gate/Where the Roses Never Fade/I'll Meet You in the Morning/When All God's Singers Get Home/Guide and Keep Us

Plus spoken introductions to each song by James Blackwood, ArtGreenshaw and Marvin Montgomery

1998 'LEARNING TO LEAN ON JESUS' CECIL STAMPS BLACKWOOD AND THE BLACKWOOD BROS QUARTET

(THE BLACKWOOD BROTHERS 154698.6)

Learning to Lean/Old Time Religion/I Love to Tell the Story/Who Am I/How Great Thou Art/You Are My Love/Old Country Church/Just A Little Talk with Jesus/HolyCity/Until Then

1998 'BEAULAH LAND' CECIL STAMPS BLACKWOOD AND THE BLACKWOOD BROS. QUARTET

God Made A Way/I Was There When It Happened/His Grace is Sufficient/Amazing Grace/Beaulah Land/Because He Lives/The Light House/O What A Saviour

1998 'THE BEST OF JAMES BLACKWOOD'

(James Blackwood 217098.8 Double CD)

Introduction/I Want to be More Like Jesus/His Grace Reaches Me/He's Still the King of Kings/Release Me (From my Sin)/I'll Met You in the Morning/the Night Before Easter/He Is My Everything/I Can Feel the Touch of His Hand/The King Is Coming/The Eastern Gate/Aloha Time/Morning Communion/Over the Sunset Mountains/Eternal Paradise/Hawaiian Wedding Song/Paradise Island/Cast Your Bread on the Water/Over the Moon/I Owe It All to Jesus/He's Coming Soon/The Sound of Music/He Touched Me/Take Away the Stone/Vessel of Honor/Easter Song/God Is Alive/Let Jesus Happen to You/How Great Thou Art/Yeshua La Mesiah/Statue of Liberty/I Never Knew/The Last Song/Keep on Singing/Happy Side of Living/Hallelujah Square/Over the Next Hill/To Remember Calvary/Come on Down/Nearing the Shore

1998 GOSPEL CLASSICS VOL.10 - I'LL SEE YOU IN THE RAPTURE

(Produced by Eric Winston)

Hallelujah Meeting/leave A Well In The Valley/Jesus Has The Answer/Restore My Soul In The Valley/He's all I Ever Need/I'm Never Going Back Again/The Joy of Knowing Jesus/I'll See You In the Rapture/I'm Unworthy/I Found Jesus Today

1998 GOSPEL CLASSICS VOL.11 - WHEN WE ALL GET TO HEAVEN

(Producer Eric Winston)

Hallelujah To The King/He's More Than Just A Swear Word/What A Happy Day/while Ages Roll/That Day Is Almost Here/When We All Get To Heaven/His Grace Is Sufficient/I'm As Poor As A Beggar/I've Been Calvary/I'm Gonna Make It

1998 GOSPEL CLASSICS VOL.12 - HE TOUCHED ME

(CSB Records Producer Eric Winston)

Redemption Draweth Nigh/Rise Again/It's Real/The Joy Of Knowing Jesus/We Shall Wear A Robe And Crown/He Touched Me/Ship Ahoy/

1998 GOSPEL CLASSICS
(RCA)
O Happy Day/Jesus, Hold My Hand/The Eastern Gate/I Can Feel The Touch of His Hands/
Precious Memories/The Lord's Prayer/Just A Closer Walk With Thee/The Old Rugged Cross
Made The Difference/Sheltered In The Arms of God/Amazing Grace

1998 HYMNS
CECIL STAMPS BLACKWOOD & STEVE WARREN
(CSB Records)
Pass Me Not/In The Garden/His Hands/Jesus Lifted Me/'Tis So Sweet/Hand In Hand/Old
Rugged Cross/Dear Jesus Abide In Me

1988 CASSETTE COLLECTION OF 8 TAPES
Containing the first 300 singing recordings by the Blackwood Brothers Quartet featuring the
voices of James Blackwood, R. W. Blackwood, Roy Blackwood, Doyle Blackwood, Bill Lyles,
Hilton Griswold, Jackie Marshall, Wally Varner (piano), Cat Freeman, Calvin Newton, Alton
Toney, Dan Husky, Warren Holmes, Johnny Dickson, Cecil Blackwood, Bill Shaw, J. D. Sumner

1999 'THE BLACKWOOD BROTHERS' HERITAGE'
JAMES BLACKWOOD QUARTET
(WORD TIMELESS CLASSICS TIME 013)
I've Got That Old Time/Walk With Me/Old Fashioned Meeting in This Place/The Keys to the
Kingdom/Just a Little Talk With Jesus/Speak His Name/Keep On Singing/Little Is Much If God
is In It/What Kind of Christian Are You/Come on Down/I Want to be More Like Jesus/I Never
Knew 'Til Now/Until you've Known the Love of God/O What a Saviour/The Last song/How
About Your Heart?/God Is Good/I Just Can't Make it By Myself/The Eastern Gate/He's Coming
Soon

1999 THE BLACKWOOD BROTHERS QUARTET SING
SONGS ELVIS LOVED
(CSB Records)
So High/Where No One Stands Alone/Where Could I Go/Stand By Me/In My Father's House/
Walk Dem Golden Stairs/His Hand In Mine/If The Lord Wasn't Walking By My Side/Peace In
The Valley/How Great Thou Art

1999 RADIO SHOWS OF THE 30's, 40's, 50's VOL.I
-(CSB RECORDS)
Radio Opening Theme/He Knows How Much You Can bear/The Keys to The Kingdom/Leaning
On The Everlasting Arms/Angels Watches Over Me/Glad Reunion Day/I'll Tell It/It Took A
Miracle/Oh, My Lord What A Time/At The End Of The Trail/There's A God Somewhere/What
A Friend/How Many Times/Bend Away Down, Low/Known Only To Him/someone to Care/
Everyday Will be Sunday/Radio Closing Theme

1999 RADIO SHOWS OF THE 30'a, 40's, 50's VOL.2
(CSB Records)
Radio Opening Theme/Rolling, Riding, Rocking/Paradise Island/Peace In the Valley/Talk About
Jesus/God Is Love/it is No Secret/Get On The happy Side of Living/The Joy Of Heaven/After
Awhile/Hide Me Rock Of Ages/when They Ring Those Golden Bells/Walk Dem Golden Stairs/
Bell Of Joy Keep Ringing/Peace Like A River/Jesus Is The Way-maker/When He Calls, I'll Fly
Away/Radio Closing Theme

1999 RADIO SHOWS OF THE 39's, 40's, 50's VOL.3
(CSB Records)
Opening Theme/Only A look/Wait Upon the Lord/How About You/Everywhere He Went/Going
Home/My God Is Real/I'd Rather Have Jesus/Joy, Joy, Joy/I've Got A Wonderful Feeling/he
Bought My Soul At Calvary/Riding The Range For Jesus/Didn't It Rain/Looking For A City/
Over the Moon/I Shall Not Want For Anything/Radio Closing Theme

1999 RADIO SHOWS OF THE 30'S, 40'S, 50'S VOL.4
(CSB Records)
Radio Opening Theme/Brush The Dust Off The Bible/Keys To The Kingdom/Old Time Faith/I Feel It In My Soul/Hallelujah What A Day/My Burdens Have Rolled Away/Cleanse Me/When They Ring Those Golden Bells/On The Jericho Road/Take My Hand Precious Lord/Swing Down Chariot/When He Reached Down His Hand/Go Right Out/I Believe/The Hand Of God/An Evening Prayer/Closing Theme

1999 RADIO SHOWS of the 30's, 40's, 50's VOL.5
(CSB Records)
Sho Do Need Him Now/Lead me To That Rock/Journey to The Sky/Is He Satisfied?/Dry Bones/ Near The Cross/He'll Understand And Say Well Done/Hide Me In Thy Bosom/What Could I Do/It's My Desire/Working On A Building/I Just Rose To Tell You/The Lord Is My Shepherd/On Step/I Don't Care/Smile, Smile, Smile/Heavenly Love

1999 RADIO SHOWS OF 30's, 40's, 50's VOL.6
(CSB Records)
The Way That he Loves/Wasted years/Those Tender Hands/Shady Green Pastures/Born To Serve The Lord/Now I Know Why/He Washed My Eyes With Tears/The Love of God/The Family of God/Inside The Gate/Softly and Tenderly/O When I Meet You/Search Me, Lord/My Desire/ What A Morning/I Bowed on My Knees/Christ Is So Wonderful/Tell I Found The Lord/I heard About A City/My Saving King/Where Thou Goes

1999 REMEMBER J.D.SUMNER
(CSB Records)
God Made A Way/Sunday Meetin' Time/Give The World A Smile/I Am A Pilgrim/Just A Little Talk With Jesus/Walk That Lonesome Road/Savior Gently Take Me Home/Peace Like A River/A beautiful Life

1999 PRESENT THEIR BASSES J.D. SUMNER & ERNIE WINSTON
(CSB Records)
J.D. Sumner: I Shall Arise/Send Me/Victory road/There's A Light/Back Home/
Eric Winston: The Lighthouse/Old Time Religion/To me He's Become Everything/God Leads Us Along/Living By Faith

1999 PRESENT "THE BASS" ERIC WINSTON
(CSB Records)
God Made A Way/Rock of Ages/Whisper A Prayer/He Touched Me/Just A Little Talk With Jesus/ At The Cross/His Name Is Wonderful/This World Is Not My Home/Wasted Years

27 BLACKWOOD BROTHERS QUARTET VOCAL PERSONNEL 1934-2000

Date	Tenor	Lead	Baritone	Bass
1934-36	RW Blackwood	Roy Blackwood	James Blackwood	Doyle Blackwood
1936-39	Roy Blackwood	James Blackwood	RW Blackwood	Doyle Blackwood
1939	Roy Blackwood	James Blackwood	RW Blackwood	Doyle Blackwood
1939	Roy Blackwood	James Blackwood	RW Blackwood	Doyle Blackwood
1939-40	Roy Blackwood	James Blackwood	RW Blackwood	Doyle Blackwood
1940-42	Roy Blackwood	James Blackwood	RW Blackwood	Doyle Blackwood
1942	Roy Blackwood	James Blackwood	RW Blackwood	Don Smith
1943	Troy Chafin	James Blackwood	Hilton Griswold	Don Smith
1943-44	Roy Blackwood	James Blackwood	Hilton Griswold	Don Smith
1944-45	Roy Blackwood	James Blackwood	AT Humphries	Don Smith
1945	Roy Blackwood	James Blackwood	Hilton Griswold	Don Smith
1945-47	Roy Blackwood	James Blackwood	RW Blackwood	Don Smith
1946	Roy Blackwood	James Blackwood	RW Blackwood	Don Smith
1947	Roy Blackwood	James Blackwood	RW Blackwood	Bill Lyles
1947	James Blackwood	Doyle Blackwood	RW Blackwood	Bill Lyles
1948-49	Cat Freeman	James Blackwood	RW Blackwood	Bill Lyles
1948	Calvin Newton	James Blackwood	RW Blackwood	Bill Lyles
1948-50	Roy Blackwood	Doyle Blackwood	Johnny Dickson	Warren Holmes
1948	Cat Freeman	James Blackwood	RW Blackwood	Bill Lyles
1949	Roy Blackwood	James Blackwood	RW Blackwood	Bill Lyles
1949-50	Alden Toney	James Blackwood	RW Blackwood	Bill Lyles
1950-51	Alden Toney	James Blackwood	RW Blackwood	Bill Lyles
1951-52	Dan Huskey	James Blackwood	RW Blackwood	Bill Lyles
1952-54	Bill Shaw	James Blackwood	RW Blackwood	Bill Lyles
1954-59	Bill Shaw	James Blackwood	Cecil Blackwood	JD Sumner
1959-64	Bill Shaw	James Blackwood	Cecil Blackwood	JD Sumner
1964-65	Bill Shaw	James Blackwood	Cecil Blackwood	JD Sumner
1965	Bill Shaw	James Blackwood	Cecil Blackwood	John Hall
1966-67	Bill Shaw	James Blackwood	Cecil Blackwood	John Hall
1967-69	Bill Shaw	James Blackwood	Cecil Blackwood	London Parris
1969	Bill Shaw	James Blackwood	Cecil Blackwood	London Parris
1970-71	Bill Shaw	Jimmy Blackwood	Cecil Blackwood	London Parris
1972	Bill Shaw	Jimmy Blackwood	Cecil Blackwood	London Parris
1972	Bill Shaw	Jimmy Blackwood	Cecil Blackwood	Ken Turner
1973-74	Bill Shaw	Jimmy Blackwood	Cecil Blackwood	Ken Turner
1974-78	Pat Hoffmaster	Jimmy Blackwood	Cecil Blackwood	Ken Turner
1979-80	John Cox	Jimmy Blackwood	Cecil Blackwood	Ken Turner
1980-83	Pat Hoffmaster	Jimmy Blackwood	Cecil Blackwood	Ken Turner
1983-84	Rick Price	Jimmy Blackwood	Cecil Blackwood	Ken Turner
1984	Robert Crawford	Jimmy Blackwood	Cecil Blackwood	Ken Turner
1984-85	RW Blackwood	Jimmy Blackwood	Cecil Blackwood	Ken Turner

Blackwood Brothers Quartet Vocal Personnel 1985-2000

Date	Tenor	Lead	Baritone	Bass
1985-86	Jerry Trammell	RW Blackwood	Cecil Blackwood	Ken Turner
1986	Donna Blackwood	RW Blackwood	Cecil Blackwood	Cecil Blackwood
1987	Donna Blackwood	RW Blackwood	Mark &Cecil Blackwood Cecil Blackwood	
1988-9	Mike Loprinze	Mark Blackwood	Cecil Blackwood	Cecil Stringer
1990	Darrin Krauter	Mark Blackwood	Cecil Blackwood	Jeff McMan
1990	Francine Blackwood	Mike Loprinze	Cecil Blackwood	Jeff McMan
1990	Francine Blackwood	Mike Loprinze	Cecil Blackwood	Cecil Blackwood
1991	Francine Blackwood	Mark Blackwood	Cecil Blackwood	Cecil Blackwood
1991-2	Francine Blackwood	Mark Blackwood	Penny Burke	Cecil Blackwood
1993	Francine Blackwood	Steve Warren	Penny Burke	Cecil Blackwood
1994-5	Paul Acree	Mark Blackwood	Francine Blackwood Cecil Blackwood	
1995-7	Paul Acree	Mark Blackwood	Cecil Blackwood	Eric Winston
1997-8	Steve Warren	Mike Loprinze	Cecil Blackwood	Eric Winston
1999	Steve Warren	Rick Price	Cecil Blackwood	Eric Winston
2000	Steve Warren	Rick Price	Cecil Blackwood	Eric Winston

Blackwood Brothers Quartet Instrumental Personnel 1934-2000

Date	Piano	Bass	Guitar	Drums
1934-36				Doyle Blackwood
1936-39				Doyle Blackwood
1939	Joe Roper			
1939	Wallace Milligan			
1939-40	Marion Snider			
1940-44	Hilton Griswold			
1944-45	Lavera Humphries			
1945-50	Hilton Griswold			
1946	Harold Bell			
1948-50	Billy Gewin			
1948-50	Ken Apple			
1950-58	Jack Marshall			
1958-64	Wally Varner			
1964-66	Whitey Gleason			
1966-69	Dave Western			
1969	Peter Kaups	Dwayne Friend		Larry Davis
1970-71	Peter Kaups		Billy Blackwood	Larry Davis
1972	Tony Brown		Billy Blackwood	Larry Davis
1973-74	Tommy Fairchild		Billy Blackwood	Larry Davis
1974-82	Tommy Fairchild			
1982-85	Jeff Stice			
1986	Darrell Williams			Robbie Blackwood
1987	Joey Cheek			Robbie Blackwood
1988	Tommy Fairchild			
1989	Tommy Fairchild			

Special Solo Vocal Personnel 1934-2000

Date	Soloist
1970-81	James Blackwood
1982-5	Rick Price
1984	RW Blackwood
1984-6	Kenna Turner
1986	Jimmy Lamar
1987	Andrea Blackwood
1989	Rick Price
1995-2000	Chris Blackwood

The Blackwood Brothers Photo Memories

Early days' photo, in the Thirties, of the original Blackwood Brothers Quartet From left to right - Roy Blackwood (Cecil Blackwood's father), James Blackwood, R. W. Blackwood, Doyle Blackwood.

Group in the Forties gathered together ready to depart in their car.

R. W. Blackwood and Bill Lyles pictured in their plane before the fatal air crash in 1954. This is the exact position in which they were seated at the time of the tragedy.

Quartet in early Fifties taking a service in church. From left to right- Bill Shaw, James Blackwood, R. W. Blackwood and Bill Lyles.

Famous gospel singers appear on programme with Blackwood Brothers in Nashville. Left to right - Denver Crumpler, George Beverly Shea, James Blackwood, Homer Rodeheaver, Roland Felps, and Hovie Lister.

Louisiana's former governor, Jimmie Davis, as he appeared on the Blackwood Brothers' concert-sing in Memphis.

Bill Shaw, James Blackwood, Cecil Blackwood, J. D. Sumner and pianist Jackie Marshall on stage performance in full flight.

The Blackwoods rose to the national spotlight in 1954 and 1956 winning the Arthur Godfrey TV Talent Scout show. They are pictured here on Godfrey's morning programme on CBS TV broadcast from New York City along with the McGuire Sisters who joined them on the programme to sing 'Lead Me To That Rock'.

1960 picture postcard featuring Wally Varner, James Blackwood, Bill Shaw, Cecil Blackwood and J. D. Sumner in the latest in the shiny suits.

Blackwood Brothers Quartet with Tennessee Ernie Ford.

James Blackwood joins renowned evangelist Dr. Billy Graham and country singer Johnny Cash.

Partners for many years in Gospel music, the Statesmen Quartet and the Blackwood Brothers Quartet.

The King of Rock 'n Roll, *Elvis Presley chatting with James Blackwood, Hovie Lister and J. D. Sumner.*

From left to right -June Carter, Johnny Cash, James Blackwood, Hovie Lister and J. D. Sumner.

Multiple Dove Award *Winners - The Blackwood Brothers Quartet.*

The Blackwood Brothers - multiple proud winners of the Grammy Awards.

Something to smile about on the TV stage-set! From left to right J. D. Sumner, James Blackwood, Tammy Wynette, Jake Hess and Bill Gaither.

Famous Christian cowboy duo, Roy Rogers and Dale Evans along with the Blackwood Brothers.

Larry Gatlin helped the Memphis chapter of the National Academy of Recording Arts and Sciences *honor the Blackwood Brothers for their many* Grammy *nominations. The special day was declared in 1980.*

The Blackwoods pose with the beloved, sacred artist George Beverly Shea during a Billy Graham Crusade in Canada beside the touring bus.

At the Garden Tomb *in Jerusalem in 1980, Cecil Blackwood leads a tour group in a brief service of thanksgiving.*

Mark Blackwood, president of Voice Box Records, *and Cecil proudly display the group's latest* Grammy *Award.*

In 1981 the group sang during a Billy Graham Crusade in Winnipeg, Canada. Pictured here in the Stadium with Dr. Billy Graham.

Francine and Cecil Blackwood outside their home.

Best wishes to James Blackwood

Jimmy Carter

James Blackwood poses with former President Jimmy Carter and his wife.